Rugby and Rationing

Rugby
and
Rationing

Growing up Through the War Years and into 1950s Britain

Sarah J Anderson

Copyright © 2024 Sarah J Anderson

The moral right of the author has been asserted.

Apart from any fair dealing for the purposes of research or private study, or criticism or review, as permitted under the Copyright, Designs and Patents Act 1988, this publication may only be reproduced, stored or transmitted, in any form or by any means, with the prior permission in writing of the publishers, or in the case of reprographic reproduction in accordance with the terms of licences issued by the Copyright Licensing Agency. Enquiries concerning reproduction outside those terms should be sent to the publishers.

Troubador Publishing Ltd
Unit E2 Airfield Business Park,
Harrison Road, Market Harborough,
Leicestershire. LE16 7UL
Tel: 0116 2792299
Email: books@troubador.co.uk
Web: www.troubador.co.uk

ISBN 978 1805145 349

British Library Cataloguing in Publication Data.
A catalogue record for this book is available from the British Library.

Printed on FSC accredited paper
Printed and bound in Great Britain by 4edge Limited

Typeset in 12pt Minion Pro by Troubador Publishing Ltd, Leicester, UK

This book is written for myself, my siblings, all our children and my father's wider family.
It is dedicated to the man himself – Tony – a fabulous father, from whom we all learnt so much.

Contents

Preface	xi
William Antony Longworth	1
Family Tree	3
Family History	4
Tony's Father's Family	5
Joseph and Mary Longworth	5
Frank and Sarah Longworth	7
The Irish Connection	8
Frank and Sarah Return to Manchester	10
Manchester City Football Club	13
Sarah Longworth's Final Years	13
Tony's Father – Bill Longworth	14
J & N Phillips & Co	14
Cycling and Politics	16
Tony's Mother's Family	17
Fred and Isabella Bentley	17
King George V and Queen Mary Visit Tunstall	18
The Swan Hotel and Retirement	19
Leigh and Emma Bentley	20
Doing the Right Thing	21
Joseph and Rachel Coe	23
Tony's Mother – Marjorie Bentley	26
Sir Stanley Mathews	27
Local Life	27
Marjorie's Interests	28

Bill and Marjorie's Wedding	30
Tony's Early Years	33
Sentimental Gifts and Possessions	43
Days Out	45
Family Holidays	46
September 1939 and World War II	50
Joe Bentley and Sunny Coe	55
Yorston Lodge School Knutsford, Cheshire	63
1939–1942	63
Sandbach School, Sandbach, Cheshire	67
1942–1946	67
Sedbergh School, Sedbergh, Cumbria	74
1946–1950	74
1946	76
First Term's Diary	79
1947	86
1948	88
Olympic Games	91
1949	93
1950	104
Family Letters	111
From School to Accountancy	187
Summer 1950–1956	187
1950 Cycling Holiday to France with Mike Adams	187
The Wilmslow Golf Club	188
The Chadwick Cup	190
Articles of Clerkship	191
Bob Neill	192
1951	198
1952	200
Cycling Holiday to France with Bob Neill	201
Wilmslow Rugby Cup	202
1953	204
Trip to Killarney – August 1953	206

Intermediate Accountancy Exam 1953	209
1954	210
Tony's Twenty-First Birthday – 12 March 1954	211
1954 and Intermediate Accountancy Exam	214
1955	219
1956	222
William Antony Longworth, ACA	227
Trip to Belgium July 1956	227
Bill Haley and His Comets – February 1957	228
Canada 1957–1960	230
1957	230
1958	243
Trip to The Caribbean	243
Other Trips in 1958	245
1959	249
Arctic Adventures	255
Homeward Bound	263
1960	263
Arrival in England	275
Marjorie Longworth's Death	276
Epilogue	280
Appendix	284

Preface

For many years I have been interested in family history and have spent much time researching my forebears. This book focuses on the more recent past – my father Tony Longworth and his family.

The idea for writing this book stems from when my siblings and I cleared out our father's house after his death in 2015. Colebrooke, the Longworth family home for over eighty years, was full of treasures. Tony and his father, Bill, were not inclined to throw anything away. On sorting through the attic, an old sports bag was found belonging to Tony. This was filled with many of his school reports, exam papers and diaries, as well as many letters from his parents, sister Maureen, maternal grandparents and friends. The letters and diaries contain a wealth of information from Tony's life, and this book is an attempt to collate it all, and to preserve the memories.

As a keen amateur family historian, I will never forget my excitement at finding the bag of letters and diaries in Tony's attic. My first read of them all was a frantic one, greedily devouring everything in no order, hungry to hear the voices and make new discoveries. I wasn't disappointed. Then my desire for organisation kicked in, and I spent time putting the letters in order of date and author, and the diaries too, and on coming to transcribe them made the decision to try to weave a story around them all.

We are very fortunate that Tony and his parents were keen photographers, and I have incorporated some of these photos, where appropriate, to help with the narrative.

Time was also spent talking to both my father Tony and his sister Maureen about their childhood memories; unfortunately, they weren't very forthcoming, but the few snippets of family life they remembered I have included.

The timespan for the book took some careful thought, and I chose to focus on the years prior to Tony's first marriage. His life was so full in his early years, that I felt this was plenty for one book, and is the part of his life about which only snippets are known.

For better readability, I have referred to my father as Tony throughout.

Please note that there are some terms in this book, used at the time, that are now thought to be offensive – they do not reflect my views.

Thank you to my good friends Sarah Draper and Anne Marie Jones for their editing and feedback; to my husband Richard, children Jen and James, their partners Hannah and Helen, and my siblings, Guy, Rob and Kate, for listening to me talk endlessly about our family tree!

William Antony Longworth

Tony was an intelligent, considerate and kind Englishman with a wicked sense of humour. He was of average height, with dark hair which was blond and curly in his youth. As he grew older and his hair started to recede, he spent many years with an amazing comb over, which the wind would occasionally catch, and the balding head would be revealed!

Tony had the most amazing blue eyes, which never lost their sparkle, as well as particularly large ears, which seem to be a family trait. His laugh was contagious and could be heard across any room.

One of Tony's favourite things was an 'early doors' pint at the local pub, initially at The Dixon Arms in Chelford and then The Dog in Over Peover. Here he would be found propping up the bar with a pint of Boddingtons, exchanging stories and jokes with the other local patrons, and especially his old friend Pete Poizer. Tony was an excellent storyteller and had a few 'old favourites' which we would hear time and again.

People of all ages were drawn to Tony, he was a good listener and often provided a kind, non-judgmental ear to whoever needed counsel. He treated everyone equally and was very level-headed. As much as Tony enjoyed company, he was equally happy on his own with a multitude of newspapers and a window with a view of the birds and wildlife.

Tony was a man of tradition, and although he didn't attend church, he was a man of prayer and a believer in God and the afterlife. He wasn't perfect and could be incredibly stubborn, especially when he felt out of control or was being told what to do. He was a very proud man who found getting older frustrating at times.

Tony's family was of the utmost importance to him, taking great pride in all his children's and grandchildren's achievements, however big or small, often with tears welling up in his eyes. He was a man of great fortitude who dealt with tragedies with a quiet dignity and strength.

Tony loved Liquorice Allsorts, duck in orange sauce, Newberry Fruit Jellies, raw peas, home-cooked beetroot in malt vinegar, roast pork cooked to his mother's recipe, chicken madras, sweet-and-sour king prawns and confectionery of any kind. He loathed onions with a vengeance!

A lover of jazz and classical music, Tony was also an admirer of Lauren Bacall, a golfer, bird watcher, gardener, collector of model boats and antique arms. He read *The Telegraph*, *The Sun* and *The Mirror* daily "to get the full perspective" and believed that a good walk and "a list of pros and cons" could solve most problems.

Tony was many things – a son, brother, husband, father, grandfather, uncle, and friend. I hope you enjoy his story.

Family Tree

I have included a family tree here, as, although this book is based on the recent past, it is interesting to see where Tony's family all came from – both paternal and maternal. Although I have gone further back in time than is shown, I have chosen to display four generations before Tony came along, as it does get a bit patchy after that.

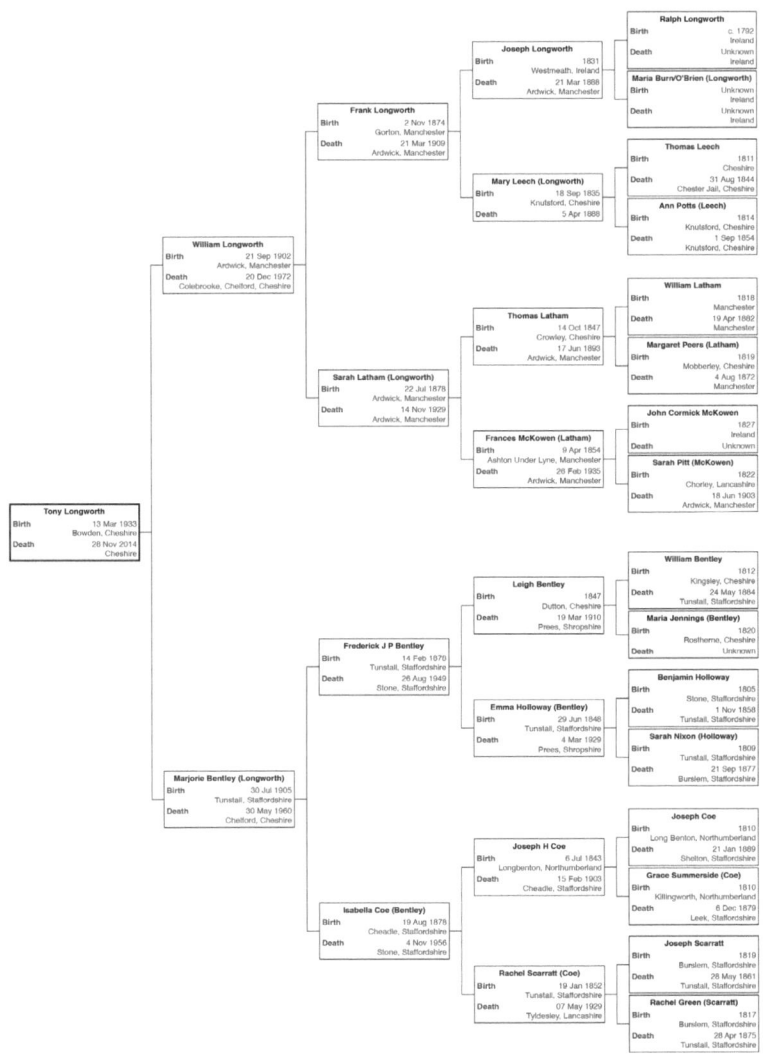

Family History

I found it very interesting that Tony was a real Northerner; as far as I have gone back, the furthest south anyone lived was Staffordshire.

Also, of great interest to me, was that Tony thought his father's family came from Manchester and Ireland, and his mother's from Staffordshire. However, originally, a great many of them came from Cheshire – Knutsford, Lower and Over Peover, Mobberley and Kingsley, going back many generations. Tony had no idea of this and was certain that neither of his parents did too. Tony's parents, Bill and Marjorie, found themselves settling back in their family's heartland – Cheshire.

I have included some of the family history that I have unearthed in this chapter and have chosen to take the family back three generations. This next section will look at Tony's parents, grandparents and great grandparents on both the paternal and maternal sides of his family.

You will also find some mini family trees as it can get quite confusing with many names appearing in different generations. If you find yourself getting confused, please refer to one of these trees which will hopefully, make things clearer.

Much of the information below has been gleaned from census records as well as birth, marriage and death certificates in my possession. As there's so many of them, I'm choosing not to include the references.

Tony's Father's Family

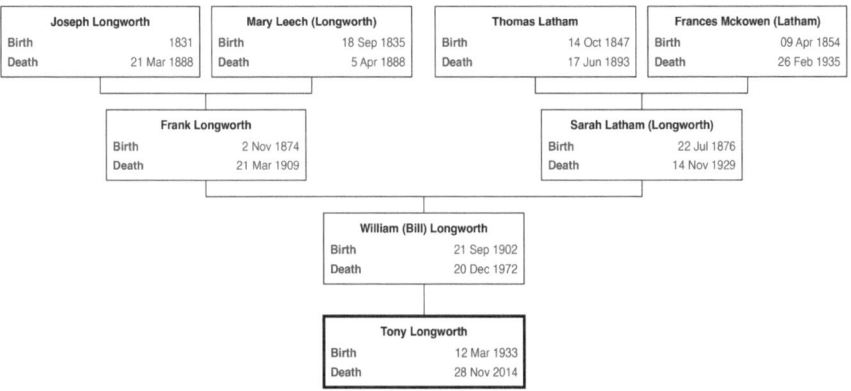

The family tree below shows three generations of Tony's paternal side of the family, which should help with following who is who. The surnames you will encounter in this section are: Longworth, Latham, Leech and Mckowen.

Tony's paternal grandparents, Frank and Sarah, were both born in Manchester. Frank Longworth in Longsight in 1874 and Sarah (née Latham) in Chorlton on Medlock in 1876.

Frank was the youngest of seven children – six boys and one girl. Only two of these children survived into adulthood – Frank, and the firstborn child, who was nineteen years his senior. Two of the boys died before Frank was born, aged three and fourteen. Then when Frank was still a young boy, two more died, aged ten and eighteen. The underlying cause of all the deaths was malnutrition. These tragedies must have had a profound impact on young Frank, not to mention his parents, Joseph and Mary Longworth.

Joseph and Mary Longworth

Joseph and Mary Longworth married in Manchester in 1855. Joseph was born in Glasson, Westmeath, Ireland and arrived in England around 1851/52. From an old notebook (in Tony's cousin, Dr K

Howard's possession), we know Joseph spent time living at Bate Mill in Over Peover, Cheshire, which, local lore has it, housed migrants arriving from Ireland due to the potato famine and it is perhaps the reason why Joseph came to England.

What was the potato famine? Between 1845 - 1852 Ireland suffered a period of starvation, disease and emigration that became known as the Great Famine. The potato crop, upon which a third of Ireland's population were dependent for food, was infected by a disease destroying the crop over successive harvests. The famine was poorly managed by the government who put the financial onus for famine relief on Irish landowners, who then tried to save money by removing tenants from their land. There followed a huge loss of life and many people emigrated to America and Canada, significantly reducing Ireland's population[1].

Mary (née Leech) was born in Knutsford, and prior to marrying Joseph worked as a servant at Booths Mill, a corn mill in Knutsford. Perhaps they met locally before moving to Manchester to embark on married life together.

Home was on Lister Street, Chorlton on Medlock, where Joseph ran a shop selling groceries; he also had a licence to sell beer. I suspect, however, it was his wife, Mary, who ran the shop, as Joseph's main occupation was that of domestic gardener. Life must have been tough for the family – this area of Manchester at the time was full of poverty and hardship with poor-quality housing (most of which was demolished in the slum clearances of the 1960s, with the housing considered to be unsalvageable).

In March 1888, Joseph, dropped down dead aged fifty-seven, on Stockport Road, close to his home. An inquest was held with the cause of death considered to be 'natural causes, accelerated by want of the proper necessaries of life'.

---

1 https://www.parliament.uk/about/living-heritage/evolutionofparliament/legislativescrutiny/parliamentandireland/overview/the-great-aminine

Staggeringly, only ten days later, Mary, aged only fifty-two, died of tuberculosis. Both were buried, along with their four boys, in the same plot in Ardwick Cemetery. The cemetery no longer exists, being closed in 1950, with the headstones removed and the site grassed over. It is now a community football centre. Heaven knows what happened to the bodies buried there – estimated at 80,000.

Frank and Sarah Longworth

Following his parent's death at the tender age of fourteen, and no doubt having left school, Frank moved to Lostock Gralam, Northwich, Cheshire to work as an 'agricultural cowboy' on a farm there. His sister Annie was working as a domestic servant at another farm in the same village. I can barely bring myself to write the next part of the story – more tragedy – in August 1889, Frank's sister, Annie died suddenly aged just seventeen years. An inquest was held, and the results written up in *The Northwich and Knutsford Guardian*:

> *Singular death of a young woman at Lostock – Mr Yates, Coroner, held an inquest at The Black Greyhound Inn, Lostock, on Thursday, on the body of Annie Longworth, aged 17, of Manchester. Frank Longworth, brother of the deceased stated that for a short time she had been staying with Mr Donovan, of Lostock. She was not well. On Monday she complained of pain in the stomach and died on Tuesday. Mr Donovan deposed that deceased came to him as servant on July 31st last but did not do heavy work. She had been ill before coming. He never heard her complain of any pain till Sunday.*
>
> *On Monday she was going to Manchester and got into his trap to be driven to the station, when she suddenly became worse, and he did not think it safe to take her. He took her to bed, and called in Dr Browne, but she died on Tuesday evening. Dr Browne stated that he attended the deceased, and afterwards made a postmortem examination. She had suffered from a*

diseased lung, but the cause of death was the obstruction of one of the blood vessels of the heart by a clot of blood. This was a most unusual thing in so young a person, and he did not think he could have saved her if he had been called in earlier. A verdict in accordance with the medical evidence was returned.

I cannot help but feel desperately sorry for Frank; so much tragedy took place in his first sixteen years, and I feel the need to lighten the mood a little, and just make the observation that Frank's parents were called Joseph and Mary, and I suspect and hope that this must have caused some merriment during the Christmas season!

Frank did, however, find happiness, and in 1897 married Sarah Latham in Ardwick, Manchester. Sarah was also from Manchester and had grown up in the Ardwick area. She trained to be a tailor's apprentice on leaving school. Sarah was one of six children, with, I think, only one dying young. Theirs must have been a busy household full of children, with her father, Thomas, working as a baker, and her mother, Frances, no doubt running the household.

Sarah's father died young, aged only forty-five when she was just sixteen. He is buried in Southern Cemetery, Manchester, in a communal, unmarked grave – a sign of their financial hardship. All is not lost, however, as Sarah's mother, Frances, remarried three years later to her husband's brother, William. They went on to have a long-lasting marriage and were supportive to Sarah and her family over the years.

Returning now to Frank and Sarah Longworth. Not long after they were married, Frank inherited the Longworth family estate in Athlone, Ireland. Before I describe how he came to inherit the estate, I'm going to explain the Irish connection in the family.

The Irish Connection

Tony's branch of the Longworth's originally came from the Township of Longworth, five miles northwest of Bolton, Lancashire. The furthest back we can trace is to a Peter Longworth who was born around 1625 in Bolton. Peter was a soldier in Cromwell's army and as such he travelled with the army to Ireland in about 1650. In 1652 he was given a grant of land under the Act of Settlement, which would have been to meet arrears of pay as well as part of the plan to settle English Protestants throughout Ireland (except Connaught).[2]

The Longworths stayed in Ireland and gradually bought up other estates, including Tubritt, in Athlone. The family had a strong presence in St Mary's Church, Athlone, and many of them were buried in the church yard.

Tony's grandfather, Frank, was not in line to inherit the Longworth family estate. However, in 1900, Frank's cousin, William Longworth, bequeathed the family home, called Tubritt, in Athlone, as well as three other farms, to Frank. Why Frank inherited and not his older brother, who was still alive, remains a mystery.

Why did William choose Frank as his beneficiary? William left a widow, and they had no children, and even though William had four sisters, three of whom were married with children, I think we can surmise that William wanted the estate to remain in the Longworth male

---

2   Dr Burgess MS, Athlone Public Library and Dr K Howard (Tony's cousin)

Window dedicated to William Longworth,
St Mary's Church, Athlone
(Photo reproduced with permission from RCB Library Gloine Collection Athlone 120070 W04 P06)

line, as was fairly common at the time. William's sisters were unhappy with the estate being passed to Frank and contested the will without success. (A copy of the case file is in my possession. King's Bench Division, Ireland, docket number 1906, No 775, Longworth and Campbell.)

After inheriting, Frank set up a memorial window to his cousin, William, in St Mary's Church, Athlone – the inscription reads: "To the glory of God & in memory of William Longworth Tubritt by Frank Longworth, Jan 1901." The window is situated in the Chancel.

Frank and Sarah moved to live on the estate, and from the 1901 census we know they were living in Tubritt House, Athlone, with the two eldest children, as well as Sarah's brother, Walter Latham, and a 'domestic servant'. Frank is described as farming the estate.

Although the family were living in Ireland, they returned to England for the birth of each child – a well-preserved family memory was that Sarah, who wasn't happy living in Ireland, wanted to give birth to all six of her children in England.

Frank and Sarah Return to Manchester

Frank and Sarah spent two or three years trying to farm the land, but it was difficult to return a profit and they made the decision to sell the estate and return to live in Manchester. It is likely that the estate was sold soon after the Land Purchase Act of 1903, which provided financial incentives to Irish landowners to sell their estates.[3]

Unfortunately, it seems that the solicitor dealing with the sale may well have embezzled much of the proceeds for himself. A letter in my possession, dated 5 February 1909, from this solicitor certainly indicates as much. There is also a family memory of the many problems settling up the estate, together with the loss of a considerable

---

3   www.encyclopedia.com/international/encyclopedias-almanacs-transcripts-and-maps/land-purchase-acts-1903-and-1909

Frank Longworth (c.1903) and Sarah with her children (c.1911). Left to right, Bill, Sarah, Sarah, Frank, Violet, Gretta and Fran

amount of money, and that Frank's wife, Sarah, blamed this loss on the solicitor.

Sadly, less than a month after Frank received the letter from the solicitor, on 21 March 1909, at home in Ardwick, Manchester, he died of tuberculosis aged only thirty-four. It seems that life had been hard on the family and from the solicitor's letter above, Frank has clearly written as much, as the reply is, "I am very sorry to hear things are not going well with you". From Frank's children's birth certificates, we know he changed jobs many times, and when he died Frank was working as a beer seller. The photos below are of Frank, probably taken around 1903, and Sarah, as a widow, with all the children, probably taken around 1911. Bill, Tony's father, is the boy standing.

Frank's will stated that he left £593 18s and 8d, leaving everything to his wife, Sarah. She also acted as an executor alongside the vicar of St Mary's Church, Athlone, Rev Richard Campbell Clark. (Calendars of Wills and Administration, 1858–1922, Archives of Ireland.) We don't know how much money Sarah eventually received, but with

Bill is seated, front row fourth from left, with Frank kneeling next to him, fifth from left

six children and a loss of income, times were undoubtedly hard. What happened to Sarah after Frank's death? From old school records held at Manchester Library, we know that Sarah and the children moved house four times from 1908 until 1914, and that their son, Bill (Tony's father), attended five different schools during this time, all within the Ardwick area of Manchester.

Remarkably, a photo survives of Bill and his older brother, Frank, at one of these schools; dated 26 April 1911. "Manchester Country School, Children of St Paul's C/M [Chorlton on Medlock] National School." From the school records held at Manchester Library – which I visited with Tony – we know that the brothers were attending this school at the time. The photograph is a postcard from Bill's brother, Frank, to his maternal grandparents. "I am sending you this photo for you and hope you are well, with love your grandson Frank."

At the time the above photo was taken, Sarah and the children were living with Sarah's mother, Frances Latham, and her family, in Ardwick; there were eleven people in total, in what would have been a small, terraced house with minimal outdoor space. Sarah was working as a "charwoman" and times were hard. This seems to be confirmed in a letter written by Bill's sister, Sarah (aka Cis), to Bill in 1960 when reference is made to their hard upbringing 'as we both agreed when last we met, we were brought up in a tough school'. It is interesting to see the siblings reflecting on their childhood many years later and confirming what the records are suggesting.

Much of Chorlton on Medlock and Ardwick were demolished in the slum clearances of the 1960's to make way for the university and shopping centres. If you have ever been to an event at The Apollo Theatre in Ardwick, you were walking where they lived.

Manchester City Football Club

For supporters of Manchester City, the family lived within walking distance of the ground on Hyde Road. Previously known as Ardwick AFC, in 1894 they reformed as Manchester City Football Club in a bid to represent the whole city. In 1920, Hyde Road became the first provincial football stadium to be visited by a reigning monarch; King George V watched City's victory over Liverpool. As the Club regularly attracted over 40,000 supporters, the King knew it was a good way to meet a large number of Mancunians. Three years later, in 1923, after a devastating fire at Hyde Road, the club moved to the 85,000 capacity stadium, Maine Road. Tony and his father Bill were life long Manchester City fans, and who knows, perhaps the family support of this club goes back further to Tony's grandfather, Frank Longworth. To this day, all Tony's children are keen supporters of the club, and some of his grandchildren too. A nice bit of continuity.[4]

Sarah Longworth's Final Years

Jumping forward a few years, by 1921 Sarah and all six of her children were living on Brampton Street, Ardwick (current site of The Apollo Theatre). Sarah is running the household and five of her children are in full-time employment. One of Sarah's daughters is married and has a little girl; they too are members of the household. Finally, Sarah's

---

4   www.mancity.com/history

younger brother, Walter, is living at the house and he too is working, so contributing to the family unit.

Little else is known about Sarah after this time, except that she continued to live in the house on Brampton Street, Ardwick, remarrying in April 1927 to William Fell. Family memory has it that Sarah was deeply unhappy in this marriage, and in November 1929 aged fifty-three, very tragically, Sarah took her own life.

Frank and Sarah are both buried in the same grave in Gorton Cemetery, with the inscription reading, "Reunited".

Tony's Father – Bill Longworth

This next section focuses on Tony's father, Bill Longworth, son of Frank and Sarah. William (Bill) was born on 21 September 1902, at 6 Gordon Street, Ardwick, Manchester, which was the home of his grandmother, Frances Latham, and the following month he was baptised in St Andrew's church, Ancoats (the church has since been demolished).

As already documented earlier in this chapter, at the time of his birth, Bill's parents, Frank and Sarah, were living in Athlone, Ireland, having recently inherited the family estate from a cousin. Both Frank and Sarah had been born in Manchester and returned to England for the birth of each child, and on this occasion they stayed with Sarah's mother, Frances.

Bill was the third child of six. His siblings were: Frank, b. 1898, Sarah (Cis), b. 1900, Violet (Vi), b. 1904, Gretta, b. 1906 and finally, Frances (Fran), b. 1908.

J & N Phillips & Co

We know that Bill attended different schools in the Ardwick area, leaving aged fourteen, which was common at the time. He started work as an apprentice with the firm J & N Phillips & Co working as a junior salesman. Some wonderful photos of Bill taken in 1919 and 1920 'at work' have survived. Bill is top row, far right in both photos.

Family History

Bill Longworth working at J & N Phillips, top row, far right

Bill Longworth working at J & N Phillips, top row, far right

Bill worked for J & N Phillips all his life. They were one of the biggest firms in Manchester, manufacturing and selling textiles. Bill worked his way up becoming a buyer for soft furnishings, blankets, bedding, etc. Part of the job was sourcing the raw materials which involved travel around Europe, especially Belgium. Bill eventually ended up running the department.

During both world wars, the firm made many items for the troops. As such, Bill's job was a reserved occupation, so he didn't go to fight. However, during World War II, Tony recalled that Bill was part of a group volunteering to put out fires, and that Bill spent many nights in Manchester, armed with buckets of sand and water on top of buildings in case they were bombed – must have been terrifying.

Cycling and Politics

As a keen cyclist, Bill was a member of the Manchester District Association Cyclists' Touring Club, and from the certificate he kept, in June 1926, he rode 206 miles in twenty-four hours, cycling through Cheshire into North Wales, skirting the Snowdonia National Park, and back again.

Bill was a member of The Reform Club in Manchester, which was established in 1867 for Liberal politicians and supporters of the Liberal cause in the city. Meetings were held in a magnificent building on the corner of King Street and Spring Gardens. Members had access to a variety of facilities including a reading room, dining room, smoking room and what was said to be the biggest and best billiards room in the city, which I am certain Bill would have made use of as he enjoyed playing and was also a member of a snooker club in Knutsford, Cheshire.

Amongst the club's members were Prime Minister's Winston Churchill and Lloyd George, both of whom addressed the people of Manchester from the building's balustraded balcony. Interesting little fact – although Lloyd George was a Welshman, he was actually born in Chorlton on Medlock.[5]

---

5   www.alexandramitchell.wordpress.com

Learning of all this family history makes Bill's success story all the more remarkable – changing the fortunes of himself and his family within one generation.

Tony's Mother's Family

The family tree below shows three generations of Tony's maternal side of the family, which should help with following who is who. The surnames you will encounter in this section are: Bentley, Coe, Holloway and Scarratt.

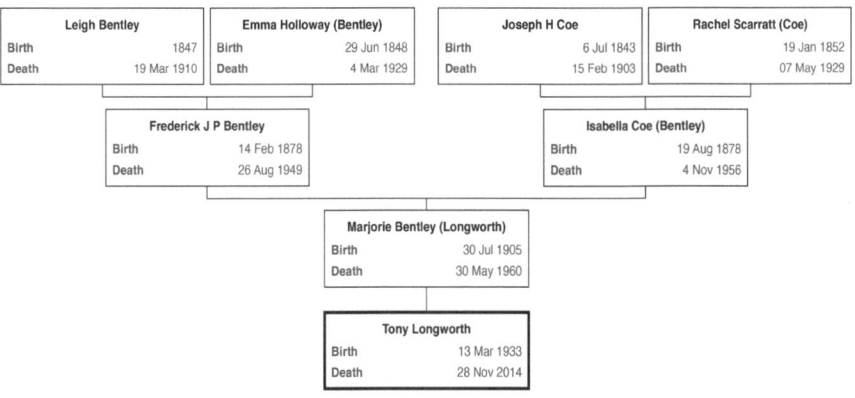

Fred and Isabella Bentley

Tony's maternal grandparents, Fred and Isabella, were both born in 1878. Frederick Joseph Parr Bentley (Fred) on 14 February in Tunstall and Isabella (née Coe) being born a few months after on 19 August 1878 in Cheadle, Staffordshire; both were baptised in Christ Church, Tunstall.

Fred was the second child of four and very tall. Until his retirement in 1940, he spent his whole life in Tunstall. Fred worked as a potters' slip maker, working in the same factory, called Alfred Meakin, as his father, Leigh. Thepotteries.org website provides a good description of his job: "A slip maker prepared the clay for production. It was an unwholesome occupation, whereby the

Isabella Coe and Fred Bentley on their wedding day, 14 December 1902

clay (or slip) is prepared by boiling the composition to a proper consistence on kilns, and during the process of evaporation, the room is filled with dense aqueous vapour. The men engaged in this work suffer severely from winter cough and chronic bronchitis."

Fred's wife, Isabella, spent virtually her whole life in Tunstall. Her maiden name was Coe, and she was also the second child of four. Prior to marriage, Isabella was a teacher and it seems she used these skills later in life as she spent many years helping to run the Sunday School at Christ Church. Isabella was also a good seamstress, and family memory has it she made all the costumes for her children in various plays and theatrical performances.

In 1902, Fred and Isabella were married in Christ Church Tunstall, with the first of their six children being born a year later. Both were very involved in Tunstall life, especially at Christ Church, where Fred was the treasurer and then the church warden; he was a leading light at charity dances and the like. Fred really enjoyed bowling and I found mention of him and his son, Leigh, taking part in various bowling competitions in *The Sentinel* newspaper.

King George V and Queen Mary Visit Tunstall

With Fred and his father both working at Alfred Meakin Ltd, the factory would have played a big part in their lives. One particular occasion happened on 23 April 1913 – King George V and Queen Mary visited the town as part of their trip through the potteries.

> *Flags flew and decorations adorned the public buildings as people throughout the towns awaited their King and Queen. Tunstall had the pleasure of their company on the final day and did them proud! Thousands of men, women and children thronged Market Square waiting for a glimpse of the royal couple as they made their way to the Alfred Meakin & H & R Johnson factories for an official visit.[6]*

From a description in the *Staffordshire Advertiser* on 19 April 1913, the entrance to Alfred Meakin Ltd factory was beautifully decorated and, as both Fred and Leigh worked at the factory, they would have almost certainly taken part in welcoming the King and Queen. There is some wonderful footage on the British Film Institute website of the King and Queen arriving at the factory; it shows the employees all lined up, looking very smart, waving and cheering their arrival. The footage is free to view and well worth a look. The occasion would, undoubtedly, have been a cause for much celebration in the Bentley household, with all school children waving flags along the route, and most people having been given a day's holiday.[7]

The Swan Hotel and Retirement

Fred probably retired from Alfred Meakin Ltd around 1935, as in April of that year he became manager of the Swan Hotel in Tunstall. He and Isabella lived there for two years along with their son Cyril and his wife Eva, who worked behind the bar. In June 1940, they relinquished the licence of the pub and moved to Stone, Staffs, where he and Isabella lived until his death in August 1949. Fred's death was announced in the *Evening*

---

6   *Tunstall* by Don Henshall
7   player.bfi.org.uk/free/film/watch-royal-tour-through-the-potteries-1913-online

Sentinel and a service was held at St Michael's Church, Stone, followed by an internment in Stone Cemetery where Isabella was also buried.

Leigh and Emma Bentley

Fred's parents were Leigh and Emma Bentley. Leigh was a potter who, as described above, worked at the Royal Albert Works in Tunstall. He must have been held in quite high regard in the company, as in October 1872, an article in the *Staffordshire Daily Sentinel* notes him making a presentation:

> *About 140 employees of Mr A Meakin, of the Royal Albert Works, sat down to tea in the St Mary's Lodge Room, Well Street, on Saturday. The object of their assembling together was to show in a tangible form the respect in which they hold the manager of the works – Mr Henry Johnson… The presentation was made by Mr Leigh Bentley, who, in the course of some remarks spoke in the highest terms of Mr Johnson, and said he hoped that the workpeople might long be under his management. In replying, Mr Johnson expressed the pleasure he had in accepting the gift… The St Mary's brass band played for dancing, and the evening was comfortably spent by all present.*

Leigh married Emma Holloway in February 1872 at Christ Church, Tunstall. They had four children, one of whom (Sarah) died young. Prior to marriage, Emma was a dressmaker, as was her mother, Sarah Holloway. Although I'm not writing about Sarah Holloway in this book, a fabulous photo of her has survived, which I can't resist including here. Sarah, born in 1809 in Tunstall, lived there all her life and had seven children that I know of. She worked as a dressmaker.

Sarah Holloway, born c.1809. Mother of Emma Bentley (née Holloway)

It seems Emma carried on her trade after their marriage, as I discovered that she ran a "drapery and fancy goods business" from their home in Cross Street, Tunstall. On searching the *Staffordshire Daily Sentinel*, I found an advert from August 1875 offering the business for sale, with "ill health sole cause of selling". It seems like they didn't succeed in selling the business as on checking *Kelly's Post Office Directory of Staffordshire* (Yellow Pages of its day) they are still trading in 1876 and 1880 as a "haberdasher".

From the 1881 census we know that Emma was continuing to run the haberdashery, and it was interesting to see that her neighbour ran a bakery/confectionery, and a couple more doors down was a grocer. Probably a typical street of its time.

Doing the Right Thing

Family memory has it that the Bentley's were a very upright family, used to doing 'the right thing', and I found a wonderful example of

Emma Bentley 'doing the right thing' way back in October 1876. The *Staffordshire Daily Sentinel* reported on a theft of bread as follows:

> STEALING BREAD – Mary Nolan, one of the defendants in the foregoing case (absconding drunkard), was charged with stealing 2 loaves of bread of the value of 1s, the property of Harriet Shaw, confectioner, Tunstall. On Monday, a young woman named Emma Bentley saw prisoner go into the shop of prosecutrix, put one loaf in her apron, and take up another to put in it. She said to prisoner "you are taking bread again, are you?" Prisoner ran away. There was no one in the shop at the time. On the previous Saturday Mrs Shaw saw prisoner go away with some bread, and told Miss Bentley, who lives next door, of it. Mr Superintendent Baker said when prisoner was apprehended, she said her husband was out of work, and she had no money wherewith to buy food. It had been ascertained that her husband was in good work, and that prisoner could earn 10s a week if she chose. Prisoner was under the influence of drink at the time. She was sent to gaol for fourteen days.

Emma Bentley was apparently very small, so I love the idea of her standing up to a drunk lady stealing bread, 'doing the right thing'.

Upon retirement, Leigh and Emma moved to Lower Heath, Prees, Shropshire. Leigh died in 1910 aged sixty-three whilst Emma lived another twenty years, living off 'private means', dying in 1929 at the age of seventy-nine. They are buried together in Pauls Holy Immanuel Cemetery, Prees, Shropshire. On the inscription Leigh is described as "one of nature's gentlemen" and Emma: "her end was peace."

Another example of a family member 'doing the right thing' and which is very important for me to include here, is my Great Aunty Jean, Tony's mother's younger sister. In 1974 my mother, Judith, died very suddenly, leaving Tony to look after Guy and me aged eight and seven respectively. Tony spoke the following words at her funeral:

Without hesitation Jean made a huge personal sacrifice, by giving up her job, shutting up her home in Southampton and coming to Cheshire to look after us. The three of us wish to record our very, very deep feeling of love and gratitude for what she did. For me it helped my recovery enormously, and the children had a great aunt to guide them.

When asked about it, Jean said, "They are my sister's grandchildren, of course I must go." An incredible act of kindness and of 'doing the right thing'. Thank you, Aunty Jean.

Joseph and Rachel Coe

Moving now to look closer at Tony's maternal grandmother's family. As we know, Tony's grandmother was Isabella Coe and she married Fred Bentley. Isabella's father was called Joseph Henry Coe, and he was born on 6 July 1843 in Durham. Joseph moved from the northeast of England, with his parents and five siblings, to the Staffordshire area around 1851. School years followed, and at around the age of eighteen Joseph tried his hand at being a cabinet maker's salesman. This line of employment didn't last, and he followed in his father's footsteps into the mining industry, first as a miner then as a colliery bailiff. By the time of his marriage in 1873 he was working as a colliery manager, just like his father – from pitman to colliery manager.

I found a reference to Joseph in the local paper in January 1874, when he became an elected member of the North Staffordshire Naturalists Field Club. During the meeting, held at The Railway Hotel in Stoke, a local vicar, the Reverend T W Daltry, "read a most interesting paper on entomology. He said that fresh discoveries of lepidoptera of North Staffordshire were made every year, and he considered that entomology was still in its infancy".

The club was established in 1865 for working naturalists; it accepted all interested people regardless of qualifications, gender, or social class. Within a decade of its founding became one of the largest and richest field clubs in the British Isles. When Joseph joined in 1874 there were 229 members, of whom seventy-two were women. The club had various sections including entomology, geology, archaeology, botany, zoology and microscopy. Various excursions were held throughout the year to places like Mow Cop, Dovedale, Lyme Park and Alderley Edge. Joseph was a member until 1883, when perhaps his busy family life and career took precedence.[8]

Joseph married Rachel Scarratt in 1873. The ceremony took place at Christ Church, Tunstall. Rachel had been born in Tunstall in 1852, the fourth of four children. She came from a family whose heritage stretches back into the Tunstall area for many years, with her parents and grandparents working within the pottery industry. As well as working in the pottery industry, Rachel's parents also worked as innkeepers and, remarkably, they were proprietors of the same pub run by Rachel's daughter Isabella and husband Fred, The Swan Inn, Tunstall, seventy-five years later. Rachel and her parents lived at The Swan Inn from around 1861, for at least ten years, with Rachel working as a barmaid there in 1871. Fred and Isabella took on the licence in 1935, a nice bit of continuity. Sadly, the pub no longer exists.

After Joseph and Rachel Scarratt married, they settled in the Tunstall area and went on to have five children. One of their sons was born at The Swan Inn in 1875, so perhaps the whole family were living at the Inn at the time, or just Rachel was staying with her mother. Sadly, this child (Joseph) died at the tender age of five, which must have been a terrible blow to the whole family. Their other son, William Henry Coe, became a colliery manager in Worsley, Manchester, and helped Tony's father, Bill Longworth, to panel the dining room at Colebrooke many years later.

During their marriage, Rachel worked as a milliner from their home on Charles Street in Cheadle, Staffs, and no doubt lived a busy life raising her children and running her business, with Joseph in a managerial role in the collieries.

---

8 www.staffordshirecountystudies.uk/page3.html

Sadly, Rachel's husband, Joseph, died in 1903 at the age of sixty. Rachel was left to raise their youngest child, William Henry, aged seven, alone. A few years later, however, Rachel remarried a widow, a gentleman of standing in the community – John Williamson. John was a Justice of the Peace and, like Rachel's first husband, he came from the northeast and worked his way up from pitman to colliery manager.

I strongly suspect John was related to Rachel's mother-in-law but haven't confirmed this – that will be in the next book! At the time of their marriage, Rachel was fifty-five and John eighty-three. They lived together in Cannock until John's death in 1916. He died a wealthy man and left Rachel an annuity of £250, a house called Meriden on Whitehall Road, Rhos on Sea and free selection of whatever furniture

Above: Left to right Fred and Isabella Bentley's children: Fred, Marjorie, Leigh, Jean, Cyril and Joe Bentley c.1921/22

and household goods she may choose. From family memory, we know that Rachel chose two ornate carved dining chairs, which I now own. On our birthdays, when we were children, we were allowed to sit on one as a very special treat, but otherwise they weren't used. I like knowing that I own something belonging to my great-grandmother, a solid connection, and I shall continue to sit on one on my birthday in the years to come.

Nothing else is known about Rachel, except that she died aged seventy-seven, in Tyldesley, Lancashire, at the home of her daughter, Ethel Walshaw.

Tony's Mother – Marjorie Bentley

This next section focuses on Tony's mother, Marjorie Bentley, daughter of Fred and Isabella. Marjorie was born on 30 July 1905 at home, which was 8 Cooper Street, Tunstall, Staffordshire.

Marjorie was the second child of six. Her siblings were: Frederick Joseph Parr (Fred), b. 1903, William Leigh (Leigh), b. 1910, Isabel Jean (Jean), b. 1912, Cyril Harry, b. 1914 and Joseph Harold (Joe), b. 1918.

Whilst I was spoilt for choice for photos of Tony's father's family, I only have a handful from Marjorie's side. Either they weren't keen photographers, or the photos have been passed down to other family members. I do, however, have one photo of the siblings below. Sadly, the photo is of poor quality, but it looks like it was taken outside Christ Church, Tunstall around 1921/22. All the siblings are in their Sunday best.

Tony spoke about his mother, Marjorie, having had a happy childhood and being brought up in a close and loving family. Her parents, Fred and Isabella, instilled in her a determination to do the right thing. Tony remembered these grandparents well. "They were wonderful, I can still see them now," he wrote in Jean's eulogy. He kept a few letters they sent during his school years at Sedbergh, and a little prayer book they gave to him as a boy.

Marjorie first attended the Forster St Junior Girls School followed by Cooper Street Board School, both in Tunstall. Alongside the entry to the latter school is the word 'scholarship', so perhaps she gained a special place at the school.

Sir Stanley Mathews

After leaving school, Marjorie worked as a teacher. Tony proudly remembered that she often talked about teaching the footballer, Sir Stanley Mathews ,who became a hero in Staffordshire. His professional career covered some thirty-three years. When he retired, aged fifty, he had made nearly seven hundred league appearances for Stoke City and Blackpool and for England eight-four times. His England career stretched from September 1934 to May 1957. In 1956 he won the first ever Ballon d'Or, which is awarded to the best male footballer of the year. Sir Stanley gained respect not only as a great player but also as a gentleman. This is exemplified by the fact that despite playing in nearly seven hundred league games, he was never booked.[9]

Local Life

Marjorie and her siblings were all involved in local life and regularly took part in pantomimes and fancy-dress parades. Isabella, their mother, made all their costumes. Jean remembered being dressed as Mother Goose on one occasion and that Marjorie used to get very nervous about appearing. Jean, as a dancer of note, gave dance performances. The photos below

Sisters, Jean and Marjorie Bentley *Jean Bentley doing the splits*

9   thepotteries.org/photo_wk/036.htm

show Jean doing the splits and the other is of Jean and Marjorie, perhaps dressed up for one of these occasions.

I found a couple of wonderful references to the family in the *Staffordshire Sentinel*. The first was from 17 February 1926 when a fancy-dress carnival and whist drive was held at Christ Church, Tunstall. Marjorie's father, Fred, was the MC of the dancing and her mother, Isabella, oversaw the refreshments and buffet. Marjorie won a prize dressed as a water lily and her brother, Joe, won a prize being dressed as a pancake in the boys section!

The second article appeared on 2 February 1927, when the Tunstall Pageant was held in aid of Parochial Funds. The Bentley family played their part in the pageant, firstly with "a solo dance by Miss Jean Bentley", and then in the production of *The King and His Knights*. Queenie Guinevere was played "by Miss Marjorie Bentley – equally outstanding and successful in elocution as acting". Performing alongside Marjorie was her brother – "Sir Lancelot, in the capable hands of Mr Leigh Bentley". Fred got a mention as being in attendance, and there is little doubt that Isabella would have been involved, not only with costumes, but with refreshments as well.

The family clearly enjoyed performing, and it is heart-warming to imagine the whole family having fun together.

Marjorie's Interests

Marjorie's love of the theatre continued into her married life – amongst the very few of her possessions that were found at Colebrooke was a programme for a performance of *The Cocktail Party* by T.S. Eliot at The Palace Theatre, Manchester, in April 1951, not long after it had won the Tony award for best play.

Marjorie enjoyed literature and reading, as shown in Marjorie's entry in Tony's autograph book, with a snippet from Longfellow:

Family History

Mummy, April 30th 1944

*The heights by great men reached and kept,
Were not attained by sudden flight,
But they, while their companions slept,
Were toiling upward in the night.*
Longfellow

After she married, Marjorie developed a love for gardening. She was responsible for creating the beautiful rose garden and rose bower at Colebrooke, as well as the planting along the driveway, which was awash with yellow azaleas, a huge laburnum tree and rhododendrons – it was spectacular in the spring; even today, the scent of azaleas takes me straight back to memories of Colebrooke. In the envelope of her possessions, I found many handwritten notes detailing the shrubs, trees, roses and bulbs that were to be planted. It is obvious that great care had gone into the choice, with notes on how to get the best of them "worth the trouble to buy tip top bulbs".

Tony remembered that one of Marjorie's favourite places to visit was Trentham Gardens, just south of Stoke. It was, and still is, a famous landmark in the area. The mansion that existed was demolished in 1912, but the gardens, designed by the eminent landscape designer, Capability Brown, remained. In 1910, the gardens were opened to the public and by 1925 motor launches, rowing boats and a miniature railway were added. It is easy to imagine the whole family having day trips to the gardens and enjoying all the facilities. I have very fond memories of Tony taking me to Trentham Gardens on numerous occasions, and I loved it too, so much so, that I chose it as my birthday treat one year. It is certainly worth a visit.[10]

---

10   trentham.co.uk/estate-gardens/history-of-trentham-gardens/

Bill and Marjorie's Wedding

Having spent time looking at Tony's parent's families and ancestors, this section focuses on Bill and Marjorie's wedding.

Tony's parents, Bill and Marjorie, married on 12 February 1930 at Christ Church, Tunstall. At the time of their marriage, Bill was living in Sheffield, working as a commercial manager for the firm J & N Phillips, a large firm manufacturing and selling textiles. Marjorie was working as a school assistant in Tunstall. J & N Phillips had large premises in and around the Stoke area, so I suspect they might have met when Bill was visiting the area on business.

Left: Bill and Marjorie Longworth on their wedding day, 12 February 1930

Their wedding afforded a large article in the *Evening Sentinel* on the date of the ceremony, together with a lovely photo of the couple shared here. The article read:

Pretty Tunstall Wedding.
Bride a daughter of Vicar's Warden.
Miss M Bentley and Mr W Longworth.

Much interest was taken in the wedding which took place at Christ Church, Tunstall, today (Wednesday) of Miss Marjorie

Bentley, daughter of Mr and Mrs F J P Bentley, of 13 Park Terrace, Tunstall, to Mr W Longworth, son of the late Mr and Mrs F Longworth of Manchester.

The bride is a member of a family prominently identified with church work in Tunstall her father being Vicars Warden of Christ Church. She is a former Sunday School teacher and has taken a leading part in work amongst the younger members of the congregation.

There was an exceptionally large number present in church, including the following officials of the church, Mr F Beacall, the People's Warden, Mr A E Parr, deputy People's Warden, and Mr A J Bickley deputy Vicar's Warden.

The ceremony was performed by the Vicar of Christ Church (the Rev A M Coxon, MA), and assisted by the Rev W M Penfold. Mr G R Wilkes was at the organ and as the guests were assembling, he played a prelude "Scena Prima" by Wagner. The surpliced choir was in attendance, and during the service which was fully choral, the hymns Praise My Soul and Love Divine were sung.

Charming Bride

The bride, who was given away by her father, looked charming in a dress of hyacinth blue georgette, with hat to tone. She wore a string of crystal beads and carried a bouquet of carnations and lilies of the valley.

Miss Jean Bentley, sister of the bride, and Miss Barbara Coe, cousin of the bride were bridesmaids. The former was prettily attired in a dress of shell pink georgette with hat to match. She carried a bouquet of pink tulips, and her diamante bracelet was a gift of the bridegroom. Miss Coe wore a dress of pale yellow georgette, with hat to tone, and she had a silver bracelet a gift from the bridegroom. She carried a bouquet of yellow tulips. The bride's mother was attired in a dress of navy *blue satin faced with grey satin and she carried a crimson carnation bouquet.*

Reception at Park Pavillion

Mr F Laws was the best man, and the duties of groomsman were carried out by Mr W L Bentley.

At the close of the service the organist played Elgar's Salut d'Armoir, and as the bride and bridegroom left the church, the Bridal March from Lohengrin was played.

A reception attended by 60 guests was held at Park Pavillion, Tunstall.

Both the bride and bridegroom were the recipients of numerous presents. The staff of Forster Street Junior Girl's School, of which the bride was a member, presented the bride with a long brass tea tray and hand painted vase, and the bridegroom was presented with a mahogany chiming clock by the staff of the soft furnishing department of Messrs J and N Phillips Ltd of Manchester.

Without doubt, Bill and Marjorie's wedding will have been a wonderful celebration, and a great send-off as the couple started their married life together in Sheffield, prior to moving to Chelford, Cheshire, a couple of years later.

Tony's Early Years

William Antony Longworth, always known as 'Tony', was born on Sunday 12 March 1933 at Langham Lea Nursing Home, Stamford Road, Bowdon, Cheshire. At the time, Tony's parents, Bill and Marjorie Longworth, were living at 23 Delahays Road, Hale, Cheshire, along with his older sister, Jean Maureen, known as 'Maureen', who had been born in 1931.

Family memory has it that Tony was late in making an appearance into this world, so much so, that Bill drove the expectant Marjorie down Tatton Mile in Knutsford, which was cobbled at the time, hoping that the jolting of the car would speed the delivery along!

I believe the family spent two years living in Hale, and prior to that lived in Eccleshall, Sheffield – 110 High Storrs Road.

Tony's father, Bill Longworth, had grown up in Ardwick, Manchester. Bill didn't have the easiest of starts in life with his father dying when he was only six years old, leaving his mother to struggle bringing up six children on her own. Bill left school at fourteen and took up an apprenticeship at J & N Phillips. Bill stayed with the company all his life, ended up doing very well managing the buying department.

Tony's mother, Marjorie Bentley, grew up in Tunstall, Staffordshire. Marjorie had a very happy and stable childhood and, like Bill, was one of six siblings. After leaving school Marjorie worked as a teacher and helped run the Sunday school at Christ Church, Tunstall.

Tony really hit the jackpot in terms of parents, with Bill's understanding of the need to work hard to get on in life to be able to provide for a family and with Marjorie's belief in a solid education and the importance of a stable and loving family life; he couldn't have wanted for a better combination.

What was going on in the world in the year Tony was born? George V was on the throne and Labour MP Ramsey-McDonald was prime minister. The film *King Kong* was released in America; *Babar the King* was published and the first photo of Nessie the Loch Ness Monster was captured. Within the next five years after Tony's birth, driving tests and speed limits were introduced, although if you were already driving you didn't have to take a test! BBC Television began broadcasting, *The Hobbit* was published and Jesse Owens won gold at the Berlin Olympics.[11]

Tony's first two years were spent living at the house in Hale, and unsurprisingly, he had no recollections from this time. However, we do know that his parents bought the family home, Colebrooke in Chelford, Cheshire, when he was about two years old. It was a detached property built around 1910, set well back from the road with roughly three acres, made up of gardens with a field at the back.

The house had three bedrooms and a bathroom upstairs, and downstairs a cloakroom, lounge, dining room and kitchen. There was a greenhouse and two sheds, one near the vegetable patch and a larger one close to the house. There was also a pond upon which, in the summer months, Tony used to sail his model boat, and in the winter, skate on the ice. I suspect the black-and-white photo of the house, was taken not long after moving in as the gardens that Bill and Marjorie planted aren't well established.

The colour photo shows the progression the house took, with the bungalow that was built in the mid-1960s, and clearly visible is the vegetable patch by the field, the rose garden and rose bough. There

---

11   Wikipedia Various

Tony's Early Years

Above: Colebrooke

Above: Bill and Harry Coe panelling the dining room, and relaxing on back lawn at Colebrooke

used to be horses on the field until the start of World War II when it was turned over to produce vegetables.

The dining room was a particularly striking room panelled in oak, with shelving on one wall for books. Tony's father Bill, together with Harry Coe (Marjorie's uncle), panelled the room themselves. I remember being told that the wood from the shelving came from the sides of an old coal cart provided by Harry, who was a colliery manager in Worsley. I'm delighted that a photo of this exists and another of the pair of them relaxing on the lawn, perhaps after they finished their endeavours. The black Wedgewood bust seen in the photo is in my possession and I believe it came from Marjorie's side of the family.

The property was situated on Peover Road (now Pepper Street) in Chelford, a small village in Cheshire. Peover Road was a quiet country lane lying on the edge of the village with The Egerton Arms at the top of the lane, which the family frequented. Chelford itself was a farming community with one of the largest cattle markets in the country, and in 1931 had a population of 341.[12]

Although it was a small community, there was a station with trains running to both Manchester and Crewe. One of Tony's fondest memories was standing on the gate at the bottom of Common Farm Lane, Snelson, waiting for his father to pass by on the train and throw sweets out of the window at him and Maureen. Walks 'down the lane' continued for all subsequent generations with great fondness.

Family life at Colebrooke was a happy one. From the photos that Tony's parents took, there were plenty of family gatherings showing bowling and tennis matches, the tireless game of running under the hosepipe and generally enjoying the wonderful large garden. Tony remembered with fondness the family dog, a golden Labrador called Peter, who was buried, along with all the Longworth family

---

12   Chelford, a Cheshire Village

Tony's Early Years

pets over the years, in the woodland near the 'green shed' by the field.

When Tony was a boy, he recalled his father taking him onto the 'big lawn' at the back of the house on a number of occasions, to watch the Northern Lights which could be seen clearly. Sadly, light pollution hinders them being visible in Cheshire anymore.

With Tony's father working long hours in Manchester and travelling around the country and frequently to Europe, help was required to run the home. Alfred Barnes was their gardener and used to chauffeur the family around in a Vauxhall 14, reg number CVT 141. From Tony's memory, his father sold the car to a man at Knutsford Fair who went to his caravan and opened up a safe, which was "stuffed with fivers" and duly paid Bill for it! I particularly like this photo of Tony on a horse with Alfred beside him.

Left: Tony in field at Colebrooke on a pony with Alfred Barnes, the gardener

Bessie Worthington was the first maid they employed – she lived in a cottage close to the post office and walked across the fields to Colebrooke. Thereafter, Ethel Tomkinson was their long-time home help, who worked for the family for many years and was held dear. Ethel lived in a cottage on Common Lane very close to the house. Maureen's son, David, remembered Ethel being very supportive of Bill's struggle with asthma and emphysema over the years.

I have included below some beautiful photos of life in these early years at Colebrooke from the stash we found:

Above: Bill, holding a hosepipe with two unknown children, probably cousins, getting drenched; Tony sitting on a haystack

Above: Maureen and Tony on the back lawn; Tony and Maureen on bikes, presumably racing around the house as my siblings and I used to do

Above: Bill (left) bowling with Fred (Marjorie's father), Marjorie and baby Tony on the bench; Bill holding Tony and Maureen

There were significant changes to the Royal Family in Tony's early years, which would have undoubtedly been a big source of discussion within the Longworth household. 6 May 1935 was King George V's Silver Jubilee, which was declared a bank holiday with plenty of celebrations across the country. Perhaps there was a family gathering at Colebrooke, and quite possibly some of the photos included below could have been from such an event.

A year later, George V died and Edward VIII acceded the throne. Not long after the monarchy was thrown into a constitutional crisis when King-Emperor Edward VIII proposed to Mrs Wallis Simpson, an American socialite who was divorced from her first husband and was pursuing the divorce of her second. At the time, the Church of England didn't allow divorced people to remarry in church if their ex-spouses were still alive, and, as Edward was the nominal head of the Church of England, it was widely believed that Edward could not marry Wallis and remain on the throne. The widespread opposition to Mrs Simpson and Edward's refusal to give her up led to his decision to abdicate in December 1936.

Edward was incredibly popular throughout Britain and the Commonwealth. Consequently, when he renounced the throne to marry Mrs Simpson, the country found it almost impossible to believe. As a whole, the population knew nothing about her until just before the abdication, which must have made it all the more shocking, and once again, the Longworth household would have followed this story with a keen interest.

Edward abdicated in favour of his brother, Bertie, the Duke of York, who took the name of George when crowned. George VI was very reluctant to accept the throne, especially as he was a shy and nervous man with a very bad stutter. However, having inherited the steady virtues of his father George V, and with the incredible support of both his wife Elizabeth and mother Queen Mary, over time he became very popular and well-loved by the British people. This was in part due to the example of courage and fortitude the King and Queen set during World War II. They chose to remain at Buckingham Palace throughout the war, which was bombed more than once. George VI was also in close contact with Prime Minister Winston Churchill and both had to be dissuaded from landing with the troops in Normandy on D-Day![13]

The photos here certainly show that the family had fun. From Tony and Maureen's memories, Marjorie played the piano and her father, Fred, enjoyed singing. Bill played the piano by ear and the concertina. Cards must have been played frequently as Maureen remembered her maternal grandmother, Isabella, always winning at whist. Tony remembered that for entertainment in the evenings Marjorie would play the piano, Bill the concertina and all would enjoy a good singalong. Maureen described her mother as being "quite strict, small, fine boned and strong".

Maureen's daughter, Fiona Birchenall, shared some lovely memories of Bill and Marjorie.

"Grandpa often took me for walks in Chelford woods to look for wildlife." Although Marjorie died when Fiona was a young girl she remembered "staying the night with them, climbing into their bed in the morning, Grandpa bringing a tray of tea up, Nannie tipping some tea into a saucer for me and stressing that under no circumstances was I to tell my mum that she'd done that [I never did]".

David Birchenall, Maureen's youngest son, remembered Bill's love of his rose beds "which were always immaculate", and the water pump on the patio which they were taught how to prime and pump. I remember being taught how to get water out of the pump – it was always icy cold. The pump continued working up until the 1980s when the water table dropped. David remembered that Bill was always calm and interested in what they had been up to. Whilst Marjorie wasn't a big drinker, just the odd sherry, they both remembered Bill's love of Bell's Whiskey, with David being made to pour Bill a drink from the age of five – the smell put him off whiskey for years!

Tony kept various commemoration mugs that he had been given over the years, these included the Silver Jubilee of Queen Mary and

---

[13] www.historic-uk.com/HistoryUK/HistoryofBritain/King-George-VI/

Tony's Early Years

Above: Tony in goal with hands on the ball appearing to have just saved a goal

Above: Tony is with Maureen and unknown child, his father is standing RHS, unknown other man

Above: Relaxing against 'the bank' on the front lawn left to right: Ted Croker (married to Bill's sister Vi), Alan Croker (Ted and Vi's son), unknown, Tony and Bill. On the ground next to Bill is a lovely leather football and a cap, perhaps they are resting after a game!

Above: The group photo in the back garden is, back row from left to right: Fred and Fran Gaskill, Vi Croker, Marjorie. Front row left to right: Alan Croker, Tony, unknown, Maureen, unknown and Marjorie Croker. Fran and Vi were Bill's sisters

King George V 1935, the coronation of King Edward VIII 1937, which never went ahead, and King George VI and Queen Elizabeth in 1937. Royal memorabilia can be traced back to the coronation of King Charles II in 1661 when ceremonial pomp was encouraged after ten years of puritanical austerity under Oliver Cromwell. It wasn't until transfer printing for pottery was invented that royal pottery became more widely available, and under the reign of Queen Victoria the commemoration market really took off, as few subjects knew what the Queen looked like, so a mug on the mantlepiece helped them to identify with her.[14]

---

14 https://www.investorschronicle.co.uk/2012/05/31/your-money/the-value-of-royal-memorabilia-6xMp25YhOyhu2zgwju6dxK/article.html

Sentimental Gifts and Possessions

This seems a fitting place to add a little section about gifts that Tony remembered receiving, some of which he kept all his life. One of these was a racing car teapot with the registration number OKT42 (photo below). He told me it was a gift for his fifth birthday, and that seems to fit as his teapot was manufactured between the years 1935–39. I think it was a prized possession as it is still in mint condition, and I remember only being allowed to use it on my birthday when it was filled with orange squash. I am now the proud owner of it.[15]

Above: OKT42 teapot and prayer book

The two photos next to the teapot are of a little prayer book that Tony's maternal grandparents, Fred and Isabella Bentley, gave to him when he was a child. Tony kept it in his bedside drawer for many years, and I read two of the prayers at his funeral.

Tony remembered that his mother once took him to a toy shop, where he desperately wanted a toy steam train, but he wasn't allowed this and was bought a bow-and-arrow set instead. He remembered really enjoying playing with the bow and arrow, but never forgot the disappointment of not receiving a much-hoped-for gift!

Another prized possession, and treated with kid gloves, was Tony's Native American outfit (at the time called a Red Indian outfit). I don't

---

15   www.okt42.info

know where it came from, but he clearly loved it as the costume was incredibly well-cared for, so much so that all his children and some of the grandchildren were able to wear it, albeit under quite strict surveillance! It is now in the possession of Tony's youngest daughter, Kate, for her boys to enjoy. The photo of Tony wearing it was taken at Colebrooke.

There is a possibility that Tony took part in the Knutsford Royal May Day celebrations wearing this outfit. Amongst the photos found was one of a boy wearing a costume in the parade but it wasn't clear if it was Tony or not. Perhaps he wore one and loved it so much he asked for his own costume, or perhaps he was watching the parade, saw the boy wearing the outfit and made the request; we will never know.

Above: Tony wearing costume at Colebrooke. Front and back showing amazing headdress with feathers, ribbons and hand-painted decorations

Whichever is true, it is a nice link to the past, as, when I was a child, there was always huge excitement for May Day weekend in Knutsford. We always watched the parade and were taken to the funfair for rides on the dodgems, Waltzer and helter-skelter. We were treated to candyfloss and toffee apples, and Tony always enjoyed a couple of packets of brandy snaps. Various goldfish were won over the years from the hook-a-duck or rifle range stands.

Very happy memories made, especially in the knowledge that Tony enjoyed it as a child too, and that I now find myself volunteering at the event.

Knutsford Royal May Day began in 1864 and is the highlight in the town. It achieved the 'Royal' prefix in 1887 from Their Majesties King Edward VII and Queen Alexandra. The parade through the town's streets culminates on The Heath with the crowning of the May Queen. A unique custom of the celebrations involves 'sanding' the streets, when various pictures and words of good wishes decorate the pavements. It is believed the origins go back to 1017, when legend has it that King Canute shook sand out of his shoes having crossed a river in the town at the same time as a bridal party walked by, and he wished them well.[16]

Days Out

As with many families, days out were enjoyed to local attractions and beauty spots – Tony remembered trips up to The Cat and The Fiddle in the Peak District. One of these trips was to the recently opened (1931) Chester Zoo. From my research, lions were first introduced to the zoo in 1937, and I strongly suspect the photos below of Tony, Maureen and Bill are shortly after the lion's arrival. You can see the unbridled joy in Tony's face on seeing said lions! Other animals on display at the time were a polar bear, a chimpanzee and a tapir. There was also a penguin pool, parrot aviaries and an aquarium. In the early days of the zoo there were very few visitors, but it has become an unbridled success and is in the top fifteen zoos in the world. Today, the zoo specialises in conservation and science, with a mission to prevent extinction.[17]

---

16 https://www.knutsford-royal-mayday.co.uk/knutsford-royal-may-day/
17 https://www.historyofuptonbychester.org.uk/zoo.html#:~:text=In%201930%20Mottershead%20moved%20to,was%20finally%20granted%20in%201931.

Above: Tony holding his father's hand at Chester Zoo, and spotting lions with his father and sister

Family Holidays

With Tony's father being in a good, stable job, the family were also able to enjoy holidays. From Tony's recollections they went to Southport, Rhyl, Borth y Gest, Abersoch and Blackpool, and although Bill travelled to Europe with his job the family never went as "no one went abroad in those days".

Some photos have been kept from their holiday/trip to Blackpool in August 1938. The family spent time on the beach, in the sea, digging sandcastles, having a ride on a donkey and most probably, a trip down North Pier, where they may have enjoyed a ride on the carousel, spent some money in the many shops or in the arcade, or simply relaxed in the sun lounge. They all seem to be in their Sunday best, with Tony wearing a tie and shorts with creases down the front, Marjorie has a smart coat on with a broach and hat, and if you look at the shoes on the steps behind the photo where Tony is lying down, Bill has his smart leather shoes on! I find the photo of Bill with Tony and Maureen in the sea particularly joyous. Old-fashioned seaside fun.

Above: Maureen and Tony on Blackpool beach and both with their mother, Marjorie

Above: Tony, Maureen and their father, Bill, on Blackpool beach

The photo/postcard below of Tony and Maureen on a donkey was perhaps taken in a studio on the pier. Printed on the back is "Charles Howell, Official Photographer, Pleasure Beach, Blackpool", a classic seaside image. The adjacent photo is of the medal that Tony is wearing in some of these photos; he told us that it was a medal for football, but I think it is more likely to be from the 'Strongman' game popular at the time, when a mallet is brought down on a puck and the height the puck reaches indicates your strength, especially as the medal is of a 'strongman'. I have memories of making Tony play this game during my childhood years and being thrilled that he could 'ring the bell' at the top. It is likely that Tony or his father won this medal on this trip for playing the game. Tony gave the medal to his grandson, James Anderson.[18]

Above: Tony and Maureen on donkey at Blackpool Pleasure Beach. Strongman medal that Tony is wearing in all photos at Blackpool.

I'm choosing to include one or two more holiday photos here, as they are just such a lovely portrayal of what a happy and loving family they were.

Left: Taken on holiday in Borth y Gest, Porthmadog in North Wales. The family are in their Sunday best for a walk once again. And Tony on the beach

18   www.piers.org.uk/piers/blackpool-north-pier

Tony's Early Years

Above: Maureen, Bill and Tony in field, place unknown. Tony, Bill and Maureen on boat off coast of Abersoch

The two photos above are from a later date and, once again, Sunday best is worn in the left photo. The photo on the boat was taken off the coast near Abersoch on the Llyn Peninsular. A family friend had let them use their holiday cottage somewhere in the area, and it was on this trip that Tony and his good friend, Bob, nearly got swept out to sea on a rowing boat (see later under Bob Neill).

September 1939 and World War II

Whilst the family were enjoying life in the northwest of England, trouble was brewing in Germany in the form of Adolf Hitler, and it is impossible to write about this time without including reference to World War I, which will have had an enormous impact on everyone and everything, and it seemed appropriate to include a brief synopsis here:

The instability created in Europe by World War I (1914–18) set the stage for another international conflict – World War II (September 1939–September 1945), which broke out two decades later and proved even more devastating. Rising to power in an economically and politically unstable Germany, Adolf Hitler, leader of the Nazi Party, rearmed the nation and signed strategic treaties with Italy and Japan to further his ambitions of world domination. Hitler's invasion of Poland on 1 September 1939 drove Great Britain and France to declare war on Germany two days later, marking the beginning of World War II. Over the next six years the conflict would take more lives – an estimated 45–60 million – and destroy more land and property around the globe than any previous war. Eight months after the start of the war, Winston Churchill became prime minister, rallied the British people and led the country from the brink of defeat to victory.[19]

Wondering how quickly this event would impact on the family's life in Cheshire, I spent some time in Knutsford Library reading the weekly local paper (Knutsford division of *The Guardian*), the answer being – with immediate effect. Two days after war was declared the newspaper was reporting on what to do in the event of an air raid or poison gas attack. It reported that all cinemas and theatres should

---

19   www.history.com/topics/world-war-ii/world-war-ii-history

close until further notice, as well as all sports meetings, although churches and other places of worship were to remain open. Petrol was beginning to be rationed, and there was to be 'no night baking'. Evacuees began to arrive in the town.

There is also a report that the Red Cross Society gained many new members to aid in the war effort. Maureen told me that Marjorie was a keen member of the local Red Cross Society so perhaps she was part of this cohort joining up to play her part and doing the right thing.

From an article in the same paper in October 1939, horses were being requisitioned for use by the army. The article made comment that owners of valuable racehorses weren't very happy as they felt they weren't remunerated enough for them. Tony remembered having horses on the field behind Colebrooke, but that during the war the horses disappeared and the field was turned over to grow crops. Perhaps this is what happened to all those horses – they were requisitioned for use in the army, with the field becoming part of the 'Dig for Victory' scheme, when people were encouraged to grow their own vegetables in gardens and allotments.

Blackouts happened very swiftly, with fines issued to those who didn't follow the rules, with their names then appearing in the paper. A drop-in facility was opened so people could check their gas masks were working correctly, and spot checks came into effect to ensure they were being carried at all times.

With the arrival of food rationing in January 1940, recipes were a regular feature as well as tips on how to 'make do and mend' in all areas of life.

Cheshire was visited regularly by the Luftwaffe during World War II, leaving behind devastation and often casualties. I remember Tony telling me that the German bombers would fly overhead on their way to and from Manchester or other nearby targets and drop unused bombs on the way back – whether this is true or not I don't know, but from a website dedicated to Cheshire and it's people during recent conflicts, there is a long list of all the air raids on the county, with hits on local villages including Ollerton, Siddington, Mere, Cranage as well as Chelford.[20]

Tony also remembered hearing doodlebugs flying overhead. Doodlebugs (V1 flying bombs) were winged bombs powered by a jet engine that had been launched from a ramp or adapted bomber aircraft. On Christmas Eve 1944, forty-five doodlebugs were launched off the coast of Yorkshire aimed at Manchester. Some of these landed in Cheshire, including one on Seven Sisters Lane in Ollerton, less than three miles from the Longworth home, Colebrooke. Perhaps this is the bomb Tony remembered. The crater is still visible today.[21]

During such bombings, the family would have taken cover in the air-raid shelter that was situated in the front garden of Colebrooke. The shelter had a large cover over the opening with concrete steps descending to an underground room, which, from Tony's memory, had bunk beds, presumably for him and Maureen to sleep in. I remember, on hot summer days growing up, Tony would, very occasionally, open the entrance to the shelter and if we were feeling brave, we would cautiously creep down the stairs to the now-flooded room, greeted by the occasional toad. I wonder who else sheltered there with the family.

Life clearly carried on, not as normal, but with determination and bravery; during the Blitz of Manchester Tony remembered his mother taking him Christmas shopping to Lewis's, the grand department store near Piccadilly (now Primark), with buildings still smouldering all around him. Not something you would forget easily. He also recalled being taken to The Edge, a local landmark in Alderley Edge with a clear view of Manchester, to watch the bombs dropping – must have had quite an impact on young Tony.

Christmas during wartime was a more subdued affair than families would have been used to. Due to blackouts, there would have been no Christmas lights in the streets, but families would still have decorated

---

20   www.cheshireroll.co.uk/cheshire-air-raids
21   www.iwm.org.uk/history/the-V1-flying-bomb-hitlers-vengeance-weapon

their homes with trees and made decorations – a favourite was paper chains made out of painted strips of newspaper. Homes would have been decorated with holly sprigs above pictures (I remember Tony doing this when I was a child), and the Ministry of Food had tips too: "a Christmassy sparkle is easy to add to sprigs of holly or evergreen for use on puddings. Dip your greenery in a strong solution of Epsom salts. When dry it will be beautifully frosted."

Many gifts would have been home-made: knitted scarfs or gloves, jams and chutneys. Practical gifts were popular – in 1940 the most popular gift was soap!

With rationing in place, families would have saved their coupons and hoarded items for weeks in advance to have a festive feast, although tea and sugar were increased at Christmas. Turkey wasn't served and Tony fondly remembered eating goose on Christmas Day. As a child I remember Tony suggesting we have goose for Christmas instead of turkey, and that he was met with a chorus of negativity. Looking back now, I can see he was probably remembering his childhood Christmas's and feeling a little nostalgic and I confess to feeling a little sorry that we didn't indulge him.

Family and friends would have gathered to play card games such as Pontoon, board games like Ludo or Sorry, and would have enjoyed listening to the wireless. I know Tony's family loved a singalong, and some of the most popular Christmas songs today come from the war years: 'I'll be Home for Christmas', 1943 and 'I'm Dreaming of a White Christmas', 1942.[22]

One of Tony's favourite stories, worth mentioning here, involves Generals Patton and Eisenhower. Their American troops were based at Peover Hall in Over Peover, only a couple of miles from Colebrooke, and Tony fondly remembered standing at the end of the drive waving to General Patton as he drove past in his car with his dog, an English bull terrier, alongside him. The Generals' local was the The Bells of

---

22   www.iwm.org.uk/history/how-britain-celebrated-christmas-during-the-second-world-war

Peover pub, and they and the soldiers worshipped at St Lawrence Church at Peover Hall. After the war, General Patton kept a promise to return to Peover for a service of thanksgiving, where his standard was presented to the church. Perhaps General Patton was on his way to this service when Tony remembered waving at him.

Returning to the wider family story; on 3 September 1939 – the day Great Britain and France declared war on Germany – the family were attending the wedding of Marjorie's older brother, Cyril, to Eva. The reception took place at The Swan Inn, Tunstall, Staffs, where Marjorie's parents, Fred and Isabella, were the proprietors. A few photos were taken, and this is the best one, captured in the back yard of the pub.

Tony's sister, Maureen, was a bridesmaid (central in the photo in between Cyril and Eva). Tony is next to Eva looking incredibly smart. Other people of note in the photo are Aunty Jean Bentley (Marjorie's younger sister) and her husband Idris Thomas on the left-hand side, looking very young and happy; Uncle Joe Bentley (Marjorie's younger brother) fifth from the right at the back – it seems to me that Tony's ears may come from the Bentley side of the family as they really do resemble Joe's! Standing to the left slightly behind Cyril, is Isabella, Marjorie's mother, and directly behind Cyril is Marjorie.

Above: Wedding party at the back of the Swan Inn, Tunstall, see above for who is who

Many years later, I took Maureen and Tony on a trip to Tunstall, Stoke, where their maternal grandparents (Fred and Isabella) lived, and their mother had grown up. The day trip sparked some memories for them both. Tony remembered the wedding, and that although it was a happy occasion, the mood was sombre due to war being declared on the same day.

For Maureen, she remembered what a wonderful voice their grandfather, Fred Bentley, had and that he was constantly singing. She also remembered that Fred would stand her on the bar in The Swan Inn and ask her to sing songs, which she did, but she couldn't remember what!

One of Fred's favourite songs to sing was 'It Ain't Gonna Rain No Mo' by Wendell Hall, which was sung at the FA Cup Final in 1925 by Sheffield United supporters, making it a popular football song of the era. Another favourite song of Fred's was 'Yankee Doodle Dandy' – the popular American song, written in 1755 by a British doctor during the French and Indian War when King George III sent British soldiers to protect the American colonists. The song was written to mock the colonists who the British soldiers thought were crude and cowardly. The tune is thought to be much older than the lyrics with European or British origins.[23] [24]

Joe Bentley and Sunny Coe

So many families suffered tragedies during World War II and Tony's did not escape. During Tony's years at Sandbach School, two tragic events were to befall the family.

On 4 August 1942, Tony's much-beloved Uncle Joe, his mother's youngest brother, was killed in action, "lost without trace", at the age of twenty-three years. Flight Sergeant Joseph Harold Bentley flew in Lancasters as a wireless operator and air gunner.

---

[23] www.kennedy-centre/story-behind-the-song/yankeedoodle
[24] www.wikipedia.org/wiki/it-aint-gonna-rain-no-mo

At the time, Joe was flying with Bomber Command Number 44 (Rhodesia) Squadron.

Tony kept a couple of cards and a letter that Joe sent him – birthday card below. From a letter written in March 1941/42 Joe writes:

How are you doing at winter sports, you should be able to bring that big chest of yours into play now and show the other boys what you can do; I've started deep breathing so that I can keep up with you.

Looking at Tony's expression on the photo below, it is very clear to see how happy he and his sister Maureen are to be with their Uncle Joe. The photo was taken at Colebrooke. No date.

Above: Maureen, Uncle Joe and Tony. Birthday telegram to Tony from Uncle Joe

Trying to expand my understanding of what Uncle Joe's role was in the war, I did a little research on the role of Lancaster planes in World War II, and gleaned a very good synopsis from the RAF Museum website, which is where the following information comes from.[25]

The prototype made its first flight in January 1941. It was the major heavy bomber used by Bomber Command to take the war to the heartland of Nazi Germany, replacing the Manchester bomber which had experienced problems.

---

25   www.rafmuseum.org.uk/blog/the-lancaster-enters-the-fray

The average age of the seven-man crew was only twenty-two years. They endured danger and discomfort, and many showed great courage in continuing to fly, knowing the odds against survival was high. Bomber Command suffered the highest casualty rate of any branch of the British services in World War II. On average, Lancasters completed twenty-one missions before being lost.

The crew of the plane had to work closely together to undertake the mission given to them and to return home safely. Uncle Joe seems to have had two different jobs during his time flying Lancasters, as both a wireless operator and an air gunner.

The wireless operator was a multi-purpose role, responsible for monitoring the wireless and communications. Part of this role would involve him activating the Identification Friend or Foe signal and giving false signals to the enemy to help suppress searchlights and the constant terror of flak. He had to check the bomb bay to ensure it was operating correctly and act as look-out through the observation dome directing the pilot and gunners in the event of an enemy aircraft attack. When a bombing run was in progress, he would spend most of his time there. He also had to have a working knowledge of the navigator's role so he could take over if necessary and was expected to give first aid to members of the crew.

The air gunner was in the last third of the aircraft. His world was the small Perspex mid-upper turret – vulnerable to night fighters and flak. This bubble contained two Browning 0.303in machine guns, each with one thousand rounds of ammunition. When strapped into the hammock-type seat, the air gunner could rotate this through 360 degrees to enable a wide field of fire to defend the Lancaster. Experienced air gunners would often remove a section of the Perspex for a better view and to combat the misting that could occur. The air gunner was recognised as a specialist in his field.

Quite a lot is known about the sorties that Uncle Joe undertook. Firstly, Tony's grandmother, Isabella Bentley (Joe's mother) gave Joe's flying logbook to Tony, which he treasured and is now in Guy Longworth's possession. Secondly, in 2007, Tony contacted the No

44 (Rhodesia) Squadron Association requesting further information about Joe. He received a reply from the Squadron Secretary, detailing "bits that would not ordinarily appear in the logbook" and he included some extracts from a book entitled *44 (Rhodesia) Squadron on Operations* by Alan White. And lastly, I contacted No 49 Squadron who were very helpful in sending through what they have. Included below are a couple of the 'bits' and extracts from the book (the pilot of the crew, Joe, flew with was Flight Officer Peter Ball):

Few operations were carried out during the first 2 or 3 months of 1942. Fg Off Ball's crew first flew a mission to Essen on 10 March followed by another on 18 April, again to Essen. At this time, six of the squadron's crews were in training for a daring daylight raid on the MAN diesel engine factory at Augsburg. This took place on 19 April and, sadly, only 1 of the six crews returned. It was on this raid that Sqn Ldr John Nettleton won a VC.

After the Augsburg setback, operational flying resumed in earnest in May and Fg Off Ball's crew took part in both the first and second thousand bomber raids on 30 May and 1 June respectively. In June the crew took part in two detachments to Nutts Corner (Northern Ireland) from where they carried out convoy support duties. It was on 15 June that they sighted a U-Boat on the surface about 5 miles from the convoy. They went into attack the U-Boat which crash dived about 15 seconds before they released their depth charges from 50ft. It is quite likely that they damaged it. He was unable to remain in the area because he was short of fuel, the total sortie lasting 10 hours 20 minutes.

The bomb loads carried on their bombing raids varied enormously from 1 x 4000lb bomb and 720 x 4lb incendiary bombs, to 112 x 30lb incendiaries or 1260 x 4lb incendiaries, depending on the nature of the target. The crew had rather a frightening experience on 28 July during a raid on Saarbrucken. Their fuel gauges showed wrong readings and, at one stage, showed that they had only 170 gallons left to get from the target area back to base. As the gauges crept towards zero, the captain ordered the crew to prepare to abandon the aircraft. After the gauges reached zero, and the engines kept turning, they realised that there was a technical fault. Very worrying!

The pace was maintained throughout August. Raids were made on three consecutive nights; Essen being attacked on the 4th and 5th, and Duisburg on the 6th. Heavy icing was encountered on the night of the 4th forcing two of the Sqn to abort; of the remaining three Fg Off Ball failed to return.

There is no indication of what happened on 4th August to cause their loss. One other crew on that raid reported considerable and accurate anti-aircraft fire.

Above: Joe Bentley, DFM, Tony's uncle

Joe is remembered at the Runnymede Memorial, which is the Air Forces Memorial dedicated to over 20,000 men and women from air forces of the British Empire who were lost in air and other operations during World War II. Those recorded have no known grave anywhere in the world and many were lost without trace. The memorial is near Egham in Surrey and well worth a visit – very sobering.

Prior to being in this squadron, Joe was part of 49 Bomber Squadron, and during this time he was awarded the DFM (Distinguished Flying Medal), which his mother, Isabella, gave to Tony. The medal is now in the possession of Guy Longworth, Tony's son. DFMs were generally awarded for good airmanship over a period of time. When I contacted 49 Squadron they requested a photo of Joe to include on their website, and the photo included here now appears on their website: www.49squadron.co.uk/personnel_index/detail/bentley_jh.

Tony kept his childhood autograph book (now in the possession of Guy Longworth), and I felt it appropriate to include the entries below. Dated 14 April 1941, Joe Bentley and the pilot Peter Ball have signed the book and included lists of some of their missions. It seems that Peter Ball visited Colebrooke on one of Joe's home visits. It is worth noting here that Peter was one of five sons, three of whom were killed in the war.

Above: Two photos from Tony's autograph book

A few pages later, written in Tony's mother's hand is the following:

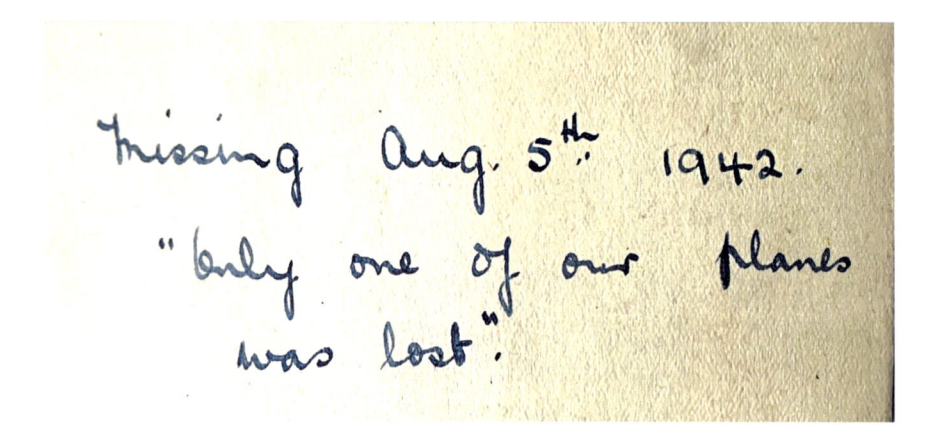

missing Aug. 5th 1942.
"only one of our planes was lost".

I do find it very difficult to comprehend the level of bravery required by the people of World War II, and have found writing about it here both upsetting, moving and extremely humbling. We really don't know how lucky we are.

Above: J H Coe (Sunny)

The other tragedy to befall the family came in July 1944. Marjorie's first cousin, Joseph Harold Coe, known as 'Sunny', was killed in action fighting in France aged twenty-one years.

Corporal J H Coe was part of the East Lancashire Regiment (5th East Lancashire's). I don't know what his movements were prior to the Normandy landings, but was able to glean the following:

Normandy 1944… by the end of June the 1st and 5th East Lancashire's took part in a renewed advance on Caen, during which their B Company fought an action at St Contest. Both East Lancashire battalions then deployed into the close bocage country west of Caen. While the 1st Battalion held a succession of defensive positions in an exposed salient, at Cheux, Grainville and Bougy, the 5th Battalion were involved in offensive action 2-3 miles further west. On 16th July ('Black Sunday') the 5th East

Lancashire suffered some two hundred casualties in an attack at Fontenay-le-Pesnil.[26]

It was in this attack that Sunny was killed, and he is buried at Fonteney-le-Pesnil War Cemetery, Normandy, France.

It was Sunny's father, Harry Coe (Tony's maternal grandmother's brother), who helped Bill panel the dining room at Colebrooke. The families were close and would have been hit hard by this second death.

These two tragic events must have dealt the family a huge shock and sadness; Tony kept photos of both Joe and Sunny on the wall at Colebrooke and whenever he spoke of them it was tinged with deep emotion.

Returning now to the family story, it is clear to me that, as a start in life, Tony couldn't have asked for more – a solid family, surrounded by people who loved him – a great set up prior to starting school.

---

26   www.lancashireinfantrymuseum.org.uk

Yorston Lodge School Knutsford, Cheshire

1939-1942

Tony, aged seven, attended Yorston Lodge School in Knutsford from September 1939 until July 1942. The small school was started by twenty-year-old Grace Brydon in 1904, in a property called The Nest on St John's Avenue, Knutsford. Grace was the daughter of James Brydon, from Scotland, who was the postmaster in the town. Sometime before 1920 the school moved to its second home, 18 St John's Road, and was given the name Yorston Lodge after Grace's great grandmother, Grizel Yorston, who came from the Shetland Isles. Sadly the school closed down in July 2023.

Grace was assisted by her two sisters, Nan and Daisy, and together they built a thriving school. Each day would start with an assembly which would include a bible story, songs and Miss Grace playing the piano. The sisters would reinforce their school motto, 'do and speak to others as you would like them to say and do to you'. Tony would have been given a good grounding in the basic subjects and would have learnt about the League of Nations (forerunner of the United Nations) of which Miss Daisy was a keen supporter.

Perhaps the most exciting part of the school day was the gym lesson, held in the kindergarten classroom where various equipment – leather-covered hoops, rope ladder with wooden slats and a trapeze bar – were lowered from the ceiling.[27]

---

27   *Yorston Lodge School* by Jill Snape

To begin with, Tony was driven to school by Alfred the gardener, until the last year or so when he cycled to school on a regular basis, having to carry his gas mask with him as it was during the war. One day he remembered being "set upon" by bigger boys who stole his Mickey Mouse gas mask. He was very upset about this and regularly recounted the tale.

In Tony's time-honoured style of not throwing anything away, he kept all his reports from his school days, and they are wonderful to read. From the Yorston Lodge reports we know that Tony was taught by Miss Daisy Brydon and that he was "very good" at maths, coming first in the form. He was always attentive in his history, geography, scripture and nature study lessons. French was more of a challenge for Tony "could be more attentive" and it seems like he enjoyed his drawing lessons: "could work well if not distracted by companions." All aspects of English Tony found hard, especially reading and spelling but he was always interested in literature. Miss Daisy describes him as "a good little worker and his progress has been very satisfactory". Reports can be found in the appendix.

There must have been music lessons of some form too, and years later Tony's sister, Maureen, taught piano at the school for a while.

I was delighted to find a photo of Tony at Yorston Lodge. Tony is bottom right, dated July 1939, looking very smart in his school blazer and cap and wearing the biggest smile.

Above: Tony at Yorston Lodge, front row, third from left

Amongst the photos found was one of Tony having won a swimming medal whilst at Yorston Lodge. It is taken in the garden at Colebrooke. He looks extremely happy with himself!

Right: Tony in garden at Colebrooke in swim apparel holding swimming medal

During his years at Yorston Lodge Tony appeared in a play – *Snow White and the Seven Dwarfs*, performed in the upper room of The Angel Pub in Knutsford. I remember so well him telling me that he played the part of Dopey, one of the dwarfs, which I thought was wonderful and promptly became my favourite dwarf when I was a child. *Snow White* was a fairy tale published by The Brothers Grimm in 1812, and it became Disney's first full-length feature film, being released to unanimous acclaim on 4 February 1938.

I like to imagine Tony being taken to see the film at The Marcliff Cinema in Knutsford which had only opened in 1935. It was able to seat 672 people and boasted a stage and two dressing rooms. The cinema is now run by Curzon and has been completely refurbished. I remember the original Marcliff very well, I saw the first *Star Wars* film there, and the cinema was so packed I was seated on an uncomfortable wooden chair rather than the plush cinema seats – I remember sulking for most of the film![28]

Tony recalled going to The Marcliff to watch the newsreels when he was growing up. The British newsreel began in 1910; it was a reel of

---

28   www.cinematreasures.org/theaters/24795

film which lasted around five minutes, showing stories from the week. Initially the films were silent but by the early 1930s sound had been introduced. With sound, the reels increased in length to ten minutes or more, covering the main stories of the day, as well as sporting events and personalities. Politics was handled with great care not to cause controversy. By the late 1950s, with the television becoming more popular, the newsreels started to die out. Many of the newsreels have survived and are now a major historical archive, used in many television documentaries.[29]

---

29   http://bufvc.ac.uk/newsonscreen/learnmore/history

Sandbach School, Sandbach, Cheshire

1942-1946

On Saturday 18 July 1942 Tony sat the entrance exam to Sandbach School, and two days later his parents received a note to say he had passed. On 2 September 1942 at the age of nine, Tony started at the school.

Tony kept the prospectus for Sandbach School, which was founded in 1677 by local philanthropists. The prospectus gives a good insight into its ethos:

> *Sandbach School is designed to provide a liberal, and at the same time, thoroughly practical education: to fit boys for business life as well as for the professions and Universities. Great attention is paid to training in the power of bearing responsibility, to the encouragement of esprit-de-corps, and to the formation of character.*
>
> *Rugby football is played during the Autumn Term; rugby football, cross-country running, and athletics sports in the Spring term; cricket and swimming during the Summer term. Boxing is taken in the Autumn and Spring terms.*
>
> *There are senior and junior literary and debating societies, a camera club (a dark room being provided for the use of the boys) and a voluntary woodwork class.*

The school stood in about eighteen acres of playing fields, with laboratories for chemistry and physics, a gymnasium, open-air swimming pool and a miniature rifle range. Assemblies were held every morning for prayers.

It is interesting that there was a camera club and a dark room – I can well imagine with Tony's love of photography that he will have made use of this during his time at the school.

Tony took the train from Chelford to school; he recounted American troops regularly sitting alongside him. He remembered that his train departed at 8:05am, and that criminals were hung at 8:00am. A gruesome memory, but as we know children love gory details.

It was at Sandbach School that his great friendship with Bob Neill began. Bob recalled their first day as new boys which, by means of an inauguration, included a head dunking under a tap in the quadrangle, and he recalled Tony saying, "I don't think much of this!". During the dunking a new silver pen that Tony's father had given him was stolen – he remembered being very upset by this.

In later years, Bob recalled Tony having a proficiency for athletics – he came third in a cross-country run of five miles. Also, that school continued on a Saturday morning with games: athletics, cricket or rugby.

The adjacent photo is a section from the whole school photo taken in 1946 – note the broken teeth – this must have been after the accident on the lane at the back of Colebrooke, when the family dog, Peter the Labrador, knocked Tony off his bike and he broke his front teeth! Standing to the right of Tony is Bob Neill. Tony is third row in the centre.

Once again, Tony kept all his school reports, eleven in

total. He started in Form I and there were thirty boys in the class. Reports can be found in the appendix.

In the spring term of 1943 Tony dropped fifteen places in the class order. He had been fourth out of thirty but was now fifteenth. This clearly caused some concern, as his father, Bill, wrote to the school enquiring what had happened. The letters are transcribed below:

21 April 1943
From H L Crockett, Headmaster at Sandbach to Bill Longworth

Dear Mr Longworth,

I have been away for a few days and found your letter waiting for me when I returned. I do not think there is any great need to feel alarm at your boy's report, although a drop from fourth to fifteenth in the form order (for no apparent reason) does look at something not quite as it should be. Personally, I think a little extra care and attention on the boy's part will soon put it right, but I shall have a talk with the boys' form master and find out if there is any reason for the falling off. If there is, I will let you know.

 Yours faithfully, H L Crockett

22 April 1943
From A R Manthorp, Form Master to Bill Longworth

Dear Mr Longworth

Your letter dated 16/4/1943 reached me today – Thursday – redirected from the school address, and I am hastening to reply.

 It is rather difficult for me – at home – to put my finger on the particular subjects which caused him to drop in the form order, but perhaps I can help you best if I summarise a few points below:

(i) Form positions are found on total term marks – and he lost 1 week out of 12 by absence. The previous term he did not miss a day and several others had long absences.
(ii) It is easier to get a place on the back line than it is to hold it.
(iii) As I know him – one of his chief troubles has been untidiness in the presentation of his work.

There is no doubt that he has the ability and promise and I don't think you need worry unduly over his drop in position this term. I think perhaps that getting so high the previous term gave him the idea that it was "just too easy", and now he finds it is not so.

As far as I know him, I always find him attentive, and a cheerful boy in class. I am sure that he will pull his weight and that it is probably a good thing for him to learn so early on that to maintain a position – a boy has to keep working.

You ask in what way you can help, and I would say that by watching his progress and by seeing that his prep is done thoroughly, you will be doing a service to him and to the masters at school. It is very pleasing to find parents who are keen in this direction – I am afraid we often get more hindrance than help from many homes.

I will certainly continue, in my usual way, to keep him "at it", and hope that next term's report will be better. Finally, I wish to finish on a note of praise. His running in the Junior Cross Country Race was a good show. 20th out of 105 from 8yrs to 14.

Yours sincerely, Alan R Manthorp

Bill, Tony's father, replied to Mr Manthorp on 5 May 1943 – he had kept a pencil copy of his letter:

5 May 1943
From Bill Longworth to Mr Manthorp

Dear Mr Manthorp

I must apologise for not replying to your very kind letter, but I have been "up to the neck" in fixing contract details and only returned this evening from a business trip to Oxford.

Allow me to express my sincere thanks for your comprehensive reply and to hear from you that my son is capable of much more with the necessary care.

During his holiday I did not discuss his studies, but I shall watch with particular interest his preparation work and you may rest assured of my wholehearted cooperation if you require anything further from me.

Again, many thanks and I hope it will not be long before becoming personally acquainted with you.

Yours sincerely

I have checked Tony's report following the above letters, and by the following term he had risen to tenth in the class, and in July 1944 he was awarded a Prize Certificate for general work and had risen to third place. I found it interesting that at the top of the Prize Certificate is "The War 1939 –", a demonstration, perhaps, of the difficult years. Support and encouragement from his parents must have paid off.

In the bundle of items from Sandbach School were many invoices for the school fees together with receipts. A terms schooling cost £3, 12 schillings and 3 pence, with extra being charged for books, games, and the Old Sandbachians' Association.

As well as photography, Tony always enjoyed art, and kept his sketch book from Sandbach School, it is unsurprising that the sketches were war related.

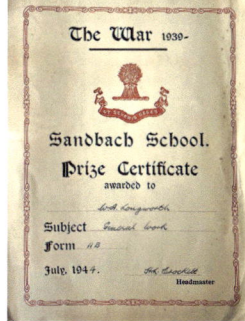

Left: Drawing from sketch book and school prize certificate

From the school reports it is clear that Tony's talent for mathematics continued, with him regularly being top in the class, and that he continued to struggle with English, as well as French and Latin.

Tony remembered his time at Sandbach School with great fondness, and the friendship with Bob Neill that began at the school, lasted his whole life.

During his last year at Sandbach School, World War II finally ended, bringing an end to nearly six years of war, which had seen the loss of life of millions of people around the world, destroyed homes, towns and cities and caused immense suffering. With Berlin surrounded, Adolf Hitler took his own life on 30 April 1945, and his successor then negotiated an unconditional surrender to the Allies. This was signed on 7 May 1945, with Churchill declaring the following day a public holiday to celebrate Victory in Europe (VE Day).

VE Day was filled with rejoicing with many street parties, thanksgiving services and parades. In London, the Ministry of Food had assured Churchill that there was enough beer in the capital, licensing hours were extended, and bonfires and fireworks were lit to mark the occasion. It was also a day of mixed emotions and reflection, and many of those who had lost a loved one felt they could not take part in the celebrations. I feel certain Tony's school will have marked the occasion in some way, as well as some sort of celebration at home too. In June 1946 every British school child was sent a victory certificate by King George VI commemorating the Allied Victory in the Second World War. Tony kept his copy shown below.

The war, however, was not yet over – it still raged in the Far East and the Pacific. Thousands of Allied servicemen were still fighting there, and many were held as prisoners of war in terrible conditions. This included Tony's future father-in-law, John Milnes, who was a Japanese prisoner of war from February 1942 until his release on 2 September 1945. With the Japanese refusing to surrender, even after multiple firebombing campaigns, including the bombing of Tokyo, which resulted in the loss of tens of thousands of lives, and

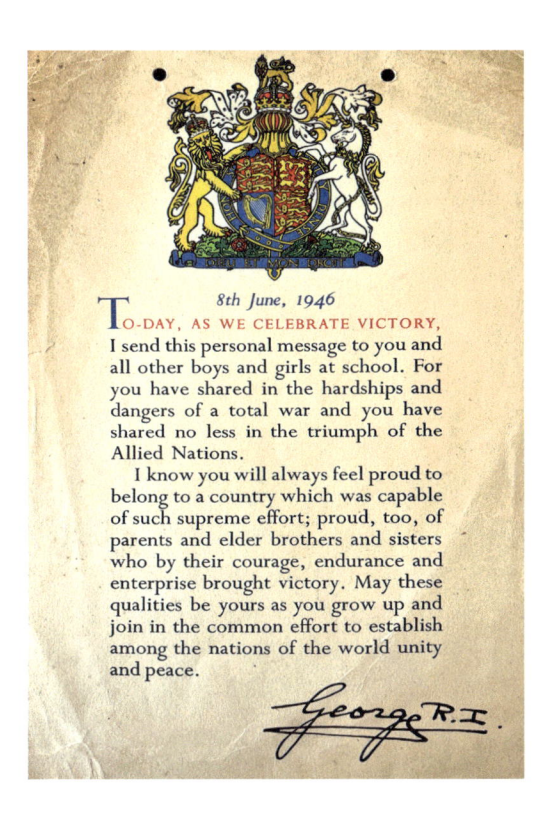

> **8th June, 1946**
>
> TO-DAY, AS WE CELEBRATE VICTORY, I send this personal message to you and all other boys and girls at school. For you have shared in the hardships and dangers of a total war and you have shared no less in the triumph of the Allied Nations.
>
> I know you will always feel proud to belong to a country which was capable of such supreme effort; proud, too, of parents and elder brothers and sisters who by their courage, endurance and enterprise brought victory. May these qualities be yours as you grow up and join in the common effort to establish among the nations of the world unity and peace.
>
> *George R.I.*

heavy casualties continuing on both sides, a decision was taken in early August 1945 to drop the first atomic bomb on two sites in Japan – Hiroshima and Nagasaki, resulting in the loss of many more thousands of lives.

On 10 August 1945, the day after the second bomb dropped, Japan surrendered unconditionally to the Allies (VJ Day), and the war finally ended. Although this meant an end to the fighting, it didn't mean an end to the suffering and hardship. Life slowly returned to normal but with the huge economic cost of the war and a practically bankrupt Britain, years of post-war austerity were to follow.[30]

---

30   https://www.iwm.org.uk/history/what-you-need-to-know-about-ve-day

Sedbergh School, Sedbergh, Cumbria

1946-1950

There is a lot of material relating to Tony's time at Sedbergh, from school reports, diaries, shooting score cards, invoices, to the prospectus and school termly diaries. However, the most exciting find was a series of letters that his parents, other family members and friends sent to Tony whilst he was at school. They really are fascinating to read, and show what a close, loving family they were. Bill and Marjorie really cared about how Tony did at school and were very encouraging. All the letters are transcribed later in this section, together with the transcription of a diary that Tony kept during his first term at the school, which is equally wonderful.

By the time Tony started at Sedbergh the family must have been pretty familiar with Cumbria as his sister, Maureen, attended Fairfield School in Ambleside. The car journeys will have been fairly slow and tortuous up the A6 as the M6 motorway didn't open until 1958.

Sedbergh School was founded in 1525 by Roger Lupton who was born in the parish of Sedbergh. Folklore has it that as there was no local school for Roger Lupton to attend, and that he walked the 270 miles from Sedbergh to London to gain an education. It was whilst he was provost of Eton College that he founded the school. He went on to become the Chaplain to Kings Henry VII and Henry VIII.

Over the years the school grew, with success often being tied to the strength of the headmasters. There was particular growth in the late 1800s with the building of a chapel, classrooms and new boarding houses. Under the tenure ship of Henry Hart, the Old Sedberghian

Club was founded (of which Tony was a lifelong member), the inaugural Wilson Run took place (more later) and the school motto was confirmed as *'Dura Virum Nutrix'* – 'Hardship is the Nurse of Man'.[31]

Tony kept the school prospectus, which just consisted of a booklet of photographs. From the prospectus, the photos below show the chapel, which will have played a large role in Tony's school life; the photo of the OTC training shows the beautiful location of the school in Cumbria, and a venture that Tony went onto enjoy. I know that Tony enjoyed being in the carpentry shop as I have a little desktop bookcase that he made in woodwork classes. Tony enjoyed lessons in the swimming bath, and on looking at the school's current website, the pool has barely changed.

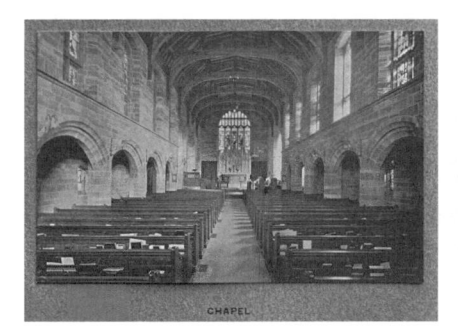

Above: Sedbergh School chapel and the OTC on the Playing Field

Above: Sedbergh School carpentry classroom and swimming bath

---

31   www.sedberghschool.org/senior/information/history-of-sedbergh-school

1946

Thursday 19 September was Tony's first day at Sedbergh School. I imagine he will have been driven to the school by his parents, along with his very smart leather trunk, inscribed with his initials. Years later, both Tony's nephews, Rupert and David Birchenall, went on to use the trunk whilst they were at Sedbergh, and then Tony's youngest daughter Kate, used it when she was at Millfield School, and everyone thought it was very cool! It is now in Kate's possession.

Above: Winder House Sedbergh 2016. Photo reproduced with kind permission, Andrew Mawby

Each pupil was placed in a boarding house and Tony's home from home was Winder House. All Tony's recollections of school were very happy ones, and there is no doubt that his boarding house will have played a part in this. Winder House was set away from the school, along a drive, with a garden and patio, affording panoramic views over the surrounding countryside.

From a postcard sent to his mother, Marjorie, by the school on

25 July, preparations are clearly underway, and with rationing still in place, coupons were being used to purchase uniform:

Blazer – 10 coupons
Jerseys – 4 coupons
Stockings – 2 coupons per pair

There are other things in the shop, such as shorts, sweaters (small size). There is a time set apart on the first day for new boys to be fitted. There should be plenty of all the above articles. The shop closes this week for the holidays. But if you need the things there will be someone there for a few days who will send off the goods if you send the coupons to the Bursar in the Bursary.

The first day of term must have been a busy one ensuring that Tony had all he needed, designed, I suspect, to alleviate pupils' anxieties when saying farewell to their families.

Tony's father kept most of the bills. By the time Tony left Sedbergh the school fees had gone up from £62.00 a term to £75.00 a term. Quite a considerable amount.

Many other things had to be bought and Bill had even kept the invoice for these items, sourced from a local shop – Jackson & Son. Economically, the town of Sedbergh must have enjoyed the business generated by the school.

During his first term Tony studied maths, English, French, geography, divinity, Latin, music and art. Typical of a new school child keenness, Tony copied out his timetable for the first term (D is divinity, SB and LB are short and long break), in what looks to be his best handwriting, and quite possibly a new ink pen!

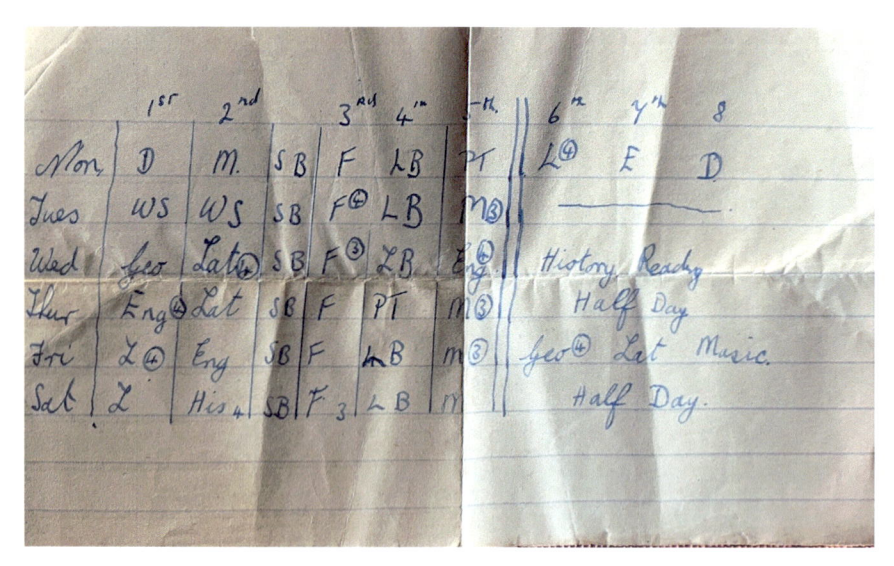

Above: Timetable for the first term in Tony's handwriting

Amongst the boys in Tony's class was Mike Adams, who was a lifelong friend, also staying in Winder House.

From Tony's first report there were fifteen boys in the class, with an average age of fourteen years. It details his height, weight and girth, as well as position in the form – he was sixth overall. As usual he was first in the form for maths, doing well with history, geography and French. Latin is clearly a struggle. School reports can be found in the appendix.

Tony's nickname at school was 'Boat', and amongst the many letters he kept, one addresses him as such.

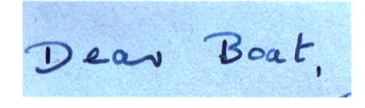

Tony remembered that school continued on Saturday mornings, not necessarily lessons, but 'Dig for Victory' when they dug up a patch of the playing fields and grew vegetables, a skill Tony took into his adult life – I can still taste the freshly picked asparagus, raspberries and peas he grew at Colebrooke.

The meals at Sedbergh clearly made a mark on Tony as they formed part of his 'favourite stories'. He would regularly recount being served whale meat, and on reading his diary from the first term, the meals are a regular feature. He also enjoyed visits to the tuck shop, also known as the grubber, and must have relished receiving parcels of food from his family – his mother once sent him a roast chicken in the post, and, written in the enclosed letter, she requested that he return the tin via the next post!

One weekend a term, parents could visit, and as Tony's sister, Maureen, was at a girl's school in Ambleside, I suspect these were happy family occasions. Chapel was on a Sunday morning, then if you got yourself a sandwich lunch you could go for a walk into the hills, usually around ten to twelve miles according to Tony, or bathe and fish in the river Lune which was very close by.

First Term's Diary

Amongst the items found was Tony's diary from his first term at Sedbergh. As it makes for such wonderful reading, I have transcribed the whole diary below. I have not corrected spellings, but to make it easier to read have added correct punctuation (he wasn't keen on full stops!). The JTC is the Junior Training Corps.

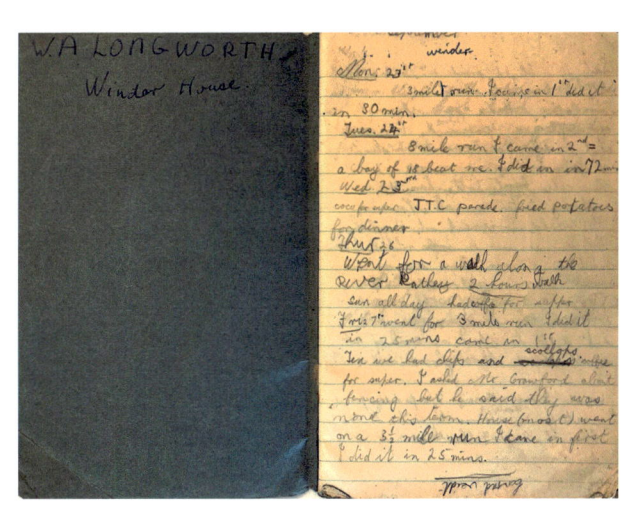

Right: Inside cover and first page of Tony's diary from his first term at Sedbergh

Monday 23rd: 3 mile run. I came in 1st. Did it in 30min.

Tuesday 24th: 8 mile run. I came in 2nd = a boy of 18 beat me. I did it in 72mins.

Wednesday 25th: Coco for supper. JTC parade. Fried potatoes for dinner.

Thursday 26th: Went for a walk along the River Rawthey. 2 hours walk. Sun all day. Had coffee for supper.

Friday 27th: went for a 3 mile run. I did it in 25mins came in 1st. Tea we had chips and scallops. Coffee for supper. I asked Mr Crawford (House Master) about fencing but he said they was none this term. House (most) went on a 3½ mile run. I came in 1st. Did it in 25mins.

Saturday 28th: Slight frost in the morning. It has been the best day so far for weather. Had a game of rugger in afternoon then went to tuck shop. Then listened to England v Ireland. England won 7-2. Man City drew with Tottenham H. Henry Cotton won the News of the World tournament at Hoylake. This evening we saw the relief of Guernsey (Channel Isles) it was in colour. King and Queen governor. Red Cross ship and an American ship which came into old harbor through a lock and had 1ft to spare on each of it as it came through the lock.

Sunday 29th: I owe Mummy 7/6 for Daddy's present. 1 went for a 10mile walk with Allen to the bottom of Bough Fell then halfway up Crook.

Monday 30th: Swam 8 length of the school baths 150yards. Went up brook it took me 36min. I came in 2nd. A very good day for weather. Sun all day.

Tuesday October 1st: We got our togs for the JTC. Not a very good day for weather.

Wednesday 2nd: Had a game of yard football. Good weather.

Thursday 3rd: Fog in the morning but sunshine in afternoon. JTC parade.

Friday 4th: We had music appreciation. In afternoon weather was good. I got a parcel from Granny and Grandpa (sweets).

Game of rugger. For tea we had chips and scallops and a piece of birthday cake from a new boy named Yeoward.

Saturday 5th: Went to tuck shop. Had a game of rugger. You spell Crichton. We went to the pictures in the evening to see 'La Fin de Jour' it was in French but with English underneath. It was about an actor who was at an old actors home. I practied in the afternoon on the piano. We had chips for tea.

Sunday 6th: Went a walk in the afternoon. Went to the pictures in the evening to see a film about the army. It was a very funny film. In the afternoon I had my first bottle of Chirres. The sun was shining all day. Went to Slah [?] Lane.

Monday 7th: Sun was shining in the morning but went dull. We had an extra half holiday. We went a walk to Holme Knott. Had blomge [presume this is blancmange] for lunch and for tea.

Tuesday 8th: Had a lovely peice of rabbit for lunch and then black cherry and apple pie. Helped Mr Crawford to weed his tennis lawn. Then went to rifle range and got a 2" and 3" group had 10 shots. We had chips and scallops for tea and we got our brown books. Weather was not very good. Mr Crawford said he was very pleased with my work.

Wednesday 9th: We had blomge for lunch I had 2 helpings. Had a game of rugger. We had chips and sausage. I do now more serving at the table.

Thur 10th: We had a feild. We were taught how to crawl the different ways and to learn the feild signals. I went to the tuck shop and had a feed. I got £1 from daddy. We had churros, I had a bottle of plums.

Fri 11th: I went up Higher Winder in 4-6 mins. We had music in the afternoon. We heard the Empire Piano Concerto and the Overture to the 'Magic Flute'. We had chips for tea.

Sat 12th: Manchester City 2 Sheffield 1. We had a lecture from Dobson and Young it was very good indeed. Dobson did all the talking and Young put the records on. He was cracking jokes all the time. He told us how they worked during the war. One of Blackburns got his shoulder blade broken and another his head cut. One was playing in a wig. Very cold.

Sun 13th: *I went to Dent. There is a shop which sells swords. We saw a fish about 1 foot long. We had icing suger on a piece of cake. Very cold.*

Mon 14th: *I had a game of rugger. We had our second lot of jam. I had apple and raspberry. Very cold.*

Tues 15th: *Had a game of yard football then went to the tuck shop. Chips for tea. Very cold.*

Wed 16th: *Blomge, chips. Very cold temp 24 degrees F.*

Thurs 17th: *Cold. I went to the Cross Keys Inn along by the river and back by the road. There was a very pretty view from the Inn.*

Fri 18th: *We had chips and scollops for tea and three ??. I had a bottle of plums.*

Sat 19th: *Had a game of rugger I scored 1 try. We had rabbit and cherrys. I went to the Sedwick Society to see 1) Locomtime 2) Story of the Wheel 3) Copper Web 4) Sea Night Mail. Braveheart. Lasted for 1.5hours. Ride 'em Cowboy. We had rabbit and blomge. The picture was about Red Indians. Went to the tuck shop and to the shooting.*

Sun 20th: *Going out. I went along the Lune it was pretty.*

Mon 21st: *I went on a run Frostrow. It took me 28mins. I came in 2nd. 8th in fortnightly orders.*

Tues 22nd: *The school had a Japanese sword presented to them. I had a game of rugger. I nearly got killed.*

Wed 23rd: *I had a game of rugger in the afternoon.*

Thurs 24th: *We had a parade and were taught all about rilifs [rifle I think!]. Then I went to the rilf range and I got 25/28 and 19/20.*

Fri 25th: *We had chips and scollops. I had three helpings of chips and 5 scollops. I went a run round quafer [Quaker] it took me 28.5mins.*

Sat 26th: 'The Broncho Buster'. 'Make it Snappy'. 'Aladdin's Lamp'. I watched a match then went round Quaker. Blanc Mange.

Sun 27th: Say what I want in my tuck box syrup, cake, apples, toothpaste. I went a walk up the Potkey?

Mon 28th: I had a lighter given me. We had an extra half. I went round Knot up a lovley valley and back by calf. She is a reservoir up the valley. Very nice weather. Sun all day.

Tues 29th: I lent my pen to Fenton LC. Very good weather sun all day. I went up calf. Went to shooting 500yrd targets. I got 14/20 and 18/20. Jackson's have a set of Monopoly. Go to Dent. My trousers have a tair in them. I want some sugar and jam.

Wed 30th: Parade showed how to clean rilfs [rifles]. Nice weather.

Thurs 31st: Good weather. Game of rugger.

Nov 1st: Had a game of rugger.

Nov 2nd: Must get tickets for chapel 2. Daddy bought me a crosbow.

Sun 3rd: Mr Crawford [Housemaster] said I am doing very well and I am to tell daddy. I went to Windermere with Maureen.

Mon 4th: Had a game of rugger. I scored a try. Lovely weather in the morning but turning to rain. Daddy went back and Maureen. I must write to Mummy and thank her for the cake and chocklats.

Tues 5th: Watched Sedbergh letting off fireworks. I had a game of rugger. Some people tried to set Winder on fire. We had blanc mange.

Wed 6th: We had a parade we were inspected by the CO. The school moto means Hardship is the nurse of man.

Thurs 7th: Very thick fog in the morning but it cleared between 9 o'clock and 5 past. I had a game of rugger. Then went to shooting 15/15 and 9/15 this was snap shooting. I also went to the tuck shop. Very heavy rain in the evening and some snow on Higher Winder.

Fri 8th: I lent Raby 4.5d. [Raby was in year above]. I went up Winder. I came in 12 out of the house. It took me 32.5mins.

> *I nearly got blown off my feet on the top. We went to a film it was called The Adventures of Marco Polo. It was a very good film, there was also a cartoon and the news.*
>
> Sat 9th: *Watched the school beat Oundle 8-6. In the afternoon I watched the school 2nd beat Lancaster 17-3, and the school 3rd beat Lancaster 13-3. The masters beat the colts 33-3. I went to the tuck shop spent 1.5d. I went a 2.5mile run it took me 16 mins. I am not at the Sedwick Society. I am going to see a film about steel. Nuneaton 14 Cheltenham 8.*
>
> Sun 10th: *Went a walk along the river.*

From here on Tony stops adding the date, just the days, but I think we can safely assume it runs consecutively, so I have added dates.

> Mon 11th: *I had my first game of fives.*
>
> Tues 12th: *I had another game of fives. Rain all day. Had chips went to tuck shop and to shooting. The under 14 beat Limehouse 15-3.*
>
> Thurs 14th: *Had an indoor parade then had a game of squash. Then saw a film. I have ordered a pair of boots. I can get them off coupons and they cost 35/. I put my name for a JTC?? It costs 2/3.*
>
> Sat 16th: *I had a game of squash. I saw 5 films one with Conrad Weidt in it. I went shooting.*
>
> Mon 18th: *House run Garsdale it took me 30min. Came in 3rd. 4miles.*
>
> Tues 19th: *Played rugger very muddy field.*
>
> Thurs 21st: *I helped Mr Crawford to mend a wall and put up a fence. I went to the tuck shop spent 1/4 ½ d [underlined heavily!]. I saw two films.*
>
> Fri 22nd: *Went up Winder took 32mins. Came in 19. Hornsby nearly got killed by an express it missed by about 6". He saw a German with a cut throat.*
>
> Sat 23rd: *Had 38 shots on range 8 were rapid, 30 were without a*

rest. 35/40 rapid!! Tuck shop.

Sun 24th: 50mile sledge 4hour 23mins 6 sec. Saw the Olympic Winter Sports [presume that's what the 50mile is referring to]. Women 2 mile schin…? 3 mins 6 sec.

Mon 25th: I went round Slack's Lane it took me 33mins which is good.

Tues 26th: Shooting. Frostrow and Garsdale 30mins.

Thurs 28th: Went to the grubber. Yard football.

Sat 30th: Went round Shorter Garsdale it took me 13 ¾ mins.

Sun 1st Dec: Went a walk. A very good sermon.

Tues 3rd: Went to grubber 1/3/5. Watched the house match. We won 7-0. Hornsby scored a drop goal. Mitchell got a try. A lot of snow on Wild Baugh Fell and Baugh Fell and Higher Winder. I came 4th in the Ladder Competition out of all the Under 15.

Wed 4th: Went to Danny Caves on the 10mile. Had a midday half.

Thurs 5th: Parade. Deminstration by troop an infantry wepons. Tuck shop.

Fri 6th: Went up Brook. 33 and ¾.

Sat 7th: House match we won 13-3. Drop goal by Appleton. Trys by Young, Swaine, Purves. Shooting. Tuck shop.

Thurs 12th: Long bridges 50mins. Exams maths and English.

This is the last entry in the diary. There are a few random notes on other pages:

Leave Crewe 2:26, Arrive Sedbergh 5:50.
If you want to come to chapel Sunday let me know.
Miss M Longworth Fairfield School, Ambleside.
Master RWK Neill, School House, Clifton College, Bristol.
Doodles of the surname Bentley, Thomas Bentley referee and Mrs Bentley
On the 8th I lent ? my compass. On 8 lent Tolfreis a Penguin

book. Picnic Lunch.

A lock for my tuck box.

Beethoven Empire Diaries. Consilio to overture to the Magic Flute.

I do not want the new pumps.

Could you please send me some Horlicks. I want a tube of toothpaste and a cake.

Above: Tony's JTC badge and a postcard from his sister, Maureen (undated). It reads:

Dear Tony,

Wishing you very many Happy Returns of the day and I hope you have a happy birthday. Lots of Love Maureen xxxxxxxxxx

1947

Lent Term started on Tuesday 21 January, and Tony was in Form II. From the form list Tony's old friend, 'Rickett', has started at the school in Form I. This was another lifelong friendship.

I have included here a handwritten letter to Tony with best wishes for his birthday (no year) from his grandparents on his mother's side. Would love to know what the "Forgive the looks, but the flavor is OK" was!

> 4 Walton Way
> Walton
> Nr Stone
>
> My Dear Tony
>
> Hope the parcel gets to you safely.
>
> Forgive the corks, but the flavour is OK.
>
> This is from Grandad & myself
>
> With Best Love & Wishes for A Happy Birthday.

Above: Photo of Winder House Sports Team in 1947. On the back Tony has written "The Winners". Tony is sitting on the end of the front row, right-hand side, wearing shorts

On 5 October 1947 Tony wrote to his parents and sister, Maureen:

Dear Mummy and Daddy and Maureen

Thank you for your letters and the parcel which has not arrived yet. Could you please send me a copy of Hamlet and the Golfing Monthly. On Thursday I had two replies from museums. One said they hadn't any, but they put me on to two more people. The other said they had two catalogues in which there were passages on arms and armour. One cost 1/3 the other 11/2 . I sent for the 1/3 one.

I have had another fencing lesson and I am getting on very well. Yesterday I played another storming game of rugger but I did not score. It was Hard Luck!!

On Friday we had an extra half and Sheard and I went up Hebbulthaite [Hebblethwaite] *Gill it is on the?. We had a wizard time. We are going for a sandwich lunch today. I am enclosing a cartoon which I hope you like. I don't know wether I told you or not but I have passed my Empire Test 1st class.*

Could you enclose some stamps in your letter next week please. I am sending you some of the replies.

I hope you are keeping well and I hope you will win on Vernons [The Pools]

Lots of love Tony [next to this is a little drawing of a gun]

It is nice to see how far back Tony's love of all things antique arms and armour goes, together with the family's enjoyment of playing The Pools. I remember well sitting down with Aunty Jean (Tony's mother's sister), trying to Spot the Ball!

Another item to have survived is a programme from a concert at school on Wednesday 17 December in Powell Hall. Tony's name appears in the choir as part of the bass section, he always had a lovely voice.

1948

Tony moved into Lower IV Modern, which, from what I can tell, allowed him to choose what subjects to study. From his report for the end of that term, Tony had been studying physics, divinity, chemistry, history, geography, English, French and maths. He has dropped the dreaded Latin, which, from reading his reports, was not a strong point! Tony's new subjects seem to suit him as he ended the term in sixth place in the form.

From Tony's diary of that year, he noted on Friday 6 February 1948, "first day we have not had sausages since the beginning of term"!

In May of 1948 Tony's father had a trip to Belgium and Holland with a colleague, and Bill sent three postcards with a nice bit of detail:

The boat is a wee bit wobbly for writing and there is a fair amount of fog. I anticipate arriving Ostend 15:30hrs. Hope you are fit and well, love Daddy x We are going by road from Ostend to Ghent.

My Dear Tony, I have been frightfully busy and I am beginning to feel the effects of the terrific heat, the trains are hot and stuffy, and nothing to be compared with ours for comfort, still one had to suffer these discomforts to do the work. Tomorrow at 6:30am I leave for Holland on business and cannot say definitely when I shall return to Ghent. Love Daddy x

Tony's French exercise book. It's the only exercise book that Tony kept from his Sedbergh days and is covered in doodles – not sure how much attention he was paying!

Above: Photo of Bill and his work companion on trip to Holland and Belgium 1948

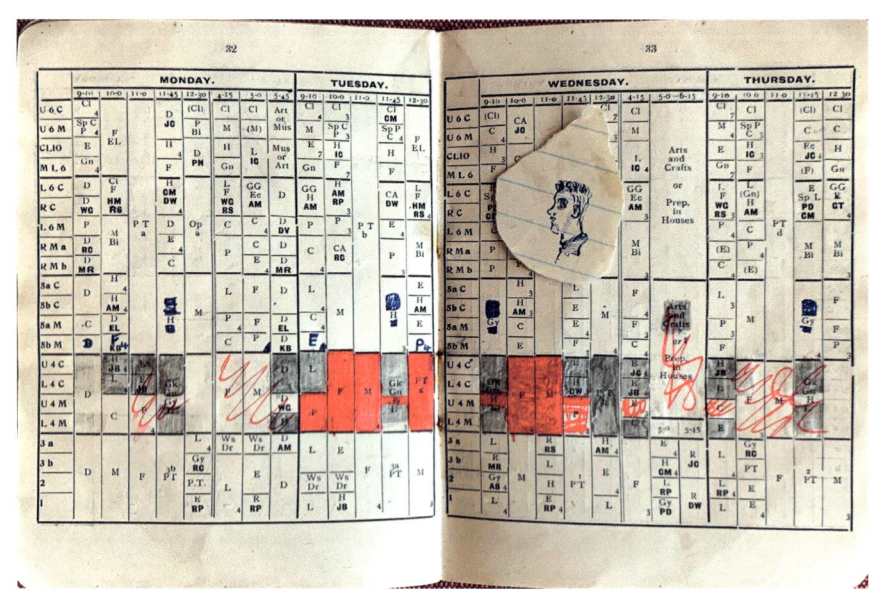

*Above: Timetable from summer term 1948,
with a lovely little doodle found within the pages*

Enclosed with the bill for the term and receipts for repairs to boots, etc. was a receipt for camera film development, so I am guessing that Tony was now in possession of a camera. There were quite a number of photos taken during his school days at Sedbergh, especially of sporting events.

At the start of each term, a booklet, known as the Brown Book, was given to each child listing which form you were in, and, as you progressed through the school which set you were put into. Tony kept all of these.

From Tony's report at the end of the summer term 1948, he was recorded as being 5ft7½ , and by the end of the term weighed 9st 7½ . His girth, which was recorded in each report as well, was 37in. There was a mixed bag of comments. I particularly like the English teacher's "some effort but is very illiterate". The headmaster gave an overall positive comment of "there is much that he has done well". A positive end to the term. See appendix for rest of school reports.

Winter term 1948 commenced on 21 September (Tony's father's

birthday). Tony was now in Upper IV Modern. Amongst the receipts for the term Tony has had his football boots and a pair of shorts repaired. From the Sedbergh School Athletic Shop Tony was bought a rugger ball, two pairs of blue shorts and a canvas scrum cap. A number of items were both purchased and mended from The K Shoe Agency.

Tony's report from the end of the winter term was pretty good. He went up from tenth place to sixth in the form. He was now 5ft8 and weighed 9st 13. It looks like he finished piano lessons as there were no comments in that section. Amongst the comments were:

Housemaster: "A promising term, in school, House, and on the rugger field. We will keep a special eye on his weakness in English."

French: "He managed to keep a fair standard of written work. Lifeless in class."

Chemistry: "Good progress though very silent."

Olympic Games

During the summer of 1948 the Olympic Games were held in London. Tony, aged just fifteen, had read about the Games in a magazine called *World Sports* and wrote to his father to see if he could go. Yes, came the reply, so Tony purchased a ticket and attended the Games on his own, staying with a colleague of his father's in Wimbledon.

The opening ceremony was on 29 July 1948 in the Empire Stadium at Wembley Park. In attendance was King George IV, Queen Elizabeth and Queen Mary. Great Britain did not fare very well in these Olympics, winning only seven medals, none of them gold, but six silver and one bronze.

Tony kept his ticket for Monday 2 August at the Empire Stadium, valid for a full day of athletics. He was seated in the North Terrace (uncovered), row 14, seat 259, and remembered watching the one-hundred-metre race from here. Tony kept all the programmes from the duration of the Games and wrote up all the results from each day, now in Guy Longworth's possession.

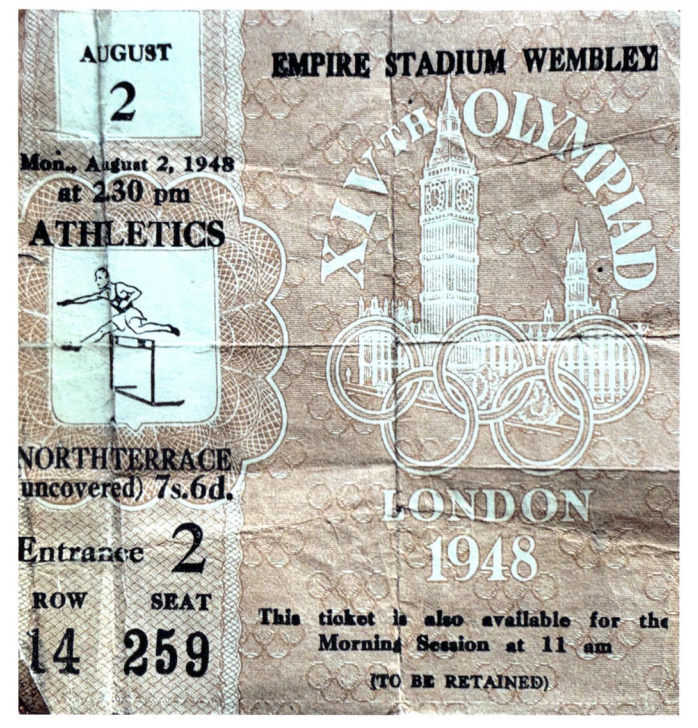

Above: Tony's ticket to Olympic Games, July 1948

On Monday 2 August, Tony will have witnessed three Olympic records and a British athlete winning a silver medal – the stadium must have been fantastically loud at that point. The events he saw were:

Men's
200m – Heats
800m – Final – Olympic record won by American Mal Whitfield
5,000m – Final – Olympic record won by Belgian Gaston Reiff
Pole Vault – Final – Won by American Guinn Smith "during the final a rainstorm came in during the jumps"
Discus – Final – Won by Italian Adolfo Consolini
Women's
100m – Final – Won by Dutch Fanny Blankers-Koen. Silver won by Brit Dorothy Manley[32]

---

32   www.olympics.com/en/olympic-games/london-1948

1949

Term began on Thursday 13 January, and Tony was in Form Vb Modern. He required his skates to be re-ground, one rugger boot to be re-studded and there was an invoice from an upholsterer for a new strap and loop – think we can safely assume this was for his leather trunk.

Amongst the books that were required for the term were Chaucer, *History of USA*, *Prose for Precis* and *Electricity and Magnetism*.

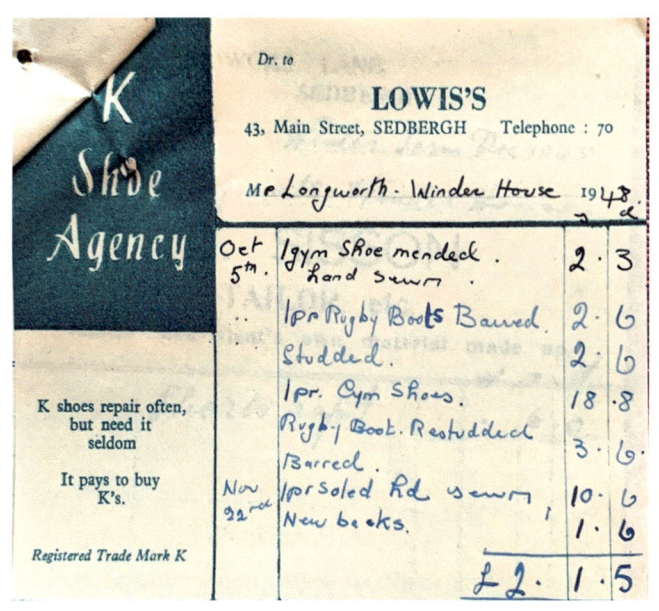

Above: Receipt from Lowis's shop, Sedbergh

In the pages of the Brown Book of the Lent term, Tony wrote "CCF Camp" (Combined Cadet Force) and as luck would have it, there is a description of the camp that Tony attended in the Sedberghian booklet transcribed below. Winder House came second.

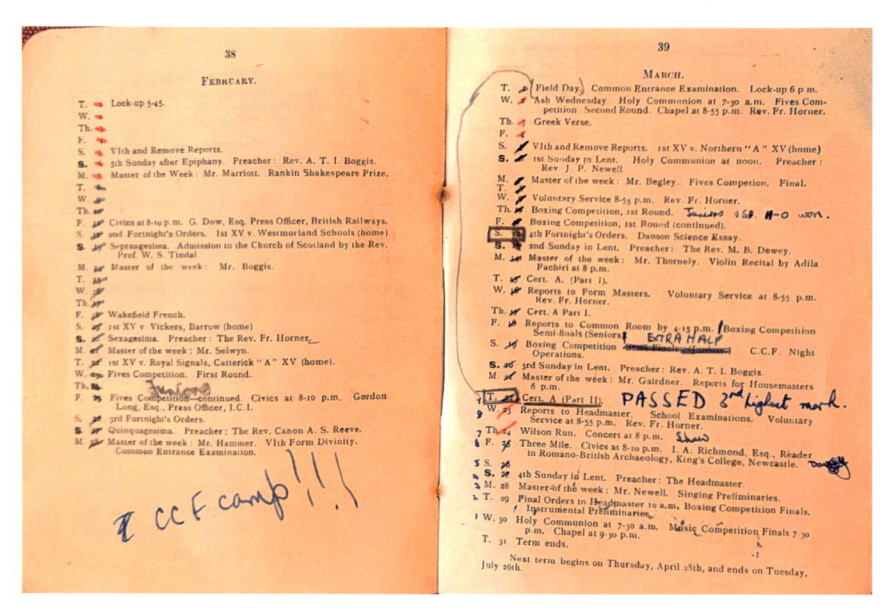

Above: Tony's Lent term Brown Book

The Drill Cup, the Annual Inspection, Field Day and Certificate "A" examinations have once more swung round in their respective orbits and have disappeared for their due seasons. And yet every year there is something, even if it is only a difference in the weather which makes these occasions differ from their predecessors and prevents them from becoming a monotonous repetition.

This term's training has differed from that of recent summer terms, since it has been done mainly in House Squads or Platoons. The Drill Cup took place on the 24th May and all parades until then were devoted to practice for it. Only five voluntary rehearsals were permitted, but two of these could be directed by members of the permanent staff. All cadets who had completed four terms in the CCF were in their House Senior or Junior Squad. This included all HQ Company and A Company instructors, who were of course only available for the voluntary parades. Despite this change from more highly trained and smaller squads, there was not much decline in the standard of the drill squads, and the general standard of the contingent at the Annual Inspection was certainly higher than for the last few years. The Drill Cup was won by Hart House whose Junior Squad was outstanding.

Close on the heels of the Drill Cup followed the Inspection of the contingent by the District Commander, Major General V Evelegh, CB, DSO, OBE, who kindly remitted the inspection of the contingent on Busk Holme on account of the intense heat [which, however, did not deter him from climbing to the top of the Riggs to see Winder House launch an assault]. The ceremonial parade was therefore limited to a General Salute and a March Past in threes. The parade was taken by U/O D M Canning. The band played well and kept a very steady step, and the excellent marching of 3 Platoon under Sgt Carr was conspicuous. In his address at the close General Evelegh congratulated the contingent on its smartness and training and stressed the importance of cadet training for potential officers, as the time available for producing offices during National Service is all too short.

Above: Photo of Combined Cadet Force. Tony is directly on RHS of troop leader, eighth from right

On Field Day, the 30th June, HQ, A and B Companies carried out training around Danny Bridge, whilst C and D Companies went to Ingmire, where the House Platoons moved round every half hour from one form of training to another. These consisted of protection at the halt, a platoon attack, compass work, weapon training and fieldcraft camouflage, a quick decision exercise and instruction on the Vickers machine gun. Protection at the halt and the platoon attack constituted an inter-house tactical competition, whilst the weapon training and fieldcraft formed a second competition. Judges for these were kindly provided by the King's Own and Border Regiments. House Platoons had been practicing for these competitions on contingent parades since the Drill Cup. The fieldcraft and handling of weapons were quite good but fire orders and verbal orders were still very weak and far too conversational. Another common fault among platoon commanders was to "lead their regiment from behind" and to make their luckless platoon sergeant lead the assault, a practice hardly likely to win them the confidence of their troops in battle. Other matters which require attention are track discipline and the position of the platoon "O" Group on the march. The results of this term's competitions are to be found below.

Twenty-three candidates passed Certificate "A" Part 1 and fifteen passed Part 2. There were no failures. Next term the shape of the contingent will have altered entirely, as boys will in future not be enrolled before they are 15½ years old. A and B Companies, as at present constituted will disappear and there will be additional employment for post-certificate cadets by the revival of a Vickers Machine Gun Section.

Tony kept some lovely photos of his time in the CCF, and most probably from the above inspections. He also kept his Cadet Discharge Certificate which shows that he enrolled in Cadet Training on 12 March 1947 (his birthday), passed his Certificate A Part 1 on 26 June 1948 and Part 2 on 22 March 1949. He also kept his badge – his Junior

Training badge appears earlier in this booklet and the one below is for the OTC, so I'm unsure which badge was awarded when.

Above: Tony in CCF uniform, and with friends. Tony on LHS

Above and left: Tony's OTC badge and Cadet Discharge Certificate

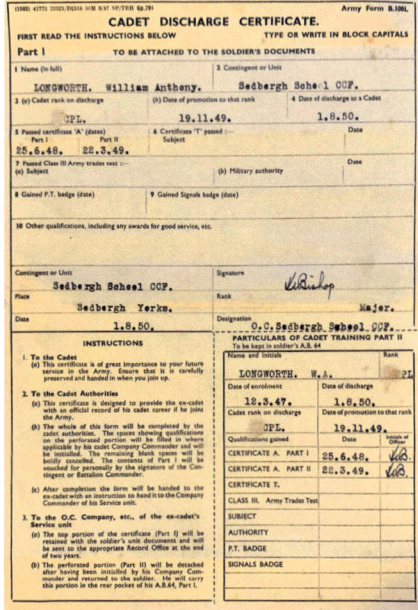

Tony's report from the term was quite mixed, with maths still being his strongest subject: "Good work and very satisfactory progress, but he ought to be becoming more spontaneous."

French and Latin were still the weakest. French: "Very weak. He must work with more determination if he is to get a certificate." Latin: "Not at all strong. A determined effort is needed to fill the many gaps in his knowledge." The headmaster summed it up with: "Good in patches but not altogether convincing."

Summer term began on Thursday 28 April. Parents were informed that the fees had gone up again from £65 per term to £75 per term to commence in January 1950. From the invoices kept, Tony required a repair to his blazer, another repair to the trunk and throughout the term numerous repairs to his boots, which included new soles, toe and heel plates, new back strap and the backs sewed up.

Tony's report for the end of this term isn't great, with the housemaster commenting, "This is depressing; he seems to have slipped back everywhere, though as a member of the House I still find him keen, cheerful, and quite effective… I find it hard to believe this is the best he can do. He certainly could improve his English if he took the trouble to".

Returning to The Sedberghian booklet from July 1949 there are a few things of interest from the headmaster's speech that resonate for today's world. He talks about the importance of not specialising to soon and keeping other subjects going:

The other thing is that we here feel very strongly that music is not a subject reserved for the odd few queer people troubled with something they call an artistic temperament but that it is the birthright of every civilized man, and that the spiritual values represented by Poetry, Art and Music are a fundamental part of his education.

He went on to give examples:

The Singing Prize has just been won by the Secretary of Football. The Art Prize has been won by, I think, the strongest forward in our XV, and, as becomes an artist and the son of a bishop, quite the most ferocious forward in the pack.

He continued:

We believe that the best way to lose sincerity is to have too much of theory and that the best advice ever given on Technique is "get on with the job". So, we get on with the job in the belief that if you have something in you it will come out one day and meantime, we keep a sense of proportion and a sense of humour.

The headmaster then turns his attention to universities and their requirements, and "the new examination set up". What he says I found very interesting:

They [universities] *have laid down two advanced subjects and three others specified by them, and not by us who teach the boy, nor chosen by the boy; and if Oxford and Cambridge still continue to insist on Latin, as I presume they will, that will mean four. Now the result of that will simply be this: that the boy will have to employ some of his very precious hours keeping up subjects which perhaps he started at 9 and which neither he nor we may think are good for him. If he is bad at them, he will have to struggle on, having lost interest and having lost hope, and if he is good at them he will have to waste time simply keeping them ticking over in order to have them ready for that examination which he is not allowed to take till 16½. And these are the precious hours which we require desperately to start him off at that age on something more inspiring, more hopeful, more educative, something which will not necessarily be examined. Now the tragedy of the thing is this: that the Universities give as their reasons for thwarting our liberty that they must stop over-specialisation and that they cannot trust the schools. Of course, they are very polite and say "Naturally we could of course trust* a school like yours, but there are a great many we cannot trust." Unfortunately, what they have done will have no effect towards their purpose at all. The unscrupulous school will simply be able to say to itself with less of a guilty conscience than before: "we have fulfilled at 16 ½ all the requirements of general education, and we will now from 16 ½ to 19 do 34 hours a week Physics and Chemistry and nothing else".

The truth of the matter is that over-specialisation, which we hate more than the Universities do, is entirely the offspring of University Scholarships. I said this at a meeting of one of the University Boards recently and got very strong support from a certain Professor. The day before he had asked the Headmaster of a Secondary School "do tell me, how many hours a week does your top form spend on non-specialist work?" "none" was the answer. "None? But isn't that a scandal?" "Of course it's a scandal," said the Headmaster, "but none of these boys of mine have any hope of going to the University unless they win a scholarship, so what do you expect me to do?" Now when you realise that in the near future the vast majority of boys will only get there on some form of Scholarship, Open, or State, or County, you can see the frightful danger with which education is threatened. But the only possible cure is in the Scholarship Examinations and what I would like to suggest to the Universities is that instead of restricting our freedom to educate they should demand that every Scholarship candidate should offer in addition to his specialist subject one serious and quite unrelated subject. Your scientist might offer English Literature, or a foreign language… If they would do this the Universities would get not only better specialist but better human beings, for the trouble is that the University does not look upon the boy as a human being but as a recruit to some Faculty. I am saying this not merely for the pleasure of tilting at the universities… But because I believe it is of desperate importance to parents. There really is a danger that the boy will cease to be looked upon as a human being but will be looked *upon as fodder for the universities, fodder for the Services, or fodder for the vast administrative machine which is threatening to take the place of father, mother, and school master.*

The final part of the speech that I am including in this document is, I think, of complete relevance today as well, with the message – let your boy do what he enjoys:

Just one more word I have to say to parents. I know that many of you are very worried because your boys seem to have no ideas as to what they are going to do with their future. You must not blame them, and you must not blame us. Thirty years ago, every boy heard his father or brother or cousin slapping himself on the chest and saying "my job is the one for you, my boy; a great life, a grand career and wonderful prospects for anyone who puts his back into it." What he hears today is generally "I'm sure I don't know what you are going to do; I don't see any future in my line for anybody." It is very hard for the boy in these circumstances to make up his mind. Above all I would ask you not to push him too far into the popular search for security. It is abundantly right that we should care greatly about security for the old, the weak or infirm, but it is not right for the young man and the strong. The world is full today of voices calling us all like cattle from the hills down to the plains where we will be provided with food, shelter, safety, pension, and a grave. Don't let your voice be one of these. You must have realized when you sent your boy here that he would get a liking for the hills. Leave him with that liking.

Winter Term began on Tuesday 20 September. Amongst the items required for the new term were the following books: *Short History of our Religion*, maths papers, science papers and *New Style Exercises in Chemistry*. The usual repairs to his boots and rugger boots were required, together with badges for the third XV team (rugger).

With it being the winter term there would have been numerous rugger matches, and Tony kept the score for each of them in the termly diary. One of the matches has an asterisk against it (5 November 1949 against Kendal Grammar School won 27–0) which reads, "I scored 1 try which was converted. I got my colours". Clearly proud of his achievement.

Tony recalled being good at rugby; the positions he played were forward, front or back row, and that he was on the first team, although from reading the letters it seems he only played for the first team on one occasion.

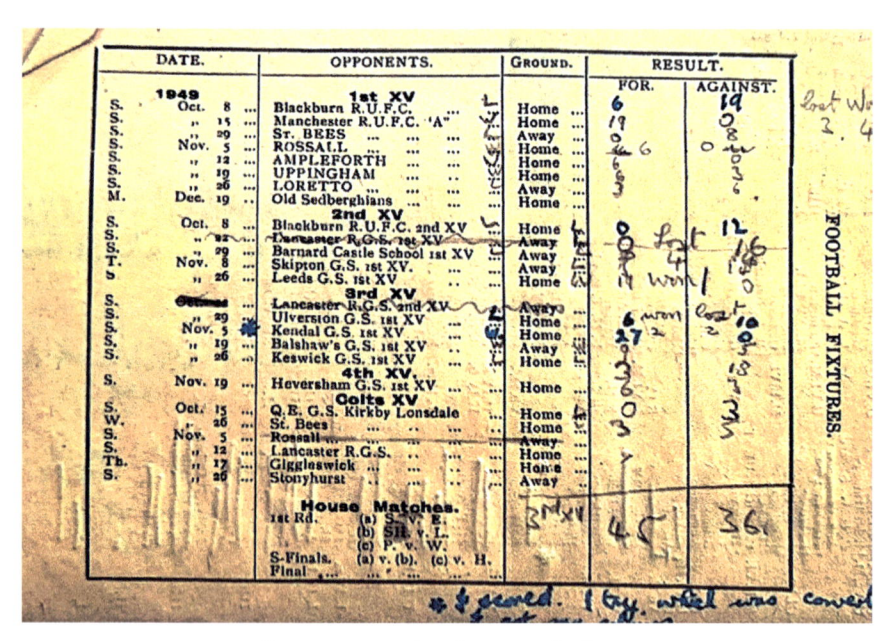

Above: Fixtures list from termly diary

Tony sat the School Certificate exams (GCSE current equivalent) on Tuesday 29 November until Wednesday 14 December, and he kept all his exam papers. On 30 November, Tony received a telegram from his parents and sister with the following message:

Dearest love and best wishes for your success, love Mummy, Daddy and Maureen.

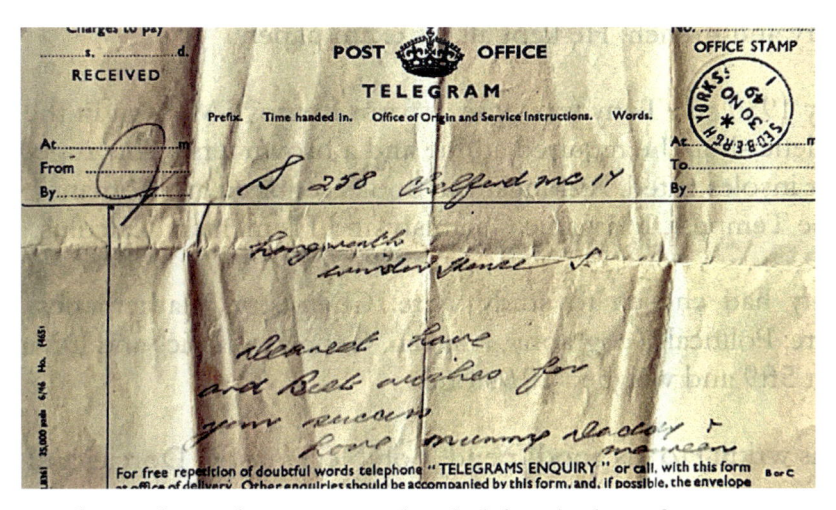

Above: Telegram from parents wishing luck for School Certificate exams

Tony's end-of-term report was much improved. Divinity: "Very intelligent and keen." Chemistry: "Much improved. A very good term." Housemaster: "He takes quite a good place in his modern subjects, anyway; and English, his old bugbear, seems improved. He is growing up sensibly in the House."

From photos that Tony kept it's clear that Winder House won the House Rugby Cup in 1949.

Above: Winder House rugby team winning house rugby cup 1949. Tony back row, second from left, taken outside front door of Winder House, and Tony's handwritten note on the back

1950

Before the start of term Tony received the results of his School Certificate in the form of a postcard from his housemaster, Mr Foster. Tony passed seven exams with credit, English language, English literature, geography, elementary maths, additional maths, physics and chemistry. Tony failed two – history and French. He kept all his exam papers.

Lent term started on 17 January 1950 and Tony was now in form Remove Modern in the sixth form. From the school athletic shop, he required a blue and a brown jersey, his rugby boots to be re-studded and leather insoles fitted. Amongst the books required are *Roman Panorama*, *Advanced Algebra*, *The Tempest*, *Inorganic Chemistry* and *Elementary Calculus*.

The principal subjects that Tony had chosen to study were: chemistry, mathematics and physics. The subsidiary subjects were: political geography, English, general classics and divinity. He was now seventeen years old and almost 5ft9 and weighed 10.9st.

From Tony's diary of 1950, he was writing to his good friend Bob Neill's sister, Dorcie, and this appeared to continue for some time as some of her letters have been kept. On Thursday 2 February, not only was he ill with flu and a temperature of ninety-seven, to make matters worse he was "chased by a horse"! Tony was still ill the next day, but he managed to read the *Lesson at Chapel*, act 18, lines 1–13. February 14 was a "good day: 2 valentines"!

Within the bundle for this term are handwritten copies of two letters that Tony's father wrote to the school to inform them that he would be leaving at the end of the summer term. Transcribed below:

To: J H Bruce Lockart (Headmaster)

Dear Sir,

I am writing this letter to intimate my intention that my son W

> *A Longworth, Winder House, will be terminating his school career after the Summer Term.*
>
> *May I take this opportunity of expressing my thanks for all that the school has done for him. I feel sure it will have considerable bearing on his future life.*

It seems to me that over the Christmas holiday Tony made a decision to leave school and not stay on to take the higher exams and go to university. We know that when Tony left school, he signed up for Articles with an accountancy firm in Manchester. I remember him telling me that he wanted to be a doctor but that his father was keen for him to do accountancy and, with a clear, natural ability for maths, perhaps this helped the decision.

Tony's report for the term was "creditable", "but nothing very striking". He finished thirteen out of seventeen in Chemistry, where "he has made a fair start with the more advanced work", fourth out of ten in Maths, "a good term's work" and twelfth out of eighteen in Physics, where "he is attentive and tries and will come on".

During the Easter holidays Tony went on a trip to Bielefeld, in the northeast of Germany with Sedbergh School CCF (Combined Cadet Force). The statement of expenses has survived which shows that the trip lasted for thirteen days, and Tony travelled via Harwich to Bielefeld.

Tony's final term at Sedbergh started on Tuesday 2 May. He required the usual repairs to his boots and to his Parker pen. The books needed included *Othello* and *Europe Overseas*. There is also a receipt for an OS (Old Sedberghian) sweater, OS blazer badge and OS wool scarf. I certainly remember seeing the sweater and scarf at Colebrooke, albeit slightly motheaten.

Within the calendar in the term booklet, Tony marked that Winder House won the Drill Cup (shooting) on Thursday 25 May, and that on Wednesday 31 May he got an "extra half and went to and past Dent on bikes".

Tony recalled being good at shooting, which was with rifles on an indoor range with two hundred and five hundred yards being the distance. In June 1950, Tony took part in a shooting competition in Altcar and he has kept the kit list, transcribed below:

Kit to be Taken to Altcar

Wear Uniform
Rifle in carrying case
Cleaning rod
Score book
Button cleaning material
Boot brushes – polish
Toilet requisites including: soap, towel, mirror etc
Pyjamas
Sheets if possible
Civilian clothes
Coat hanger
Mug, knife, fork and spoon
Lock up suitcase

Tony kept two of his shooting score books (Alfred Parker Score Books), one from 1948 and one from 1950, in which can be found the scores from the competition at Altcar, shown below.

Tony also took part in the Lord Robert's Cup on Thursday 6 July; he underlined it in his calendar) and wrote underneath, "we won by 8 points from SH. We were 7 points ahead after 200x and gained 1 point at 5x".

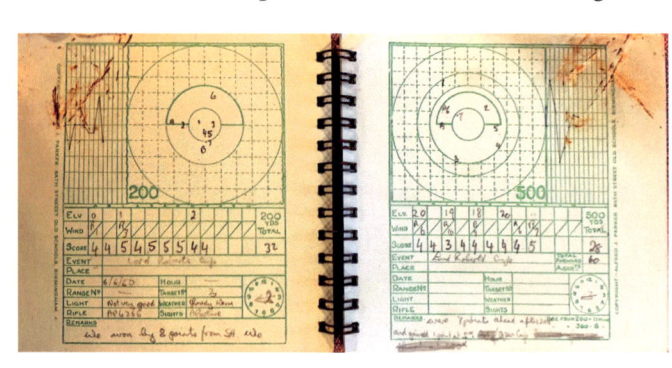

Left: Score card from shooting competition

The photos below are of Winder House boys, with cups they have won. On the table are the two trophies that Tony won at the Lord Roberts Cup. (Tony is in the middle row, fourth from right. Tony recalled that on a return visit to Sedbergh some years after leaving, he tried his luck in the range and got ninety-nine out of one hundred.

Left: Winder House boys with trophies from shooting competitions. Tony is back row RHS

Above: Photo of Winder House pupils with cups they have won. Tony third row, fourth from right

At the back of each term booklet is a list of names of all the boys in the school within their respective houses. There are a total of 397 boys in the school and Tony has made a note in pencil which reads, "105 boys I don't know". To know so many of the boys in the school he may well have been a popular child and certainly always spoke with great fondness of his time at Sedbergh School.

Tony was a talented runner and made frequent reference to his running in his school diary. In March 1950, Tony took part in The Wilson Run, which was and still is a major part of the school's history and tradition. It has been raced over almost the same route since its beginnings in 1881 and has only been cancelled four times. The event is the oldest, and arguably toughest, school run in the country. "It is a brutal cross-country race that has followed the same up-and-down, lung bursting, ankle-twisting, nerve-shredding 10 mile course in its 140-odd year history."[33] Tony finished in thirteenth place, in one hour, twenty-three mins and thirty-three seconds – a huge achievement, and his parents were there to cheer him on. Tony recorded his achievement in his diary of that year. The winner finished in one hour, fifteen minutes and fifty-nine seconds, and sixty-two boys took part. Below is the school report from the day, I especially like ,"from our special correspondents, by bicycle and walkie-talkie"!

Above: Going up Thrush Gill, Tony at back

---

33   Martin Love, The Guardian 4.4.2014

Above: Tony on home stretch, he's at the front

As a nice bit of family continuity, Tony's nephews, who both attended Sedbergh School, took part in The Wilson Run years later, with Rupert coming in third and David twenty-fifth. Very commendable efforts.

Above: Tony's diary entry for The Wilson Run

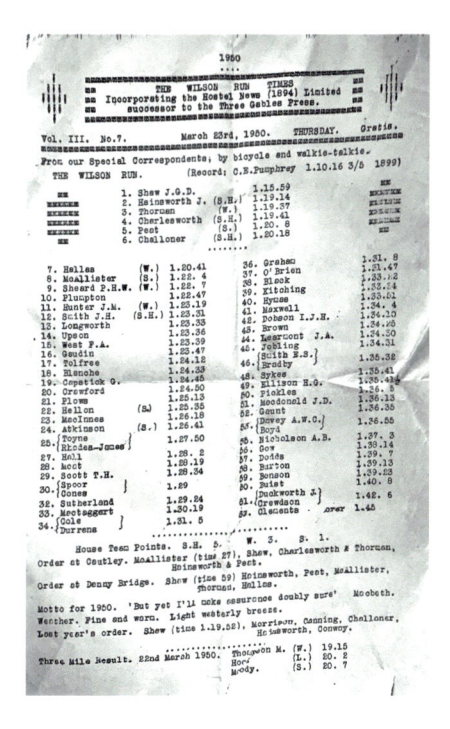

Tony's final report was a mixed bag. He had encouraging words from the housemaster: "He has always tried his best, and it is a pity that he is leaving before his efforts have had quite time to be crowned with success."

From the headmaster he received: "A very good last lap is always a sip of the right spirit. Good luck and good wishes to him."

It has been a real pleasure to read through all the documents that Tony kept from his time at Sedbergh. Tony spoke so fondly of his time at the school, and how happy he was there, and from the documentation and photos it is very clear how true this was.

Family Letters

Amongst the documents found in the sports bag in the attic at Colebrooke were many letters Tony had received, mostly from his parents, but some from his sister, Maureen, his grandparents (Fred and Isabella Bentley) and Ralph Birchenall (Maureen's fiancé). They are nearly all from 1949, when he was starting to prepare for his School Certificate exams. I have transcribed them all in date order. If I have been unable to read a word I have 'best guessed' and included a question mark. They are typed exactly as written, so may not all make perfect sense, but it's how they appear. To add interest, I have included photos where they seemed relevant.

When Tony started at Sedbergh, his sister Maureen was attending Fairfield School Ambleside. By the time he finished she was studying music at the Northern College of Music in Manchester. Maureen was a very accomplished woman who taught the piano, played the flute and, to a lesser extent, the cello. She started a nursery school from her family home on Knutsford Road, Wilmslow, which continued when they moved to Davenport House in Alderley Edge, and went on for about thirty years. Maureen's youngest son, David, attended the school, as did my brother Guy, myself and my sister Kate. My memories of the school are tremendously happy ones made up of my own peg with my name on it, wonderful wooden toys, miniature tables, chairs and toilets, pots of crayons and glue, brightly coloured pictures on the walls, Maureen playing the piano and all the children singing along. I also remember being cast as Mary in the nativity play – I like to think this was on my own merit but suspect a bit of nepotism was involved!

Maureen was a force of nature, full of energy, eccentric and way ahead of her time with a move into studying and then teaching meditation and mindfulness in the 1970s.

7 February 1949
Colebrooke, Chelford, Cheshire
Phone. Chelford. 26

My Dear Tony

Very delighted to hear you are feeling very fit and trust you continue building up both strength and health. The weekend weather here has been simply marvelous very frosty but plenty of sunshine to go with it, I thoroughly enjoyed my golf and played quite well taking the conditions into consideration.

What a pity the Lancs V Warwickshire Rugger match had to be cancelled, it should be a ding dong battle when they do meet. The Scotland V Ireland must have been a very close match 6 pts to 5 pts and no doubt an exciting game to watch.

Well M/c United are still battling with Bradford but I am certain that at Maine Rd today M/C will decisively beat the Bradford boys. Huddersfield losing to Newport must have been a severe blow to the Yorkshire boys, there was no fluke about it either.

It was rather singular that you should suggest "The Jungle is Neutral" for a birthday present. I had already placed an order with Barber and took delivery last week, I cannot pass any comment on it yet having had no time to peruse it; I shall post to you for your Birthday.

You do not state how the English is progressing this term? Good reading and a constant use of the dictionary for spelling and definition will be your greatest asset, are you receiving any preparation from Mr Begley.

Good to hear you are in the scoring with two tries and wish you all the best. I sincerely hope the effects of the black eye have worn away and trust it was nothing like the one Idris received a fortnight ago I've never seen an eye in such a state.

Maureen is still spending hours practice on the piano, in addition to extensive work on the flute and rehearsals for the Green Room play, A Room without a Thorn.

All my best wishes,
Your Loving Daddy xxxxx

Monday 8 February 1949
Colebrooke,

My dear Tony,

We were very sorry to hear about your knee and I do hope it doesn't incapacitate you for much longer. Write again and let me know if there is any improvement. I sent you a small parcel on Friday which should have arrived by now and today I have sent you another. As we have not heard anything from Dr Hill I have enclosed the brown suede windjammer along with some fruit, jam, dripping and milk.

I've seen "Mr Deeds goes to Town". [In the letter 'town' is underlined three times.] *In a title all nouns have a capital letter. The frost has gone now and the pond has thawed. Hoping you are better.*

With love from all, Mummy xx

Thursday 11 February 1949
Colebrooke,

My dear Tony,

We were pleased to receive your postcard this morning saying your knee was better. It looks as though the small parcel I sent *you has gone astray although I put a label on it as I usually do. Fortunately, it didn't contain anything really valuable – but it was ½ my ration and ½ Daddy's sweet and chocolate ration!!*

What a day it was yesterday! The wind was simply terrific and the small Rose Arch on to the tennis lawn was broken in two.

Daddy has had two days in bed with a high temp and chesty cold. It is down today but he is in bed feeling a bit weak. We went to see "Miranda" last week but neither Daddy nor I enjoyed it very much. Maureen went on Saturday with a boy name Graham Ellis from Alderley and they enjoyed it. R Birchenall – the boy with whom she is going to the Dance plays rugger for Wilmslow.

The Green Room are very busy. Maureen had a postcard from Barbara Cox who is enjoying the Winter Sports in Switzerland for a month. Lucky blighter! Fairfield School Choir broadcast next Tuesday conducted by Miss Stephan at 6.30pm (if you want to listen).

It is Grandpa's birthday on Feb 14th and he will be 71 and on Saturday Daddy and I will have been married 19 years.

I think that is about all the news now. So, here's hoping your parcel may arrive.

With love from us all, Mummy xxxxxx

There is regular mention of rationing throughout the letters, with many foods being hard to come by. Rationing was introduced by the British government in January 1940 during World War II, to ensure a fair supply of food for all at a time of national shortage. Every man, woman and child were given a ration book with coupons which were then used to buy rationed foods.

What was rationed? Basic foodstuffs like sugar, meat, fats, bacon and cheese, with priority allowances of milk and eggs given to those most in need. Other items were rationed according to availability.

One way to buy rationed foods without coupons was on the black market, with prices greatly inflated. People also traded coupons and goods within communities, and within rural communities like Chelford, farmers helped support families 'on the quiet'.[34]

Tony remembered being sent to a farm behind Colebrooke for a dozen eggs, but on walking back home through the field he fell and broke them all – he was devastated and cried all the way home understanding how important they were to his family.

Friday 14 February 1949
Colebrooke, Chelford, Cheshire,
Phone. Chelford. 26

My Dear Tony

No wonder you passed a comment on the pen I used last week – it had a twisted nib!

Daddy is better again now but I have a dreadful cold and yesterday I stayed in bed until 3pm and then got up as we were going to see "Rose without a Thorn". Maureen was very pleased with your telegram. It was a remarkably good show – Maureen doing quite well. I will send you an Advertiser and later on a photograph.

Thank you very much for the Anniversary Card but as I had had 5 teeth out on the Friday and Daddy was only just recovering, we couldn't celebrate it at all.

I had intended sending you another parcel this week, but I have not yet been to the shops. Couldn't you get it at the Chemists instead of me having to pay postage on it. If not – I'll send you some next week – so, please let me know. Did the sweet parcel turn up by the way?

We have been having lovely warm weather but this morning there is a strong cold wind blowing.

---

34 https://www.iwm.org.uk/history/what-you-need-to-know-about-rationing-in-the-second-world-war

I'm sure Grannie will be delighted with her wool winder. She has always envied me mine.

I have looked again for your programmes – but all I can see are the two swimming ones. Maybe they have gone into the playroom, have they? You will have to have a good look round when you come home.

Do your school arrange any holidays abroad – because if you are thinking of one, I should say that is the best way of going.

Mr Smith is probably coming up for the OB's meeting on the eve of the race.

In the dining room I have a lovely bowl of yellow hyacinths and in the lounge a glorious bowl of deep yellow daffodils, a bowl of blue hyacinths and the pink azaleas are still in bloom although they are beginning to fade a little now. Hoping you keep free from these wretched colds.

With lots of love from Mum xxxxxxxx

14 February 1949
Colebrooke, Chelford, Cheshire
Phone. Chelford. 26

My Dear Tony

Sorry to relate but I have been indisposed with the flu since Tuesday last and I still feel very groggy on my legs.

I have made the effort to come to business for a few hours today to clear up a lot of detail.

IGJ called to leave some Chambers Journals whilst I was in bed and again last night when unfortunately, I had to leave him after a few minutes conversation to collect Maureen at Alderley, she had been rehearsing for the play from 3.0pm until 9.30pm. IGJ may be up for the 10mile if of course the Old Boys Meeting is held at that date.

The enforced stay in bed gave me an opportunity to read

the "Jungle is Neutral" a very fine human story in fact almost unbelievable. I sincerely hope you are feeling really fit and well and now free from the knee trouble. Keep hard at it and may God Bless You.

With lots of love, Yours Ever xxxxxx Daddy

Enclosed with the letter were two newspaper articles, one on new putters the other a comic strip rugby.

19 February 1949
Colebrooke, Chelford, Ches

My dear Tony

Thank you very much for the telegram – it was very good of you to send it. Were you feeling rich? The Play has been a howling success since the 1st night. Everyone has enjoyed it. On Thurs the crits were in the papers. Evening News and Evening Chron. The news was the best as it mentioned everyone. This is the Advertiser's effort (enclosed cutting). Quite good for them. The photo isn't frightfully inspiring. On Tuesday night 'Navana of Wilmslow' took photos. We saw them last night and they are really very good. The set of 12 costs the mere flea bite of 157/-!! The cheapest sizes are 25/-! So, I think the society will buy them in dozs which will be cheaper and distribute them to individuals.

Last night I had a different dress which is much nicer than the one in the photos which is rather a pity. After the show tonight we have a party to round it off. And then down to hard work for me! Until the wretched ? in Altrincham which will put things out a bit. I'm supposed to be taking a p.forte exam at the end of March – Lord only knows how I'll do it!

Nancy Mayson is the girl whose party I was in at the Hunt Ball. Did Mummy tell you that Sally's father is going to get married before Easter? I don't think there's any more news. Keep the rugger going.

Hope you are well. Jim is in bed with flue – Daddy has just gone round with a book.

With much love, Maureen

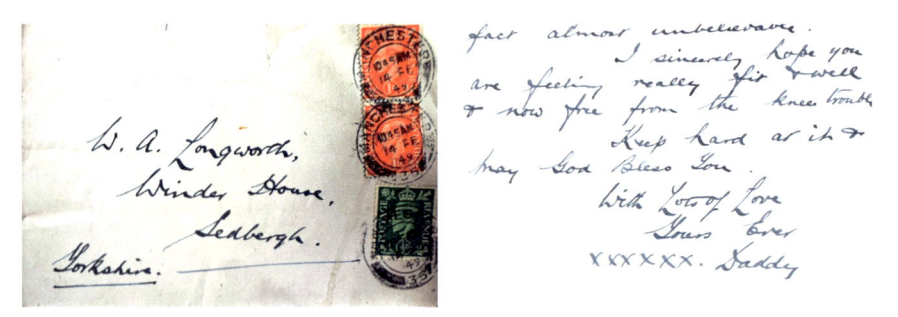

Above: Letter to Tony in his father's handwriting

21 February 1949
Colebrooke, Chelford, Cheshire
Phone. Chelford. 26

My Dear Tony

I am feeling much better with the exception of a severe attack of fibrositus which believe me is an exceedingly painful condition of muscular rheumatism, my hand will scarcely hold this pen and I have the greatest difficulty in keeping my head straight. I smell like the dressing room of a football team, all liniment and thermogena, here's hoping for some relief this week.

G Martin finished 3rd with 91 less 13. 78 in the monthly medal. Neville Young was the winner with 79 less 4 75 nett. Very excellent score. Fred Banks second with 80 less 4 76 nett a very fine effort indeed. Needless to say, I can hardly lift a club but carried on with the game to complete the card for Mr Martin.

The garden has every appearance of Spring with Primulas, Crocus Snowdrops etc in bloom and the grass is growing rapidly. By the way I have bought a Motor Mower so you can get busy at Easter.

I ache too much to write any more, lots of love xxxxx Daddy

Friday 25 February 1949
Colebrooke, Chelford

My dear Tony

Many thanks for the snaps. I like the bowl of roses very much and the truss of tomatoes looks jolly good. I have put in a claim for the sweet parcel but as it wasn't registered, I don't suppose I shall get much satisfaction. On Tuesday I sent you another parcel registered so please let me know if you have received it.

Maureen received one Valentine, but she has no idea who sent it. Adrian is home now but he hasn't been round – no doubt he realizes he's "had it". Maureen has gone to Windermere for the week-end and next week-end Patricia comes here.

I went to the Dentist again yesterday and I am hoping to have my new lower dentures in soon. I have still 11 more top ones to come out.

It is another lovely day but a cold breeze. Did Daddy tell you he has brought a Motor Mower so I can see you having a good time with it when you come home. When is that – by the way?

Yesterday, in Knutsford I saw Mrs Partington. Bill passed School Cert 2 years ago and now he has a motorbike and works for his father. He will be 18 in July. He nearly came over to see you during the Winter holidays, but his mother said you would probably be back at school anyway, you can give him a ring during Easter hols.

Richard has the flu now but is recovering. We won a bottle of Gin in a raffle for the Conservatives – whew!!

Hoping you are AI, with fondest love, Mummy xxx

27 February 1949
4 Walton Way,
Walton, Stone, Staffs

My Dear Tony

Thanks very much for the birthday card which I appreciate very much. It's very nice indeed to think you are in someone's thoughts when your birthday comes round, especially on my 71st birthday.

Sorry to say I have had a nasty attack of bronchitis and it's affected my heart somewhat and I got to take things very steady and quietly, but I may say I am feeling a little better now and trust when the warmer weather comes it will buck me up a bit. Of course, I must not grumble, it must be over 50 years since I had a week in bed.

I sincerely hope you are going on well at school and everything OK. Learn all you can and make the best use of it. School days only come once!

Pleased to say Grannie is keeping well and sends her love. Peter is coming on fine, a real lad. There's not much news things about as usual. So, Cheerio! And all the very best

With love, GranDad. [This is Marjorie's father, Fred Bentley.]

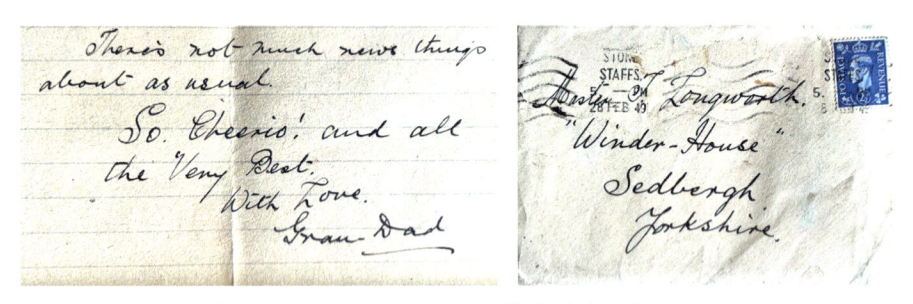

Above: Letter to Tony in grandfather's handwriting

28 February 1949
Colebrooke, Chelford, Cheshire
Phone. Chelford. 26

My Dear Tony

We have experienced a frightfully rough week-end. It blew a gale force from Saturday am until Sunday evening and this morning the ground is white with keen frost.

Yesterday am it was the greatest effort to stand on your feet, needless to say there was some very peculiar golf, you would be already set for a putt and your knees would buckle throwing the putt off the line or topping it; despite all this I set off Sunday am 10/5. 11/4. 12/5. 13/6. 14/3. 15/6. 16/5. 17/5. 18/6. 1/5. 2/7. 3/6. 4/5. 5/6. 6/4. 7/6. 8/6. 9/4. Which, taking all things into consideration was quite good.

As an indication of what was happening in one foursome match semi-final the players halved the 15th in TEN. I must admit I felt really fit well and was glowing all over when I had been in the clubhouse a few minutes.

Sorry to hear you have had beastly weather this last week, it was reasonably good with us considering it was the last week in February.

Some of the snaps are quite good. I particularly liked the bowl of roses, I trust you are now more experienced with timing, developing and printing, don't be afraid to ask all the questions you can, it will be of great assistance.

Maureen travelled to Windermere last Friday for a week-end with Patricia and returns today, I hope the weather was kind.

M/c United still in the Cup but they have a stiff assignment to win it two years in succession.

Great show for England against France and generally agreed upon that the result was unexpected. Have you played since your knee was bumped? I sincerely hope it is absolutely fit again.

More interesting kinds of qualities of sweets and chocolates may come on the market later in the year after the rationing ceases, do you think by that time you will be "fed up" with them????

Au revoir, lots of love xxxxxx Daddy

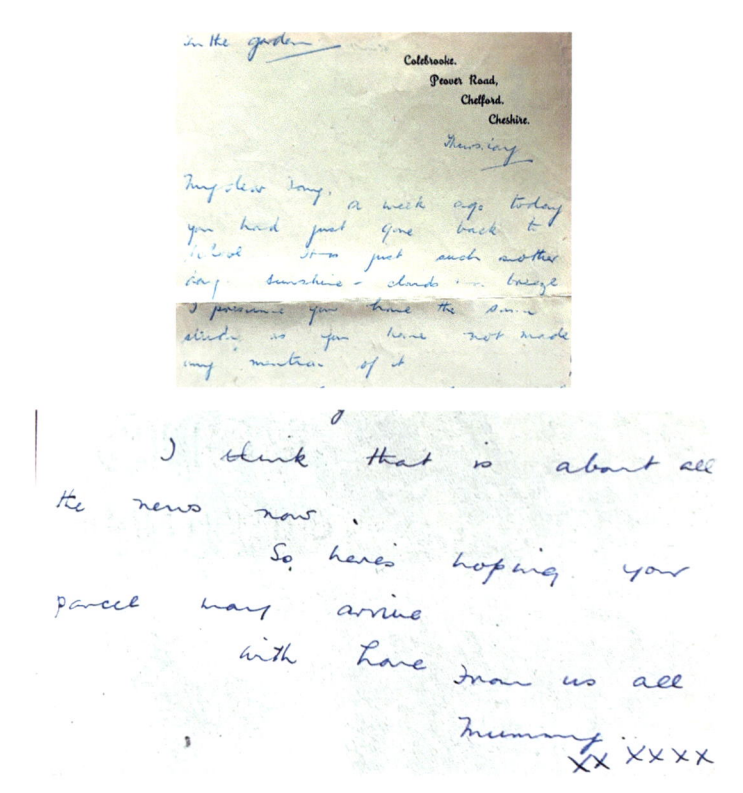

Above: Letter to Tony written in mother's handwriting

3 March 1949
Colebrooke,
Chelford

My dear Tony,

Thanks for your belated letter received on Wednesday. Although mine didn't reach you until Monday (it was posted early Fri afternoon) you should have written on Sunday, nevertheless, as you had had a letter from Daddy to reply to. I have sent you some jam as requested.

Yes, you can go to the JTC camp at Eaton Hall if you wish. You have been round it – with Daddy, Maureen and I after we had had a trip up the river. I wonder if you remember it.

We are all feeling a lot better now thanks. We had a severe frost last night and I daresay you will soon be having some skating if this keeps up much longer.

Patricia comes tomorrow for the week-end. On Saturday night they are going to the Rex with Ralph Birchenall (Wilmslow rugby player) and Brian Walker (Green Room member) to see the Southport Repertory Players give GB Shaw's play "Night Must Fall".

Richard is getting better but hasn't been out yet, as his ear has been troubling him again.

There were two lovely hares in the field this morning. I wish you had been there with a gun.

I am hoping to have my new lower dentures in by Tuesday as all being well, we are going to the Green Room Dance on the 11th.

Hoping you are keeping up with all your work – as well as you are doing with rugger (good show).

Lots of love, Mummy xxxxxx

7 March 1949
Colebrooke, Peover Road,
Chelford, Cheshire

My Dear Tony,

It is rather singular that the enclosed cartoon should have been published shortly after receiving your letter, a rather amusing drawing. Delighted to hear you are keeping fit and well may you continue to build up your strength, are you still OK for the Adexoline capsules?

You will be interested to be notified I have increased my weight by 11lbs since last July and I am confident that the Adexoline have been the cause and effect.

Patrician Hewitson arrived Friday evening. She and Maureen should have attended a Play at the Rex Wilmslow with

Brian Walker and Ralph Birchenall, unfortunately Pat went down Saturday 5.00pm with flu and a temperature 103 degrees and is still in bed; Dr Evans has called and twice and will be here again today. Hard luck but cannot be avoided.

The boys came for Maureen about 7.30pm amid the snow and blizzard arriving home 11.15pm with a car covered with frozen snow. Brian Walker is evidently a careful driver, so they were trouble free, Ann Goodyear Stood in for Pat a very fine gesture.

Ralph plays for Wilmslow 1st and scored a try last Saturday when they beat St Helens by 5pts to 3pts what a day for Rugger.

Will you advise me if you will require any financial assistance for Altcar and the date you are going and date of return home. Also, when do you start the Summer Vacation? If we are going away it is high time we commenced to negotiate accommodation. Note these requests and reply to them in your next epistle.

No golf to report except an attempt to play and being blown up snowed up frozen up and etc etc 2 balls lost and four holes scrambled. Snow being about 1½ to 2" deep it was foolish to give a putt of 6". I must be crazy but wanted some fresh air and a blow, and did we get it.

Lots of love, yours Daddy xxxxxx

Adexoline capsules were taken for vitamin D deficiency, and was important during rationing when, perhaps, people weren't getting the correct nutrients.

9 March 1949
Colebrooke, Chelford, Cheshire
Phone. Chelford. 26

My Dear Tony

Wishing you a Very Happy Birthday and Many of them.
Lots of love and best wishes from all of us xxx Daddy The

Birthday Cake is in this parcel. Take Care [doodle of skull and crossbones]

PS I thought it advisable to keep my present of Spencer Chapman at home until you return, I trust you are agreeable.

Maureen went down with the flu on Monday am and Mummy is in bed also. Pat was allowed to come downstairs this afternoon for a short period. I don't think Mummy will be fit enough to write but you know full well all her thoughts and good wishes are with you.

I am hoping to send some fruit, chocolate, sweets and a tin of fruit if at all possible, tomorrow.

10 March 1949
"In bed"

My dear Tony

Many Happy Returns! I'm afraid you're getting rather a raw deal this time as we've all been at death's door with flu. Patricia is up and doing, answering the telephone etc. Mummy is taking the normal course and so am I except for a positively vile cough. Ben came again this am and said my tonsils weren't so good.

The Green Room dance is completely 'off' and so is Altrincham next week – which is rather a blow. But I certainly won't feel up to it. Mrs Savage has been telephoning and they've managed to find someone else.

It's surprising how many people have been enquiring about us. Mrs H rings up and asks how we are and when D says "oh Patricia got up for lunch today – she'd reply "oh! Well, you're all feeling much better", (with great relief after offering to do things for us and not meaning it at all). From what I can gather from M he said to her (Mrs H) last night "It sounds like it doesn't it?" and slammed the receiver down!!

Richard has had another draining of one of his ears but is home again now. Hope the fives ball hasn't ruined your beauty. Trish's Pa is coming down in the car on Saturday to take her back.

The latest catch is a chap called Ralph Birchenall (friend of Cedric's). He's not a bad old stick really. Had a good lunch of goose etc in Cullens only this Tues with him.

Hope the cake arrives OK. It looked rather good. I can't recognize Thorman on your photograph. Mummy's getting you an archery target (she apologises for not writing) from a chap who started the Macclesfield Archery Club. And it if suits you I'll get you something the same. Or perhaps you can suggest something? Daddy's bought you that book.

With lots of love from Maureen.

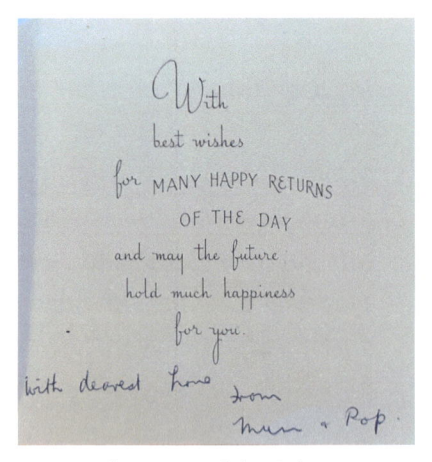

Above: Birthday card to Tony from his parents, on his sixteenth birthday, 1949

14 March 1949
Colebrooke, Peover Road,
Chelford, Cheshire

My Dear Tony

My letter this week must of necessity be short and I hope sweet. We all hope you enjoyed an excellent Birthday and I trust the parcels arrived safely and in good condition, again "many of them".

Last week I was head cook and bottlewasher, having to prepare trays of light foods and many liquids for the invalids; it would happen of course that Elsie [housekeeper] should be away at Prestatyn and still staying for a least another week. I managed quite well but was frightfully tired by the week-end.

Up early to prepare breakfast for four with 3 trays and running up and down the stairs and many other jobs. Off to business on the 8.33am and at it again when I arrived home.

Delighted to say "Trish" returned home last Saturday, Mr Hewitson driving over to bring her home, he left Windermere 5.0am, breakfasted at the Royal George, Knutsford taking a long rest and arriving for Trish at 9.30am and leaving at 10.00am

Mummy came downstairs for a short time yesterday and will most likely be up when I return this evening. Maureen relapsed a little last Thursday and Friday and Dr Evans advised bed for her until he arrives today, she appeared much better this am.

I have re-posted "Golfing" I hope it arrives with this letter. Enclosed please find Four Pounds which will be all you should require, don't throw it away on trifling objects, anyhow it is yours to please.

A longer letter than I anticipated, Lots of love, Yours Daddy

PS Please acknowledge – all the best and stick at that English etc. Pop

PPS Lancashire Rugger Champions Heaton missed the match after 75 appearances for the County.

I've added two photos here for interest, the first is Tony in the garden near the drive at Colebrooke, the laburnum tree can be seen in the background. The other photo is of Tony's grandparents, Fred and Isabella Bentley – they are the authors of the letters from Grandpa and Grannie.

Above: Tony in garden at Colebrooke and his mother's parents, Fred and Isabella Bentley

March 1949 (just after birthday, but no date)
Colebrooke, Peover Road,
Chelford

My dear Tony

Many thanks for your two letters. I was so glad the cake arrived safely and the other parcels too. I had to leave it to Daddy to pack them this time.

Maureen and I are up now but still feel very shaky and bar doing just the necessaries the rest of the work is having to wait. Needless to say Elsie is away and has been now for 3 weeks.

Daddy sent you £4 on Monday and he asked you to let him know if you received it safely. Up to now we have not heard so please send a card by return of post. You did quite well for Birthday cards! Fancy one from Dorcie – she must have an eye on you.

Your target has arrived in Macclesfield and will be fetched as soon as we can get it. Mr Whiting formed an Archery Club in Macc and he is willing to give you any tips or information you may require.

It is suggestions not surgestions by the way.

We were fully pleased Winder had won the Junior Cup. Did you play for them or not?

With being ill we couldn't go to the Green Room Dance. Maureen hasn't been able to play her part this week at "The Garrick" Altrincham. Barbara Pownall took it on instead.

A Heywood has asked her to go to a Dinner Dance on Saturday but as she hasn't been out at all yet, we told her she couldn't go and she specially wants to go to a dance with R Birchenall at Lyme Hall, Disley next Friday 25th with a party from Alderley and Wilmslow.

Daddy has gone to Witney by car today and I had hoped to go with him but as I haven't been out yet either I didn't feel up to it.

When you come home at Easter bring any English books that you are studying for S Cert and don't forget. Hoping the flu keeps away from Sedbergh and that you are putting in a lot of really hard work.

With lots and lots of love, Mum xxxxxx

2 May 1949
Colebrooke, Chelford

My Dear Tony,

I am sorry to have to advise that Mr Martin blew up last Saturday and had to tear his card, a great disappointment to myself and many others, he appeared to me to be a bundle of nerves, so much so that I was giving more thought to his game than my own and lost quite 5 or 6 short putts to be out in 49.

After he tore up I settled down to finish 45 gross 94 – 16 = 78. As you will see JGS pipped me by one stroke 94 – 17 = 77. It was a pity I had to play with George, I feel in the morning I would win the over 10s for Saturday's medal round and must admit I was disappointed at the score.

Even in the afternoon foursomes he could not hit a ball off the tee and when I got him out of the difficulties back he pushed the ball again, I will not add any more except to say it took us 9 shots for the 16th (foursomes you take alternative shots). R G Potter 80 – 10 = 70 well won the under 10s.

We are all well at present and the weather still holds fair, trust you are fit and well and now settled down. No further news at present.

Lots and lots of love, Daddy xxxxxx

PS £1 enclosed I owe you for your pull over. Do you want any golf shoes?

Golf scores:
10 and under
RB Potter 80 – 10 = 70
AG Southern 81 – 9 = 72
D Eadie 77 – 3 = 74
F Banks 78 – 4 = 74

Joint best aggregate for the 2 days: D Eadie 75 & 74, A G Southern 77 & 72 = tie 149 to be played off.

Over 10s medal
D Handford 90 – 13 = 77 to be played off with below
J G Smith 94 – 17 = 77
W Longworth 94 – 16 = 78
Foursomes medal
Holden & Partner 73 ½ – 1st
W Robinson & son 77 – 2nd

Scratch medal
Roger O Booth 76

Tuesday May 1949
Colebrooke

My darling Tony,

Here are your golf shoes and nuts inside them and a box of chocs.
    We went to see Grandpa last night. I'm afraid he is very poorly, and his heart is very weak. He sent you his love. Grannie was very pleased with the wool winder and she will be writing to you if she can find time.
    Grandpa thinks you have grown into a fine young man, and he is very proud of you indeed, so try to live up to it my love because Grandpa is a fine example of an English Gentleman who has lived a good life with the highest principles.
    I hope CA soon puts on some weight and height for you. Good show. Having someone else to compare notes with.
    Hope you are working hard, with dearest love, Mum xxxxxx

Thursday May 1949
Colebrooke, Peover Road,
Chelford, Cheshire

My dear Tony,

Another parcel has been sent off this week which I hope you will enjoy. Sweets are scarce here too. There were none in Knutsford so I had to put in the honey toffee until I can get some. You made several spelling mistakes this week by the way!

Scored of golf shots – correction off
Sherburn – Sherborne

Streight – straight
Pleasent – pleasant

No, Ralph didn't go to Sherborne but Silcotes near Wakefield. They had a very enjoyable day at the opening of the new cricket ground. Wilfred Rhodes (71) bowled the first over. Maureen was introduced to him. Ralph took 2 wickets, one of which was A B Sellars. An account would be in the Yorkshire Post (Thursday) and photographs etc.

Have you increased in weight yet? If not, you'll have to be telling CA about it.

The enclosed came yesterday re the Rugger Club. Can you spare the 5/-?

The Hills are having a glorious time at Rhosneigr. We have had 2 PC's from them.

I am expecting Mr Bailey to come today although the fridge doesn't arrive until Saturday and then whoopee!!

I saw some white shorts in Wilmslow yesterday, but they were £3.6.9 so I didn't buy them.

Grandpa is still apparently holding his own. I haven't been able to go this week as the decorators are in doing the landing, stairs and hall. We do look 'posh'.

Yesterday I put in the tomato plants and strung them up – I hope they do well. This drop of rain has made the plants – and the weeds grow so we are busy coping with them.

If you have time to write to Grandpa again.

Hoping the work goes well, with fondest love from us all, Mum xxxxxx

Thursday May 1949
"In the garden"

My dear Tony

A week ago today you had just gone back to school. It is just such another day sunshine – clouds and a breeze. I presume you have the same study as you have not made any mention of it.

Maureen, Ralph and I went to see Danny Kaye at the Odeon Cinema last night. The picture was not as funny as it might have been though Danny was of course very good.

We had a meal at the Princes Restaurant and Ralph brought us home in the car. Later Daddy came in with Mr Hampson, Mr E Pownall and Mr G Gill so they putted on the dining room carpet and then played dice. After they had left, we four went in the lounge and had a sing song. Ralph has a very clear high tenor voice – very pleasing indeed.

Here is some news for you! The Heywoods are leaving! Mrs Hill asked me if I knew about it but as I haven't seen Heywoods except Adrian – who didn't say anything – I didn't know. Apparently Mr Heywood has a job probably as Bursar at some school in Hertfordshire and they are going in June – so I believe. I'll give you all details when I know.

The Hill family is off to Rhosneigr on Saturday for a fortnight, so I hope they get some nice weather.

It was a pity you didn't shoot that rabbit – the wretched thing has eaten practically all the Spring cabbage.

We had a letter from Grandpa yesterday written by himself to say he was feeling a bit better but wasn't able to get up yet.

The lawn wants cutting and what about it? I expect Dick Camine [?] or Daddy will do them tonight as they have almost finished the rose bower.

Work extremely hard this term, at all your subjects there's a good chap. I'm relying on you.

With all my love, xxxx Mum xxxx

9 May 1949
Colebrooke, Chelford

My Dear Tony

"Good Shooting" a very good score but would have shown to greater advantage on a golf card whew!!!

We are still having fine weather, but the garden now sadly needs some rain and whilst I should prefer the fine spell to continue the rain would be greatly appreciated from a utilitarian viewpoint.

You will no doubt be sorry to hear Grandpa is very poorly indeed, Mummy was there last Friday and the Doctor reports that his heart has completely given out and in view of his age it is now only a question of time. Mummy requests you write to him, I should pen a cheerful note and a description of your activities shooting etc, etc, he will greatly appreciate having a letter from you. I should also express your sympathy with him in his sickness trusting he will soon recover. I hope to go to see him this evening.

A great score by Dewes and Doggart for Cambridge and a pity they could not be given time to beat the World Record 2nd wicket stand, but their captain Insole has declared the innings in the hope he may force a win. Had Essex not been 20mins late (their coach broke down) they may have achieved the record before close of play.

I had a good round yesterday am: 10th 5, 11th 4, 12th 5, 13th 5, 14th 3, 15th 5, 16th 7, 17th 3, 18th 5 = 42. 1st 5, 2nd 5, 3rd 5, 4th 5, 5th 5, 6th 3, 7th 5, 8th 6, 9th 5 = 44. Gross 86.

I was in the pond at the 16th second shot and picked our losing a stroke 4 short of the green and an approach too strong and 2 putts, I should have played my second shot down the middle short and 3 to the green. The 9th I was in the brook under clubbed 3 on the green and 2 putts.

Have you started cricket yet?

Keep hard at your studies and give your English a real good whacking.

Lots of love, Yours xxxxxx Daddy

Monday 9 May 1949
Colebrooke, Chelford, Cheshire

My dear Tony,

This photo arrived from the Stockport Advertiser this am and although they are not the ones I wanted I've decided to keep 'em so here is one. I thought you might like to have it. It's not particularly good – I look rather like Brer Rabbit. (Photo not with letter)

Last Wednesday I saw "The Secret Life of Walter Mitty" which was very funny in parts but could easily have been much funnier.

Above: Tony and friends in school uniform, Tony on LHS

Ralph came yesterday and brought his gramophone and some Caruso records. We spent all the time playing records. Our pick up has been taken away to be mended.

Uncle Harry, Aunty Sallie and Barbara [Coe] arrived about 7ish and stayed till 8. They had been to see Grandpa who is not at all well. Mummy and Daddy are going tonight, and I am going to the dentist! I rang up this am and the first booking was July 7th!! Or 6.30 tonight – so I thought I'd better book both!

The Heywoods are leaving about June 7th. Mrs H came round last night and was apparently (I didn't see her) most embarrassed because M said she knew already that they were going.

I received my 'Advanced" Certificate on Friday. It's rather vast!

The invitations have come for Marjorie's wedding but of course none of us can go.

On Friday I'm dragging Ralph to Altrincham to see "Faust" done by an amateur company. Two chaps from the Matthay (NSM) are singing in it and wanted me to go. I can't imagine what it will be like.

Mummy will try and get you some nuts tomorrow. Is this all for CA's benefit? Is the other CA chap a Winder boy? Do we know him?

Fluffy's kittens are absolutely sweet a la mo. She has moved them into the playroom – they're growing rather fast. According to the Heywoods she had 4 – they said there was a dead one lying about near the rest. I thought she only had 3 – didn't you. I don't think the other 5 have got their eyes open yet. They are not nearly so nice as Fluffy's.

Well, I must away and get some work done. I've been presented with a piece by Melan-Geioult, to do with another student with a view to playing it in the Houldsworth Hall in June if its good enough. I hope so – so here goes. Trills octaves etc!! Hope you're working hard too. We have yearly exams this term, so I've just got to work!

With lots of love from Maureen

13 May 1949
Colebrooke, Peover Road,
Chelford, Cheshire

My dear Tony,

I hope the parcel arrived safely. I am sitting in the shade on the lawn as it is so hot. It seems a pity that there is a change coming although the gardens are bone dry.

I hope you wrote to Grandpa. We have not heard anything since Monday, so he is still apparently holding his own. He has had letters from the Dean of Tamworth who used to be our vicar at Tunstall and the vicar of St Martins in the Fields – who was a curate there too.

The Hills are having a glorious time at Rhosneigr.

Mr Benton from Exeter was here on Tuesday night, and he is going to Sidmouth next week to see what he can do about rooms for us although he thinks we have left it very late. I have still not heard from that wretched Town Clerk. J Kitching also called last night just for an hour before his meal.

I went to a sale at Alderley yesterday hoping to buy a clock, but it fetched £10 2 – so I didn't bother! I bought you a nice leather blotter.

I was glad to hear you had scored 17 runs – keep it up. I should love to see you playing a good game. All being well Maureen goes with Ralph next Wednesday up to his old school for that cricket match, so we hope the weather is good for them. Tonight, they are going to hear "Faust".

We had the electrician yesterday and we are hoping to get a "fridg" in the very near future. We have been measuring to see if we can accommodate a large one or not – with a few adjustments we may be able to. Both sizes make Ice Cream!!!! Whoopee.

Daddy, Maureen and I have had an invitation to Dorothy Dunkleys wedding on June 8th at Astbury Church (near

Congleton). We have also had the invitation to Marjorie's wedding but fortunately I had written beforehand and said we should be away at that time.

As there is a lot of gardening to do and I want to write to Grandpa again I'll finish now. Hoping you are putting every ounce of energy into your school lessons.

With dearest love to the best son in the world, Mum xxxxxx

16 May 1949
M/C (Manchester)

My Dear Tony,

At last, the weather has broken and we have had a few showers of rain this am but for the good of the garden we shall require very much more volume. The lawns were looking very brown, and it was far too dry for planting out I can only hope for a continuance for a few more days.

I played the first round of the singles KO last Saturday against PG Armitage and he had one of those good days when everything went the right way, he had only 3 straight drives in the 18 holes but each time he found the ball sitting up and in no trouble at all, I would have a good drive or second shot and be in a divot hole or buried and in 2 bunkers my ball was buried six inches in a deep heel made hopeless for me to play from. I lost 4 & 3.

Yesterday George and I played the four-ball against Roger Booth and F Banks. We lost 5 & 4. Booth's figures alone were 72gross. He played very good golf indeed never off the line and if in any bunker he pitched out dead, Banks said he had never had an easier passage in any competition game just our luck to strike a player at the top of his form. Nevertheless, I thoroughly enjoyed it.

What do you think 10th drive and seven, 11th ditto, 12 driver and 6, 13 driver and 6, 15th driver and 4 at the back of the green, 18th driver and Brassie back of green ace from the back tees. We were never in the picture. Won 1 hole the 4th where I got a 4 nett 3 against his gross 4, perhaps 5 & 4 was not a disgrace.

Sorry to write that Grandpa is still very poorly, we had a letter from Grannie last Saturday and the Dr had been on the Friday and said his condition was extremely low.

I do hope you are polishing up your French and English etc. Keep hard at it and I know you will get the results.

Very little news, I was just thinking this letter is all golf maybe Mummy will have a more interesting letter for you later this week. No news from Sidmouth it looks a bad egg.

Lots of love your loving Daddy xxx

20 May 1949
4 Walton Way,
Walton, Stone

My Dear Tony,

Thank you very much indeed for the lovely wool winder. You may guess I find it very useful now that I have Grandpop to hold it for me.

Grandpop is about the same, still very poorly. This is the 7th week in bed, and you may guess he is getting tired of it, but still there is nothing else for him but complete rest.

I had Uncle Joe's logbook sent to me last week and I thought you might like to have it. Would you like me to send it on to school to you or wait until you come home?

Peter is just having his bath and squealing with laughter. He is doing fine. We do not see much of Uncle Id now the cricket season has started. He made 60 runs on Sunday. I suppose you will be pretty well occupied with the shooting and cricket.

A change on the weather was very good for the gardens. We have a lot to do in ours, but Uncle Id has put some beans, peas etc in and the rain has done good to start them. Not much news here. Trusting you are keeping fit and well.
With love from us all, Grannie

23 May 1949
M/C

My Dear Tony,

We received a letter from Grandpa last Friday in his own handwriting and he says that he is feeling slightly better. He had had letters from the Vicar of St Martin's in the Fields London and also the Dean of Tamworth, both old friends of

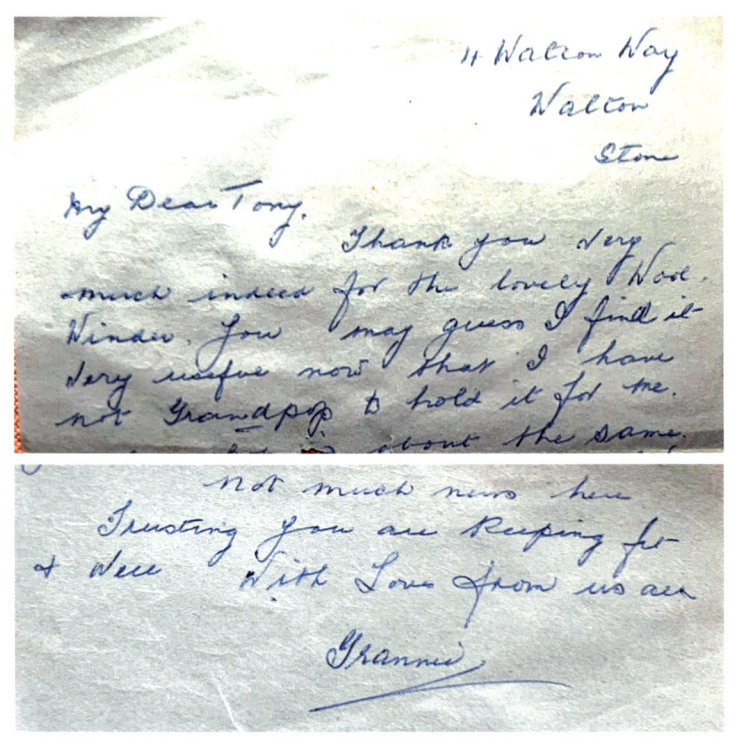

Above: Letter to Tony in his grandmother's handwriting

the family, they appear to have given Grandpa the greatest of pleasure; I have great expectations that he may now steadily recover.

The garden is looking very well, and the rain has done an immense amount of good work, the drive is an absolutely glorious blaze of blooms azalea, rhodo and red hawthorn and laburnum. Maybe the gardening I have been doing has stiffened my golf, if that is the case it is just too bad; I cannot neglect the garden.

We hope to play a few holes at Knutsford on Wednesday evening. It is a 9 hole course in Tatton Park. Being a member now of the Cheshire Golfing Society permits the use of this course otherwise you may only play at the invitation of a member, no ordinary visitor is allowed.

GM was playing his KO last Saturday and I fixed a singles with Hieldrup losing at the 18th after a tough battle. I was 3 down at the 14th and won 15, 16, 17th losing by the last putt on the 18th a good scrap. GM lost 5 & 3 to Bullivant in his KO then latter going round in 76 gross off 8 whew!!

Sorry the sweet situation is so difficult, but you may be better without (I am waiting for your storm of protest).

Mr Benton phoned on Friday last saying he had tentatively booked accommodation at The Victoria, Sidmouth. We confirmed the booking by telephone on Saturday evening. It is frightfully expensive, but I promised Mummy a nice holiday and may we now hope for fine weather.

How's the cricket etc. I trust you are doing well. Do write and let me know how your studies are progressing, would it help if Maureen corresponded in French?

Lots of love and all the best, Yours Daddy xxx

Cricket match at Sedbergh, and Tony (RHS) with, I think, his good friend Peter Sheard

26 May 1949
Colebrooke, Peover Road,
Chelford, Cheshire

My dear Tony,

I'm so glad you received my letter after all. It probably had a tour round somewhere. I hope this comes direct to you. We are having fun with the painters!! There were 4 painters and 2 plumbers here yesterday and the place was a beehive of activity.

The Refrigerator has been installed in the back kitchen so yesterday I made our first cream ices and very good they were too. I'd send some only I'm afraid they would only be a drink of water when they arrived. Anyway, you will be able to enjoy yourself when you come home. We come up on the Friday by the way. Sometime in the evening as Maureen is doing exams until Friday afternoon.

What a pity you couldn't go to Rossall! We were as disappointed as you were – but we hope you'll be chosen sometime soon.

Do watch your spelling and writing Tony. These last two weeks they have both gone "off" considerably. I only hope it isn't so in your schoolwork. Remember that these two terms mean a pass or not for SC.

I hope the questionnaire on Chaucer proves helpful. Answer all the questions fully and carefully with the aid of your book. It will be most useful and give you some idea what type of question to expect.

Did I tell you we had a letter from Grandpa written by himself so he must have been feeling a little better to do that!

Our rooms are booked at The Victoria Hotel, Sidmouth from Aug 20th to Sept 3rd at (whisper it) 2 guineas a day each! This includes early morning tea – breakfast in bed if wanted – choice of newspaper, free garage, dancing every week-day, 18 hole putting green and bedside telephone and radio diffusion and tennis court. We shall have to keep our spends down to a minimum.

Hoping you are benefiting from CA. With fondest love from Mum xxxxxxxx

Above: Photos from the trip to Sidmouth. Left to right: Bill, Marjorie, Tony and Maureen

30 May 1949
Manchester
My Dear Tony,

Delighted to hear you are fighting fit and trust you will continue to be so; we are all fit and well at present and enjoying the sunshine between the rain.

Last Friday we had a torrential downpour for hours on end which resulted in flooding in parts of Salford and Manchester. No doubt you would see photographs in the weekend papers; yesterday there was a strong breeze but a very pleasant and refreshing one.

Sunday was the day of the G Chadwick Challenge Cup. 36 holes medal the best aggregate of the morning and afternoon rounds. I played in the am medal round but not the pm. At the moment I have not the result, but I should imagine G Mather to be the eventual winner, off the Tiger Tees his score in the am round was 69 nett. Extraordinary good figures in that wind. I think his handicap is 6 and his margin of shots in hand of the field should have been good enough for him to finish in reasonable figures in the afternoon to win the cup.

Cheshire Wayfarers beat Cheadle Hulme yesterday. Fyffe the rugger player getting another 50 odd runs for the winners, Ralph's team have knocked up some big scores:

175 against Knutsford – Drawn

206 against Macclesfield – Lost (just imagine 415 runs in one afternoon)

179 against Alderley Edge – Drawn

204 against Cheadle Hulme – Won

They are a very sporting side and knock up the runs quickly and declare giving their opponents a chance to win.

Haywoods are leaving this week for Torquay. Mr H has accepted a berth as Bursar so they are selling everything. We hope to have cocktails with them this evening.

Sorry to hear you missed the trip to Rossall. Have you lost your sniping eye? Come on now get weaving. More news next week DV

Lots and lots of love, xxx Daddy

2 June 1949
Colebrooke, Peover Road,
Chelford, Cheshire

My dear Tony,

Thanks for your very interesting letter which contained the good news that you had been given a credit for the Chaucer and Precis papers. Do keep it up Tony and from now on polish up your English especially the use of relative pronouns etc. When you have two short sentences think of a suitable word to join them into one. Example from your own letter, 1) 'the acting and entertainment was excellent. ^for which^. I enclose a programme.' 2) 'This is the only pen that I have at the moment. ^as^ The other has just broken.'

You should have long passed the stage of using simple sentences.

Well now – on to the news. On Tuesday night Jimmie Kitching and his wife and Ralph came for the evening and we had quite a jolly dinner party which broke up at midnight. On Wednesday morning I went into Manchester to buy some new shoes and a new white flower to wear at Dorothy Dunkley's wedding next Wednesday.

In the afternoon I went to the sale at Haywood and bought a Butlers tray and a folding stand. We had drinks there on Monday evening by the way. Today they have gone to Torquay. Meanwhile Adrian is living with his aunts at Alderley.

I have been busy this morning planting out and hoped for a nice gentle shower but instead I have been landed with a hailstorm which I hope will soon stop.

The painters have finished, and we are now waiting for the plumbers to finish off the roof tiles.

At the moment we have a family of cats and kittens living round the back door. One ginger kitten has been given away and at the moment Maureen is sitting in the lounge with a very pretty grey one asleep on her shoulder.

All being well Maureen should play at the Houldsworth Hall on either June 23rd or 24th.

I have been lucky enough to get you some sweets this week so go carefully with them as I don't know when the next will come.

I had a letter from Grannie this morning saying you had written. Grandpa is about the same – no better but no worse. It must be very tiring for Grannie, but they have brought the bed downstairs which makes it easier for her.

> *We are thoroughly enjoying the 'frig' and I have put it to good use making some lovely ice cream dishes and setting fruit in jelly etc. Is that making your mouth water? Your turn will come though. The 16 guinea jacket is still in Reeds and likely to stay there I should say.*
>
> *Hoping you are still as fit as a flea, with dearest love from Mum xxxxxxxx*

An extra pencil note included which reads: "Fruit, choc, sweets. Will bring more next weekend. Surely you want a few other things don't you? Love Mum xx Jam, beans, jelly, apple pie, tart, tin milk evaporated and condensed. Yes! Buy the shorts but keep them clean for the holidays."

The arrival of the family's first fridge in May 1949 caused great excitement for Marjorie, how it must have helped with the management of food storage.

Prior to the arrival of electric refrigeration, some people in Britain used ice boxes to keep things cool. These wooden boxes were lined with tin or zinc and insulated with material such as sawdust, cork or seaweed. A large block of ice was held in a compartment at the top of the box and the cold air then circulated down to keep the contents cool. A drip tray collected the melting ice and had to be emptied daily.

Without an icebox many homes, including Colebrooke, had a pantry, which was a cool, small room, usually next to the kitchen, sometimes with a stone or marble slab, where foods such as bread, cheese, milk, meat, eggs, etc. were stored.

Fridges as we know them today started arriving in British homes in the 1920s, but it wasn't until after World War II that they were mass produced. Only a very small percentage of households would have had a fridge in 1949 – when Bill and Marjorie got theirs – and even less owning one with a freezer compartment.[35]

---

35   www.historyofrefrigeration.com/refrigeration-history/history-of-fridges

20 June 1949
Colebrooke, Chelford

My Dear Tony,

We have had a glorious spell of fine weather this last week and the prospects this am appear bright enough for its continuance.

I read in one Sunday newspaper that F Stranahan had been searching for a place to exercise his weightlifting and eventually some weight lifter has loaned him bar bells 2 ewt ? each for his use and FS's idea being to strengthen both back and shoulder muscles for his golf.

You will be gratified to hear that your efforts on the rose bower have produced highly successful results. The rose that was intermingled with the gooseberry bushes has produced the most marvelous show we have ever had from it, masses of orange cream roses and still plenty of buds coming along. We must have pruned it right.

Mummy and I saw some excellent bowling by a young boy about 17½ from the naval home base at Warrington, they were playing Alderley Edge who turned out the first team containing 3 or 4 varsity blues. Darran the star batsman was clean bowled for a 0 and the Edge were 57 for 7 then they made a stand 133 for 8, one left handed batsman could not be moved and the navy appeared to have only 2 bowlers, the fast bowler had taken 5 wickets and almost bowled out his heart for 1hr 35mins too long a spell. With Alderley 142 and 10 or 15 minutes they looked certain winners only needing 16 runs. The left hander was at last bowled 147 for 9. He made 70. The fast boy came again and with his second ball clean bowled the last man, the navy winning by 10 runs with about 3 minutes to spare. I must find out the boy's name from next week's Advertiser. Just imagine 6 clean bowls.

I sincerely hope you are fit and well and sticking hard at work. All being well we shall soon be seeing you.

Yours with lots and lots of love xxx Daddy.

27 June 1949
Colebrooke, Chelford, Cheshire
Tel. 26. Chelford

My Dear Tony,

I was delighted to receive a message from Mr Smith saying he was fortunate enough to meet you personally and how fit and well you looked, the parcel was received with acclamation I have no doubt.

Yesterday he passed quite a crowd of Sedbergians who had been bathing at Waters Meet, the weather has certainly been ideal this year, but evidently you appear to have a very poor cricket team, it is about time you took a hand in setting an example.

Maureen has gone to stay with Trish Hewitson this week-end and returns home to-day, they had plans all arranged for bathing in Windermere Lake, I sincerely hope it was warm enough for ML.

In the Captain's Prize Comp last Saturday I returned a 74 nett to gain 3rd place. C Hodgson off 19 came in with 70 nett, a young fellow and long hitter. I cannot understand the system of handicapping, I have played against him previously and he was 15 h'cap??? And he beat me 2 & 1. So what!

Roger Booth had an excellent round 73 less 1, 72nett. We were all playing from the Tiger Tees he required a 72 to beat the amateur course record.

Mummy just arrived so I must conclude. More news this week-end.

Lots of love yours xxx Daddy

Above: LHS Tony at Sedbergh with his good friend Peter Sheard

11 July 1949
Colebrooke, Chelford

My dear Tony,

I'm writing this at the NSM [Northern School of Music] as Daddy is in bed with a chesty cold and I doubt if he could be bothered. It was so stifling at home yesterday that I wished we were at Sedbergh once more tickling trout!

The flute exam was awful – I failed. He said my breathing was very unsteady – well of course it was I was shaking like a leaf. However, it's not important in that it is connected with LR. I haven't told Daddy yet so I hope that by the time he is up he will have forgotten all about it. Anyway, I've decided I don't like Charles Groves anymore!

We had a pleasant time on Saturday evening. At least Mummy and I did – we went to Hills for a cocktail party to meet some American friends who were staying with them for the wkend. Mrs Austen was very American and it wasn't always easy to understand her. He wasn't so broad. The Carruther's were there and Mr C's brother. They are all Canadians and live opposite the Vicarage in the ivy covered house. Mr and Mrs Hubble were there – she tried to rope me in for her beastly garden fete next Saturday. I expect I shall have to go as Mummy is doing something. The Howarths were there too. He plays cricket for Chelford.

Yesterday we had it all arranged at last to go to the Lowe's. Of course, we had to cancel it. We've been trying to fix up a day since they came to us for my birthday wk end last year!

At the moment I'm awaiting a sight singing aural exam. Ghastly. Have to do all sorts of foul things. On Wednesday I have Keyboard Harmony and one day next wk my piano exam. Except for Elocution on Thursday of this wk I shall be jolly glad when they are all over.

Jim called the other evening and stayed for hours. He brought us a cutting and photos from the paper recording Speech Day. He's been round twice with his Chambers and things to see Daddy. He's a very decent fellow at heart and is always eager to hear any news of Sedbergh.

On Sunday Wilmslow Rugger Club are forming a cricket team and playing Old Birkmions (I think). After they are holding a dinner party at The Royal Oak, Alderley Edge. Should be quite good fun. On Wednesday I'm going to the ballet to see Coppelia.

Have you done much river bathing lately? I do wish there was somewhere to bathe at home. When do your exams begin? We finish on July 22nd but there is a holiday course the following week and Louis Kentaer (?) is coming for 2 days. I haven't decided whether or not to go yet.

Must away to a lesson now. How is Richard? Send him my regards.

With love from M & D. Lots of love Maureen

14 July 1949
Colebrooke, Peover Road,
Chelford, Cheshire

My dear Tony,

Today I have sent off to you a box of ripe gooseberries. Divide them up among your friends. I thought we might have heard from you sometime this week knowing Daddy was ill. He is dressed today but still feeling rather groggy after a rather nasty attack of flu and congestion of the lung.

Maureen and I went to Hills on Saturday evening 6.30pm to 8pm for cocktails to meet the American people. It was quite a nice party.

We were pleased to see Sedbergh had done quite well in the Bisley shoot. I hope Winder does well in the House match. Are you entering for any of the sports? Let me know what you are doing.

Please write a more interesting letter this week – last weeks was a poor effort, quote "I had to has a stitch… But I is healing rapidly" What careless mistakes Tony. Do read your work over and make any necessary alterations.

I hope your hand has healed up by now. I have done the same thing almost. First, I cut deeply into my 1st finger and then the next day I did the same to my thumb. Fortunately, they are both practically better – although now I have two huge lumps made by insect bites, and they are hard and red and fiery and altogether a jolly old nuisance.

Please make further enquiries re my gloves – cream lace ones, let me know the result.

The rain has come at last so it looks as though Mrs Hubble's Garden Fete on Saturday will have to be held in the Parish Hall. I am having a stall of remnants.

The Hills are going to see the "Craig" on Monday to see if suitable for Richard.

No more news for now and don't forget I want a thoroughly interesting letter… or else…!!

With lots of love from all xxxxxx Mum

15 July 1949
Colebrooke, Peover Road,
Chelford, Cheshire
Friday morn.

We hope to leave here 2.30pm next Friday.
Wear not "ware" (this means cups etc)
My dear Tony,

Enclosed is the programme of last night's concert. It was very good indeed and Maureen played confidently and well. Ralph came with Daddy and I and Mary Lane brought a friend too. She was pleased to receive your letter, but you failed to say whether you had received my parcel which I sent on Monday.

Maureen is going up to Windermere tonight for the week-end as it is The Craig Fete.

What a poor cricket side you have this year! Last Sunday Daddy and I went to Alderley and saw some marvelous bowling by a boy from a naval training centre. He skittled 6 wickets and 1 caught!!

Ralph is off on Sunday with a few friends to Buckingham to see a Compton Benefit match. Richard Hill has gone to Cheltenham today to sit for his entrance.

I do hope you are working hard. Put all you know into it.

See you next Friday. Lots of love Mum xxx

18 July 1949
Colebrooke, Chelford

My dear Tony,

Just a hasty note as Daddy is busy doing some work with James. He's up now but feeling pretty rotten as he's bound to after flu or whatever it's been.

I've had all my exams now except piano (the most important to me) which is tomorrow at 10.44. Hold thumbs! (That will have to before the results as this won't arrive in time!). I've passed them all except flute, (Daddy doesn't know about that one!). I didn't do any work for it. The only results that aren't out are 'Appreciation'.

We give our Summer Concert on Friday evening, orchestral, choral, solo items. I'm singing in 'Hiawatha's Wedding Feast'.

On Wednesday afternoon I had a swim in town, but it wasn't terribly nice. You never know whether the baths are really clean or not. In the evening I went to see 'Coppelia' at The Opera House. On Thursday I had a speech training exam and came out 2nd with 81.

Saturday was the day for Mrs Hubble's Garden Fete. It started to pour with rain at about 3.15. I didn't go but Mummy did as she had a remnant stall and sold everything, making £13.0, which I thought was pretty good. The whole fete got £102.0.0 which was pretty good for a wet day.

In the evening I went to Knutsford and saw a grim film definitely to be avoided "No Room at the Inn". Very soul destroying. Sunday afternoon Wilmslow Rugger Team played Old Birkonians (rugger) at cricket and won by about 20 runs. Ralph was Captain. We had tea in the Badminton Hall. After the game we had a dinner party there. Agar's, a Manchester firm, catered. Cedric brought Shirley Hamon along. John Leese (wkt keeper) was there with Ann Seymour and heaps of other members of the rugger club. Brian Walker was there. Quite recovered from his operation. It was great fun.

We break up officially on 23rd and the holiday course starts in 4 days next week; but I don't think I can be bothered to go.

The cats continue to catch an abundance of rabbits and various other beasts.

The Hills called on Saturday to see Daddy – they've gone up to Windermere today to see the Craig.

Joan Smith is home, but Pat doesn't come for ages. What date do you come home – 4th?

Must away and practice now. Pity about the holiday on the Broads. Glad Richard can come anyway. Lots of love Maureen. M & D send their love.

Above: Tony by the playing fields at Sedbergh and Tony on a walk in the hills above the school

21 July 1949
Colebrooke, Chelford
My dear Tony,

We were pleased to receive a more interesting letter from you this week, but you failed to mention my gloves. Have you made any further enquiries about them or have I "had it"?

We see in the paper that parents are asked to come to visit the Camp on Sunday July 31st. Will you let us know what time in the afternoon to meet you and where. If we have to have chits send them to us. We shall be able to bring home your golf clubs for you too.

Daddy is feeling much better but is soon tired if he tries to do anything. He will not go into town this week.

The times of the sports events are very slow aren't they? A ¼ mile in 59 secs!! Ralph says he did it in 50.2 and this week in the sporting events it was 48.9 or 49.8. I just forget which.

Daddy says the condition shouldn't have made much difference as the record mile was run in the foulest of weather on a muddy track. We hope Saturday's events show some improvement.

"Practice" is a noun – such as a Doctor's practice. You should have said "I practised – verb – for the Lord Roberts' Cup". These are tricky words you are likely to have for SC.

What a pity you had to refuse the Broad's offer. Daddy once had a very enjoyable holiday sailing up there. I think you will have seen the snaps of them cooking sausages etc.

Grandpa, I am sorry to say, is still very ill and it doesn't seem likely that he will ever get up again.

We had the Garden Fete at Mrs Hubble's on Saturday, and although it rained, we made £102. I took £13 worth of remnants and sold them all.

Maureen and Zoe Mason have made a recording of their duet. Now don't forget to let us have all the information about

Camp etc. Hoping you have a good time.
   Your affect Mum xxxxxx

15 October 1949
Lower Key, Rushworth

Dear Boat,

I'm afraid that I have not got your various articles of missing clothing. I should think the most likely people would be the two in the next door cubes to you.

I had quite a good time with, or rather most of the time without dear Peter. There were some smashing dames there, two of whom use to live in Halifax and now live in Harrogate and I know them quite well. There was also David Crowther who was a friend of mine at Cliveden House, and I see him occasionally, and Roger Moores, so I was not at all dependant of PY. I also got on very well with a girl who I met by chance there – in fact I nearly missed my train home saying goodbye to her, after having been at her house till well after midnight the night before!

I was sleeping at a hotel and Yeoward was usually dragged home to bed soon after 10pm so I had late evenings to myself. I'll tell you more about this, in just a week's time. What a thought.
   Yours aye, Luke

10 October 1949
Colebrooke, Chelford, Cheshire
Tel. 26. Chelford.

My Dear Tony,

Just a brief note to say we are all keeping fairy well and sincerely hope you are again feeling fit and well and putting some weight on again.

I am certainly feeling the benefit of my abstinence from smoking and maybe in a few days or weeks or months I shall be fighting fit.

You will be surprised and delighted to hear JGS scooped the prizes during the Autumn meeting. The 1st day 1/10/49 he returned a 70 nett to win the Jubilee Vase and last Sat 8/10/49 a 76 nett which with the 70 = 146 for the best net aggregate to win the Ashford Cup, in addition he and partner won the foursomes with 75's net.

JGS had prizes of cocktail shaker, table petrol lighter and 12 65s in addition sweep money of about £9 for the two weeks, there is no doubt he has been training for it and practicing at home as well, jolly good show.

I was disappointed at being away for the 1st Oct and on the 8th Oct Alan Croker was married at 2.0pm, which meant my rushing round the course like a scalded hen and not being able to play in the afternoon.

Old James certainly has the power to concentrate and also patience to wait the golden opportunity.

Kindly convey my sincerest thanks to Mr Bishop and I do hope you are cramming and paying every attention to your lessons. We want and will have that School Certificate.

Went to Tyldesley yesterday to see Granny and Aunty Ethel and met some ghastly fog on the way home. Grannie looks quite well, and we hope to have her with us this week-end for a sojourn of a week or two.

Poor rugger show against Blackburn, Ralph by the way is ill with pleurisy after a nasty bump in the chest.

More news next week. Lots of love xxx Daddy

17 October 1949
Colebrooke, Chelford, Cheshire

My dear Tony,

I fully expected a reply to the card I sent you on Tuesday asking if your parcel had arrived. If not, I must put in a claim for the contents. It contained collars, opener, needles, cakes, biscuits, sweets, choc and chestnuts. I'm not sending one this week until I know.

We were all delighted with your maths paper. It really shows you are putting up a good show and I hope your other subjects show a good improvement too. Let me know your fortnightly place as soon as you know.

Wilmslow inflicted their first defeat against Shrewsbury winning away 17-8 and the A team beating the A Shrewsbury team at home too. A jolly good show.

Your rugger tie has arrived – do you want it sending on?

Grannie is looking a lot better and sends her love. We went to see "Bless the Bride" on Wednesday and enjoyed it very much although P Brooks wasn't in it!!!

Oh!!! Michelle [next-door neighbour] came round on Wednesday evening to ask about the boundaries and hedges etc and Daddy soon told him where he got off as regards the wire netting. He explained that his wife was frightened of Peter. [Peter was the family dog – a golden Labrador.]

I am sending you these 2 collars in case the others are lost, which seems to be the case as your empty tin arrived on Tuesday afternoon.

We go to the Green Room show tonight and hope to enjoy it.

We are taking Grannie home on Sunday. What fun your CCF night "do's" are – I guess you were all beautifully clean after it all.

Ralph called at 8.20am and picked up Maureen to take her into town by car. It is 12 months since they were first introduced.

Hoping you are still feeling fine. With dearest love from all Mum xx

Above: Rugby match at Sedbergh

17 October 1949
Colebrooke, Chelford, Cheshire

My Dear Tony,

Delighted to hear you are again feeling in the best of health and may you go from strength to strength.

There is very little exciting news to report this week, Grannie arrived on Friday evening and no doubt you will be delighted to know she looks very well indeed.

RWB [Ralph Birchenall] *will be unfit for rugger until November 6th, that is according to his medical advisors, the fluid has gone but the ribs are still badly bruised; needless to say, Ralph is very annoyed and disappointed at missing his opportunities for Captaining; the worst feature is that the tackle was totally unnecessary and unfair. RWB had kicked the ball – with arms outstretched for balance, was barged into with the opponent's shoulders crashing across his unprotected ribs and chest.*

How nice to have your note stating progress is fairly good, keep it up and as they say "get stuck into it", the essay must have been very good to have such excellent comment from the Master.

My golf being only week-ends when possible has deteriorated somewhat, many holes quite good but insufficient concentration on the few holes making a poor total.

I am still very busy and quite unravelling in the volume of work which keeps me more than fully occupied.

From the gloomy speeches this week-end by various Cabinet Ministers I gather the impression we shall have more taxes, more ? and possibly a resumption of clothes rationing, what a life! 4 ½ years after the war.

Keep smiling and may you enjoy life. All the best, with lots of love xxx Daddy

PS I detest these pens and cannot write legibly with them.

14 October 1949
Colebrooke, Chelford, Cheshire
Friday morning

My dear Tony,

I was very pleased to hear that you had gained 2 places in form and that you had written such a good essay. Do keep it up there's a good chap.

Yesterday I sent you another parcel – not too many gramaphone needles as I want you to spend any spare time swotting.

Dick Camm brought the chestnuts from Heyworth's where they are falling off the trees.

Grannie comes today from Tyldesley to stay a while. Ah! "all right" not alright. Do not confuse with "already" which is an adverb meaning "quite ready" as against "all ready" meaning is "every one ready".

I hope your rugger team bucks up a bit. We would like to hear of a few wins. Ralph will not be able to play until Nov 5th the doctor advises.

I didn't write last night as I had a nasty headache due to some lotion getting in my eye at the hairdressers and giving me 'jip', so I'm writing it now at 8.30am. Elsie isn't coming either so I shall have to get to work. Hoping you keep fit and keep up the good work.

With fondest love from Mum xxx

16 October 1949
Falmouth

My Dear Tony

I was more than delighted to learn about 14 days ago through the Bush that you had earned, deserved, received your first team colours for Sedbergh – unfortunately I have been somewhat unwell otherwise I would have sent my congratulations to you earlier. Nevertheless, I am just delighted and no doubt great pride will also be derived from and by your progressive achievements – by those who are near and dear to you – it is a great spur to ambition to realise the pink of happiness that such success give to our parents, sister and others who all hold dear to one. Continue in your progress Tony, nothing is out of reach of determination if it is supported with those principles of faith, truth, loyalty and cleanliness.

Good fortune with you, if you continue to earn it as I understand you are doing.

Funniface [name illegible]

The Top of Winder Hill is a great place for aspiration and resolution. F

October 1949 (no date)
Colebrooke, Chelford, Cheshire

My dear Tony,

Today I have sent you another parcel and hope it arrives safely. Daddy and I were exceedingly pleased with the effort you are putting into your work, and we hope very much that it will be sustained all through the term. It certainly has proved that you can do it if you put your mind to it.

Mr and Mrs A Cox and Mr Dundenny are staying at the Egerton this week. Daddy has had a game of golf with the men folk whilst I had a day in town with Mrs Cox. I came home really worn out, so I went to bed early. The Hills are in Windermere this weekend.

We had a delightful surprise on Tuesday. Ralph took us to Belle Vue to hear Gigli sing. It was a very lovely concert and I only wish I had heard him when he was a little younger and in his prime.

Tomorrow, we go to the Rugger Dance at the George, Knutsford. It will be an important night for Ralph – so Maureen has had a new evening frock for the occasion. I shall wear my black lace and Papa has paid a visit to Moss Bros and brought home some "tails".

For the first time I have started a fire in the dining room as there were a few degrees of frost last night and this morning the garden was white over.

I hear Benson is in the 1st XV and weighs about 12stones. He must be huge! Wilmslow lost to Sale last week, but it was a very good game. They haven't a fixture for this Saturday so will be having a practice instead.

The little black kitten has vanished – so now we are 3!! Please write a little longer letter than last week – after all its only once a week. Lots and lots of love Mum xxxxxx

31 October 1949
Colebrooke, Chelford, Cheshire
Tel. 26 Chelford

My Dear Tony

I had just commenced to pen these lines when the telephone rang, Mummy saying she had just received your letter and its contents stated you had still not received my letter.

I have given instructions for enquiries to be made at this end and I am only too thankful that there was no enclosure in this instance. Maybe someone has had a look and then destroyed same.

Sorry to read the football result St Bees 8 Sedbergh 0. You will have to show them how it is done, by the way I understand that Benson is now in the 1st XV.

We all had a most enjoyable time at the W Rugger Dance last Friday but what a pity the main course duckling was ruined by inefficient cooking, good food spoilt. I managed to obtain a perfect rig out, full evening dress from Moss Bros and it fitted OK.

My golf as I have written to explain has recently gone under a cloud, the tee shots OK better than ever, but any distance within 120 yards of the green I am hopeless and if it were possible, I should leave nearly all my irons in the locker, I do hope I shall improve before the Winter KO starts.

Frank Robinson beat Roger Booth 3 & 2 in the final of the ECC Hunter Trophy. All players start off scratch. 16 entered and the final was over 36 holes. In the Winter four-ball my partner is Mr Eric Steward.

Business is still brisk despite the jitterbugs of the Government, but the effects of devaluation have not yet been fully felt, and I am sorry to say they will not be pleasant these coming months; we shall have increased prices for all wool, cotton and many other textiles and minerals and believe me somebody is going to feel the pinch.

More news next week. Keep fit and concentrate, the efforts since the holidays are showing results.

Lots of love your loving Daddy xxx

Telegram received 1 November 1949
Longworth, Winder House, Yorks

Maureen and Ralph engaged. Love Mummie and Daddy

Above: Tony's sister, Maureen, with her fiancé, Ralph Birchenall, sitting on the bank of the front lawn at Colebrooke. The rug they are sitting on was still in use when my children were small

The joy and excitement of Maureen's engagement to Ralph Birchenall is wonderful to read; he was welcomed into the family with open arms. Maureen and Ralph's daughter, Fiona, remembered that Ralph spent the war years in Canada as a flying instructor, and only returned to England on his father's insistence, to join the family firm – Beresford and Birchenall – who were spinners and weavers of narrow fabrics. Years later he ran a pet shop on Princess Street in Moss Side, Manchester and lived in a flat above the shop. I remember visiting – he had kitted out the basement with wall-to-wall fish tanks and, very excitingly, had some piranhas for sale. Sadly, in the Manchester riots of 1981, many shops were looted and destroyed. Fiona remembered that after the riots insurance companies wouldn't provide cover for the shops, so Ralph made the decision to stop trading.

On a personal note, Ralph was my favourite uncle – I adored his company. He had the most infectious giggle and when I was little would sit me on his knee and pull my hair bunches until I was crying with laughter. For Christmas his were always the biggest presents under the tree – I remember the excitement now.

3 November 1949
Colebrooke, Chelford, Cheshire

Ralph thinks you ought to have been consulted first – but hopes you approve.

My dear Tony

Many thanks for your interesting letter. You seem to have been having a very busy week. And so have we!! Weren't you thrilled with our news? Ralph came on Monday evening to ask Daddy's permission to be engaged and we celebrated with a bottle of muscatel. On Tuesday they went to buy the ring – 2 diamonds with a sapphire between. Very nice indeed. In the evening Ralph bought his mother and father over to meet us.

On Wednesday I went to town to do a little shopping. Daddy and I bought Ralph an engagement present of a silver inkstand which he liked very much. Maureen bought him a full set of cuff-links, evening buttons and studs.

Today at the Rotary Club luncheon Ralph was the guest of honour and was asked to sit by the President. He called on everyone to drink the health of Ralph and Maureen.

They have had lots of phone calls and letters and good wishes after the announcement in the Guardian on Wednesday – a cutting enclosed. It was in the Telegraph today. By this morning's post we had two advertisements from press photographers and one from a dance band – in case we want a party I expect.

All the waitresses in Fullers restaurant wanted to see the ring and told Ralph to let them know in good time when the wedding was to be, and they would have a cake for him.

On Saturday we go to Birchenalls for a meal. Ralph is playing at Rochdale in the afternoon. On Sunday Maureen is going with Birchenalls to see some wealthy relatives at Derby. So, from now on I can see they will be very busy.

Yes! You can go to Ascrofts in January and see you bring a ham home with you!

The Havana? Photographer is coming here on Monday to take Maureen's photograph!!! Hoping you are still working very hard. With dearest love from all Mum xxx

Additional note attached:

Mr E Stuart rang Daddy and said Robin would be home on leave probably Dec 10th and that you must fix up a game together. He is in the Black Watch and stationed at Fort George.

Maureen sends her love and thanks you and Peter for the telegram.

You have only one month now to School Cert to put all your heart and soul in the work to get it.

Love M

7 November 1949
Colebrooke, Chelford, Cheshire

My Dear Tony,

Well! I suppose you have again, burned Guido Fawkes. We all went on invitation to Birchenalls on Sat evening for a meal and passed a few bonfires during the journey, but I did not notice anything spectacular or noisy, I have missed the pleasure of creating a bang this year.

Now that we have experienced a week of tumult and excitement I am hoping we shall be allowed to settle down to a more or less steady routine; as you may well imagine Mummy has been equally as excited over the engagement as Maureen.

We were quite pleased with Ralph's parents and after the meal his pater entertained us to a very fine cine show. The pictures were taken on a 16mm Kodachrome and the colourings portrayed on the screen of Ralph and his friend climbing the rocks for Seagulls, Herring Gull, Tern and Kestrel nest and eggs, were simply exquisite and must have required the maximum amount of patience and care in timing and adjustment. I do hope you will see it later.

Mr B remarked that he had studied and read the instruction book for weeks and weeks before deciding to risk shooting the film, they cost 35/6 each and at that price you cannot afford to make a mistake.

Golf washed out last Saturday am when I should have played in the monthly medal, it didn't just rain it was a complete deluge.

Cheshire 6pts Lancs 3pts. What a terrific surprise, before the match the result was a foregone conclusion according to the experts but the final result was a real tonic for Cheshire. It was a pity that D Rothiman? [Wilmslow] had to stand down, being indisposed at the last moment.

R says Wilmslow played well against Rochdale to lose 9pts to 8pts and with less injuries and a little luck may have turned the tables.

Poor show on the part of Oundle. Yes, OK for you to fix up with Ascroft if you wish to.

Mr Eric Steward asked me to advise you that Robin is now at Fort George Inverness in the Black Watch, he has plenty of work to do which keeps him fully occupied; he anticipates commencing a leave about Dec 21st and would appreciate your fixing a game of golf; will you note your diary and contact him on your vacation.

Lots of love your Daddy xxx

PS I keep buying fruit etc and no doubt Mummy sends it on.

7 November 1949
Sunset, Hough Lane, Wilmslow

My dear Tony,

It is just a week ago today since Maureen and I received your father's blessing and official approval to shock the local population with the announcement of our engagement. Whether or not it shocked you I can't say, I can only hope that you approve. You will have heard I expect from Maureen the full cycle of events, and our only regret was that you were not there to join in the celebration, but we'll have another one when you come home don't worry.

Of course Maureen and I both felt that as well as asking your father's permission – that Monday's wait until I saw him in the evening was quite an ordeal – we should both have consulted you as well, but if we had had to wait for a wire from you as well as waiting for your father's consent we should probably both have been hospital cases with nervous breakdowns. I think there's a moral here, when you come to the same point for heaven's sake don't go and waken the old man up at 11.45 – particularly when he's been in bed since 6.0 with a rotten cold and then have to chew your nails all the next day waiting for his reply – grab him, corner him and don't give him time to keep you in suspense.

On the Tuesday Mum and Dad came round for the official visit and in the morning Maureen and I got the ring and I know she'll be dying to show it to you, we both like it very much indeed and everyone else seems to admire our choice. Anyway, perhaps the stories will still be there when you come home though JM has practically worn the ring part away already taking it on and off to have a good look at it.

I think the part Maureen dislikes most is that now, when we might be making plans and perhaps buying in the odd bit of antique furniture at sales, she should be working harder than ever. Of course, we both realized this, but now that it is an actual fact I think she finds it rather harder to face up to than she anticipated. I shall I suppose, have to play my part by only seeing her at weekends and that will be far from easy.

On Saturday after an absence of six weeks I got back on the rugger field again only to see the side beaten by Rochdale 9-8. Unfortunately we were 7 short of the original team picked – Mike Rhodes off with fluid on the elbow – Constant ill – Tim Hough ill (so we hardly got the ball from the set scrums at all) Roach (prop) ill, Massey playing for Cheshire, Poizer (2nd row) ill and David Rollinson who should have been playing for Cheshire, but is now off for a month with fluid on the knee.

Next week we play Davenport and Massey and Rhodes will both be back anyway. The Sale game we lost a bit unluckily 12-6. Each side scored one try, but Griffiths of Sale kicked 3 penalty goals to one by Wilkins – although another ?? from the halfway line hit the post and just bounced away.

On the phone at lunch today Maureen gave me a graphic description of a try by Longworth v Kenal GS following a forward rush and then asked me to explain it! These women who don't understand our games! Anyway, good work, keep it up and see what you can do in the Christmas School Boy Games at Wilmslow – or will you be away?

Cheerio for now, give my regards to Dicky. I'll look forward to seeing you before long and for heaven's sake don't bother replying, I know you haven't got time.

All the best, Ralph

9 November 1949
Colebrooke, Chelford, Cheshire

Darling,

Just a very hasty note in reply to yours this morning. Needless to say, I was delighted that you had your 3 XV colours and I phoned Daddy to tell him too. He was very very pleased indeed.

Enclosed re WRC (Wilmslow Rugger Club) if you are chosen to play you would have to return home either the 8th or early train 9th. What a pity Vaughan dropped.

Parcel sent off to you today. More news later. Lots and lots of love Mum

Put a scarf round your neck when you go to the "DENTIST".

9 November 1949
Colebrooke, Chelford, Cheshire

My Dear Tony,

Mummy has just telephoned to me giving details of your letter. I am delighted to hear that your form position at half term is so much improved, and I do hope you will put on the pressure to still further improvement. You can do it as these results prove.

Hearty congratulations on the selection to the 1st XV, may your tries be many and your feet sure.

Enclosed is a £1 for a celebration in the grubber with your friends, and a £1 for the usual expenses.

Lots of love, in haste, Daddy x

10 November 1949
Colebrooke, Chelford, Cheshire
Tel. 326. Chelford

My dear Tony,

I have had a trip to Manchester today in the hope of doing a little shopping but who should I meet in Kendals but Mrs Mitchell (Kathleen's mother) who used to come to Ambleside when we were there. Do you remember her? We stood and chatted quite a while and then decided to go for a coffee and so my morning was cut very short indeed.

Daddy made a mistake when he thought you were in the 1st XV but is nevertheless very pleased indeed and hopes that you will eventually be chosen.

Ralph phoned so I was able to tell him, and he said "oh good o! We will soon be having him playing for Wilmslow."

Tonight Maureen and Ralph have gone to a reception and dance at the Grand Hotel Manchester. It is Ladies Evening at the Rotary Club.

We had a busy morning on Monday when the photographer came from Navana photographers, Wilmslow. When they saw the announcement in the Guardian they wrote and asked (among several others) if they could take the photographs. They suggested it was much better to have them done at home and it certainly was. They bought triple lights and single lights – in fact the lounge looked like a studio. In all they took 9 plates, so we ought to get a good one or two out of that total number.

By the way you put "I was glad to here". Come come!! You know as well as I do that it is hear, connected with the "ear", wear a badge. I was a bit disappointed that you had dropped back in fortnightly place so do try to step it up again. Your ½ half term position was quite good but would have been better if you had maintained 8th place. Go to it again with renewed vigour.

Last Saturday we went to Birchenalls for a meal and Pa showed us pictures from his cine camera. They were lovely and you will have the opportunity of seeing them too sometime.

I hope your tooth is OK. With dearest love from Mum xxxxxx

Tony (LHS) and unknown friend at Skating Pond, Sedbergh

14 November 1949
Colebrooke, Chelford, Cheshire

My Dear Tony,

So sorry I misunderstood Mummy's telephone message in reference to the mention of rugger in your letter, nevertheless I am very pleased to hear you are fit well and capable of selection; hope you enjoyed a "beano".

Wilmslow had a good game and a hard fight to bear Bramhall but according to RWB the result was a fair reflection of the run of play.

Laburnum Grove I have seen both on the stage and screen and heartily endorse your remarks "a good show" and I only hope your fellows gave a good show.

The week-end weather has been a real mixture. Saturday, we had a terrific gale, I have never experienced a worse one in Cheshire; Sunday calm but showery and this am rather cold.

My golf at the present time is in such a deplorable state I would rather draw a veil over it until I discover my form again. Do you suggest bowls or skittles as an alternative.

We are pleased with your scholastic progress, keep it up and may you have every success.

Really Tony I am at a loss for words this week, nothing exciting or extraordinary having occurred.

In conclusion may God bless you and keep you, your loving Daddy xxx

21 November 1949
Colebrooke, Chelford, Cheshire
My Dear Tony

You will no doubt have already read that Cheshire RFC are equal with Northumberland in the top positions of the table, and the play off between these two should be rather exciting.

Wilmslow won 9 – 8 a good hard game says RWB, and the visitors were cheered on by Mr John Guest who now resides in Southport and is a member of both clubs but a soft spot for his old associations. Ralph scored his first try of the season.

We had quite a good game of golf last Saturday and I played a little better on Sunday am. I had a match arranged KO singles against Morris Armitage (Drummer Boy) and it was heavy with fog, anyhow we started at the first where visibility was about 120yards and varied down to about 80 yards. I managed to win 9 & 8 by playing as straight as possible and by a very poor display by my opponent, you may imagine how badly he played when I say I won the first 8 holes halved ninth and won the 10th and match, he plays off 12 but was nearer 24. I cannot take any credit for such a win but I had to take advantage and rub the advantage in at every opportunity.

Yesterday pm we attended the christening of Barbara Birchenall's baby daughter, had a cake, cocktails, later a bit of food and a colour film show by Poppa B, arriving home about 10.40pm. No fog but a howling wind.

The Messiah was a very very excellent performance and most enjoyable.

I send you my very best wishes for your continued success in your studies and hope you are giving the job the "works"!!

Keep fit and well and look after yourself.

May God bless you, lots of love your loving Daddy xx

PS Hope you had a good feast, let me know if you are broke. Dad

24 November 1949
Colebrooke, Chelford, Cheshire

My dearest Tony,

Many thanks for your letters. When you read your rugby fixtures it said Southport – A, which means Wilmslow were playing away – so they didn't pass on the road. Wilmslow won 9-8 Ralph scoring a try. They then went to have tea at Uncle Billie's.

Daddy will make some enquiries from Taggart re woods for you but says you should try some out before buying.

You seem to be touring the countryside on these rugger trips and having a jolly good time. What happens to your Saturday morning lessons? Do you manage to squeeze them in? I hope so.

I was glad to hear from you that you were working hard – but was naturally disappointed that your position was down. So have a good week looking up anything that you are not sure about.

Last Thursday when we went to hear the Messiah someone tried to get in the car. They managed to wrench the handle off, but as there was a special screw they apparently gave up. Fortunately, Daddy had taken the Rator? arm off so they wouldn't have been able to start it. We all went to Birchenalls for a cup of tea with Aunty Ethel.

We had a very enjoyable day at Birchie's on Sunday when Baby Helen – Ralph's niece was christened. Ralph was here last night for a meal – while Barbara and family and Mrs B had been for tea in the afternoon.

Mrs Cookson and 2 youngsters came to tea this afternoon and so we have been busy.

Maureen's photograph proofs have come and out of 9 taken we like 4.

We will see about a timepiece for you and send it off soon. Is it the 1st Dec when you start?

I have sent you another parcel off today.

On Dec 21st you are booked for a party at Mary Lowe's. Tomorrow, Maureen and Ralph go for a meal and then on to the theatre as it is Mary's birthday. Brian McGee is also in the party. On Saturday Mr R go to Barbara's at Nelson for the week-end.

That is about all the news now and quite a bit I think. So, here's hoping you have a very successful week. With dearest love Mum xxxxxx

28 November 1949
Colebrooke, Chelford, Cheshire

My Dear Tony,

Short and sweet is the motto this week; I am fortunately up to the neck in work.

No report of school in rugger columns this week so I presume the first team did not play, Wilmslow with seven reserves managed a good win at Warrington.

Mike Rhodes's brother at Rossall was mentioned in the account of their match against Fettes, he must have played well.

In the foursomes knock out round yesterday Mr Stewart and I just managed to win one up against Tom Marriot and Mr McCrae, we were 3 up at the turn and began to ease up and believe me we were really struggling in the end to win.

The weather has been cold and showery this weekend and it is rather cold this am.

With references to the golf clubs (woods) it is most inadvisable for me to purchase them, and I have no doubt it is your intention to try the feel of different sets before making your final choice.

Mummy thought I should get them or order some, but I explained to her the difficulty or impracticability of choosing clubs for other people, you will be ok with Freddie I have no doubt.

Robin Stewart passed the Selection Board and DV should be transferred to Eaton Hall Chester on Jan 4th after his leave.

Maureen and Ralph spent the week-end at Nelson with R's sister Barbara. Cedric Keene engaged to Shirley Hampson Friday 25th.

Every good wish for the exams. Confidence in yourself and concentration and may the Lord be with you. Lots and lots of love xx Daddy (x) for luck

Above: Firm evidence of Tony hard at work at school. The photo of golfer Bill Cotton on the wall behind him, Tony kept all his life

30 November 1949
Colebrooke, Chelford, Cheshire
Tel. 326. Chelford

My dear Tony,

The great day has dawned at last, and you may rest assured that all our love and hopes will be centered on you this coming fortnight. Just do your best darling and think carefully before committing your answers to paper. A few hints:

Don't cross out – just put a bracket round anything that should go wrong and rewrite.

Spellings hints – 'I' before 'e' except after 'c'. 'Ful' at the end of a word and not 'full'.

If not sure how to spell a word, try to find a substitute.

When doing maths make sure each answer is correct before writing down.

Set your work out neatly.

Make good drawings to illustrate – faintly at first and when correct outline them.

When answering English, History, and Geography – write all you know about the subject that relates to the question. Don't leave the examiner guessing.

Keep to the point and don't ramble.

When writing your essay try to make a vivid picture of your choice and use good well chosen adjective.

Read over the instructions very carefully doing the 'must' questions first.

I went to Manchester yesterday and bought a few Christmas presents. Hankies, ludo, snakes and ladders, dominoes, truck of bricks for Peter and a set of 4 pewter measures for Ralph.

I don't expect you will get much more rugger in now your exams have started – but get some fresh air when poss. Which day do you come home? I could probably meet you in town if you want to do some shopping.

I will send you a final parcel at the beginning of the week – so if you want anything special included, please let me know.

I have ordered Maureen's photographs and Navana want to send one to Cheshire Life.

Barbara – Ralph's sister – has given her a very beautiful bed jacket in pale pink wool trimmed with marabout fur – a new home will be acceptable I should imagine.

I brought some lovely Chrysanthemums on the day they were engaged, and I still have some of them and they are now 1 month 2 days old.

Dick Camm brought us a chicken last night as a little gift for "being so kind to him" wasn't that thoughtful of him? The Hill family wish you all the best and so does Ralph and Maureen too.

So, here's wishing you every success for your School Certificate

Tony dear, with my very dearest love and thoughts xxx Mum X for good luck

1 December 1949
Telegram

Good luck, Grannie, Uncle Idris, Aunty Jean

1 December 1949
Colebrooke, Chelford, Cheshire

My dear Tony,

Just a short note to give you our very best wishes for School Certificate. Go to it fearlessly and you'll be all right. One important tip is don't write what you are not asked for. Even if you're not very full of knowledge on one point it's much better to write a little of what is good than a lot of irrelevant stuff. Anyway, we are all holding thumbs.

By the way when do you come home? Mary Lowe has a party on 21st and has asked you, Ralph and me to go.

Tomorrow night R and I are going to the Green Room dance and Barbara and Donal, Ann and her boyfriend.

On Tuesday 6th I take my driving test. 12.15. So, if you're not busy you can hold thumbs for that.

I'm writing this on the train so there are innumerable distractions. I don't usually go down on Thursday but I've a flute lesson ce matin.

Next Thursday we have to play piano and flute in groups to Miss Collers. On Friday 9th we have the end of term concert and so is the end of term. After which I have an elocution exam either 12, 13 or 14th. Then Christmas shopping starts in earnest. I suppose you've no idea of what I could get you. I tried to do some shopping yesterday – but everything worthwhile is so expensive that I didn't buy a thing. It's most disheartening.

Shirley Coops has started at the Lucie Clayton Mannequin School in King Street. This is her 2nd week, the course lasts a month. She comes home on 18th, so she can't be doing v much. Shirley Broom of Alderley Edge (ugh!!) also goes.

I've just sent you a telegram from Oxford Road so I'm finishing this at the NSM.

Last Friday we went to Mary's for a meal and then to the Opera House to see "The Merry Widow". The place was empty – but the show was passable. On the Saturday we went with a friend of R's to Barbara and Donal's for the wkend at Nelson – north of Manchester. This was after the game at Warrington which we just managed to win 14 – 12. It was 14 – 6 at ½ time and we had the wind with us in the 2nd half. The rugby was appalling!

Must go and tune up the old tin whistle. Good luck old boy. Regards to Peter. With lots of love, Maureen

3 December
Colebrooke, Chelford, Cheshire

My dear Tony,

We are all wondering very much indeed how you are doing in SC. Do please let us know as soon as possible how the papers are. You didn't mention them at all in your letter.

Mrs Hill rang on Monday morning very anxious to know how you were doing.

I have sent you two parcels this week. There are no oranges allocated yet in this area. I bought you a chicken and roasted it yesterday, so Daddy took it to post this morning. That is parcel no 2. Please return tin box as I need it to put a Xmas cake in.

I shan't be able to meet you in M/c on Dec 20th as that evening we are having a cocktail and dinner party. So you can imagine how busy I shall be.

Ralph is coming to spend Xmas with us as his parents are going to Nelson to stay with Barbara (Ralph's sister) on Dec 21st. You go to Mary Lowe's party, so you are going to be quite busy. If possible, bring your suit home with you as you can't be at a cocktail party in a tweed jacket.

You will have to buy Ralph a present – I know he has bought you one. We have the cocktail measure for you to give Daddy – the one I bought in Glasgow. I must read some of the recipes ready for the 20th.

We are hoping to have a television set soon. But the type we want "Bush" is being held up for some unknown reason – so we must just hope for the best.

Cedric and Shirley Hampson are engaged and they and M & R and Mr and Mrs Hampson and Kearns are going to a dance at Alderley on Friday.

I have made 3 Xmas cakes and 4 puddings, so we shan't go hungry. We go to dinner to Wallis's on Dec 13th.

Do try to send a short note if possible about SC. We are constantly wondering and thinking about you. No more news for now. With heaps of love, Mum xxxxxx

In early December the family were looking to acquire a television set. The arrival of the television in the 1920s and 30s brought the outside world into the living room. They were a rare sight before World War II with only around 20,000 sets in Britain. During the war, broadcasts were discontinued and sets could only be used for their radios.

After the war, the technology became cheaper and by 1949 television ownership had risen to 90,000, a tiny fraction of a population of around 40,000,000.[36]

---

36   www.televisionheaven.co.uk/tv-history

5 December 1949
Colebrooke, Chelford, Cheshire

My Dear Tony,

You will no doubt be well into the exam fray ere this, with nose to the grindstone and maybe burning pencils and pen nibs, we are all thinking of you and our good wishes always there.

I am still frightfully busy and enjoying it, I certainly like being fully occupied, the brain is more active and the intellect more alert.

The less said about the weather we have suffered this weekend and the better rain, hail, gales and goodness knows what, there is no improvement this morning.

We managed 18 holes foursome Sunday am, this is much speedier than a four-ball, consequently one can keep moving and warmer, it was hardly a match. G Martin and T Ward v WL and JGS. We finished the match 8 & 7 and played the remaining 7 holes.

I had 9 holes with Freddie Saturday afternoon 10 to 18, he won 2 up with a 34. You may imagine I did not so badly to be only 2 down; it was pouring with rain – no one would turn out, I had a difficult task persuading Fred; but really I wanted some exercise.

Wilmslow played well to beat Liverpool 14pts to 3 pts and RWB said it was a good sporty game. I see Rimmer (Sale) got a good write up for his play in the Trial.

"World Sports" I have posted under separate cover a little relaxation will do you good.

More news next week DV. May God bless you and keep you, your loving xxx Daddy

13 March 1950
Colebrooke, Chelford, Cheshire

My Dear Tony,

Many, Many Happy Returns of your Birthday.

I charged the wine glasses and had them all rise and drink your good health etc after which we enjoyed a piece of birthday cake. I am sorry we were not with you, but I am sure you know that if we were not there in the flesh we were with you in spirit, hope you had a good party and are feeling fit and well.

Last Saturday I made the journey to Birkenhead Park to see Cheshire win the final of the County Championship. It was a lovely day with a cold north wind, which made the ball lively, fortunately the stands (covered) had their back to the wind, and we did not feel its full effects in the same way that the crowd on the opposite side of the field.

No doubt you will have read all the reports, and I can only add to them that the first half was scrappy with the Cheshire Pack tackling fiercely and without any quarter on either side but East Midlands were in that period playing the better football, unfortunately for them Gray did not kick too well and missed 3 penalty kicks with a strong wind behind.

The second half was a real thriller and the last 20 minutes of the game Cheshire showed their strength and covering ability by repeatedly smashing very forceful attacks by EM.

Tindall played better than his opposite number and Bartlett (17st 6ft 4) was a tower of strength and unbounding energy. Massey (Wilmslow aged 20) played a very fine game indeed and I feel sure with Michael Rhodes at full back in place of Shone we should have had a better first half, a good hard game and a good result (KH Jones incidentally was crocked early on an hardly in a fit condition to continue hooking) still after a wait of

73years I don't suppose any Cheshire player would have left the field except on a stretcher.

Enclosed is the programme which you and others may like to read. Some interesting tit bits in it. Please retain or return it.

Again, all good wishes and may God bless you, your loving xxx Daddy

Above: Last photo of Tony taken during his time at Sedbergh

Wednesday
Colebrooke, Peover Road, Chelford, Cheshire

Dear Tony,

Letter received this morning. Shan't you be coming out Friday evening as usual. All being well we should arrive in Sedbergh about 5.45-6pm. Could you be by the church then or would you rather be walking towards Cross Keys. Perhaps the latter would be better. So, if you are not at the church we shall expect to see you on the way. If you can't come out let me know by return. Yes! Ask Sheard or who you like. In haste, love Mum xxx

This is the last of the letters that Tony received whilst at Sedbergh. They demonstrate what a close and loving family they were, and, in particular, how much Bill and Marjorie cared about Tony's success with the School Certificate, with Marjorie's background as a teacher shining through with her incessant corrections of Tony's mistakes!

From School to Accountancy

Summer 1950-1956

This next section focuses from when Tony left school to when he qualified as a chartered accountant. It includes some golf triumphs, a section on his oldest friend, Bob Neill, playing rugby at Wilmslow Rugby Club, a variety of trips, accountancy college/exams and his twenty-first birthday, amongst other things. Where possible it is in chronological order.

1950 Cycling Holiday to France with Mike Adams

The first of Tony's cycling trips was with his school friend, Mike Adams. From his recollection, they went along the south coast of France calling at Seté and Agde. Tony remembered the terrain being very flat and that they were cycling straight into the Mistral wind, so it was quite challenging. On this trip they visited Carcasse, where Tony purchased a pair of pistols for 3,000 francs, roughly £3.00 at the time, and he kept the receipt, which roughly translates as:

> *This is to certify receipt of the sum of three thousand francs for the sale of a pair of small pistols uncovered during the 19th century. I acknowledge and guarantee that these pistols have been a thing of intrigue in the past – they date back to earlier than 1830.*

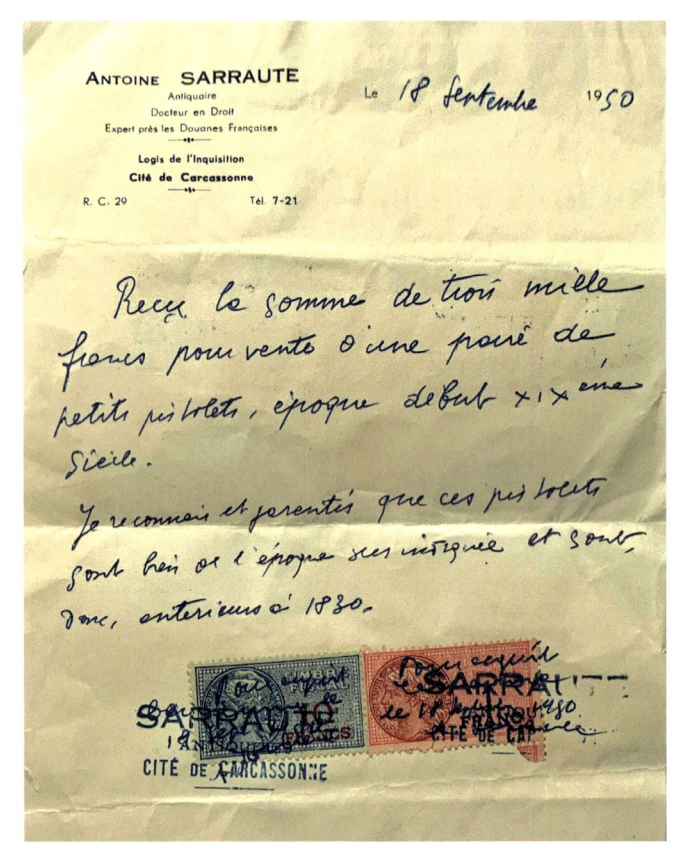

Above: Receipt for pair of pistols

These pistols are now in the possession of James Anderson, my son.

The Wilmslow Golf Club

Tony had a lifelong love of golf, encouraged, no doubt, by his father, Bill. From the age of seven, Tony started playing at home with one club – an eight iron. As his father was already a member of The Wilmslow Golf Club, Tony must have been delighted to become a junior member. From a young age, Tony took part in many competitions and in a letter from the Hon Secretary in May 1948 the following was written:

From School to Accountancy

In reference to the competition for School Boys at the Club in which you took part, I have pleasure in informing you that the Captain, Mr Donald Eadie, has agreed to pay for you to have three lessons from Taggart during your next holidays.

In 1950, Tony took part in the Boys' Amateur Golf Championship at Lytham and St Annes Golf Club. He kept the entry form, the receipt for £2.20 as payment, his competitor badge, and the score card.

Tony recalled playing against a boy who was on the English Boys' Team, and in the write-up in *The Daily Telegraph* after the competition, Leonard Crawley wrote, "Gordon Clark of Whitley Bay had an easy victory over Tony Longworth of Wilmslow." Despite the loss it must have been an exciting event to have been part of.

From Tony's diary of 1950, on 12 November he wrote, "beat Daddy 3/2". This will have been a pretty big deal, especially as not much else was in the diary for 1950.

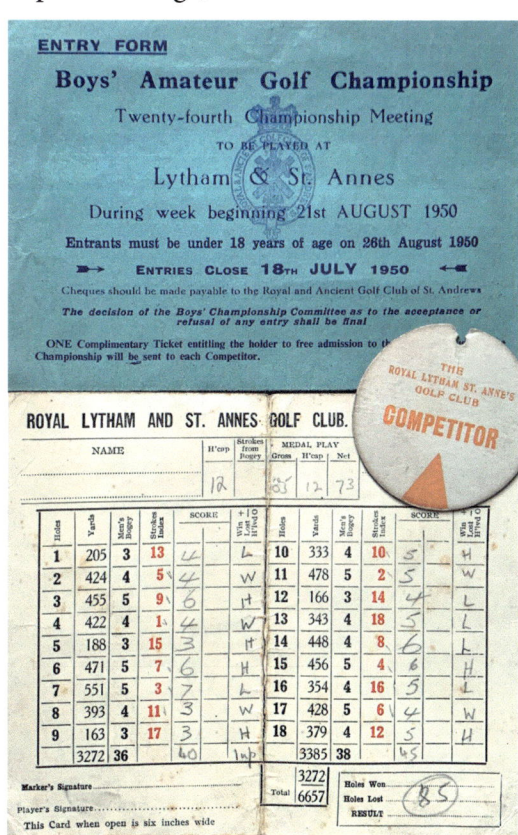

Entry card and score card from competition at Lytham St Annes and Tony playing golf, roughly sixteen year old

The Chadwick Cup

In July 1950, Tony's father, Bill, won the Chadwick Cup at Wilmslow Golf Club. This must have been of huge excitement for everyone, and a number of photos were taken to mark the occasion. The Chadwick Cup is a major competition of thirty-six holes. Tony went on to win it four times, in the years 1952, 1955, 1961 and 1975. A photo of the board bearing both Bill and Tony's names is below.

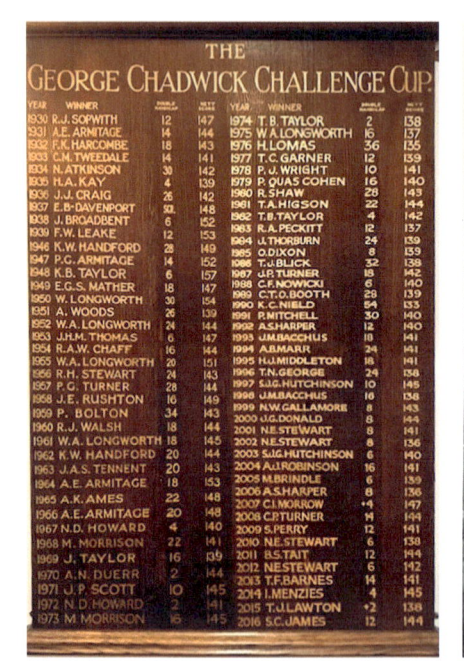

Above: Chadwick Cup board at The Wilmslow Golf Club and Tony holding trophy in back garden at Colebrooke in front of his mother's round flower beds, planted with wallflowers and dahlias, her favourites

Above: Bill Longworth with golf trophies, and pictured by the rose bough with Peter the Labrador

The beautiful golden Labrador pictured next to Bill is Peter, who was buried in the wood near the pond, which is where we went on to bury all our pets when we were children – I remember ceremonies for various cats over the years with little headstones, and a few goldfish!

Articles of Clerkship

Having left school in the summer of 1950, Tony made the decision to become an accountant. Bill made arrangements for Tony to become an articled clerk, commencing on 22 November 1950, at a cost of 150 guineas, to the firm of chartered accountants called Jones, Crewdson and Youatt, at 7 Norfolk Street, Manchester. The term of indenture was five years.

Tony was exempt from the preliminary exams at the Institute of Chartered Accountants because he had completed his school certificate. During the next five years Tony undertook his training whilst working at Jones, Crewdson and Youatt, as described in his CV from 1960:

Articled for five years. Institute of Chartered Accountants Final Examination May 1956. Varied range of audits mostly limited companies both large and small, plus taxation, trusteeships, estates etc. After intermediate exam, working alone or with staff as assistant to principals.

Bob Neill

This section looks at Tony's friendship with Bob Neill, whom he met in 1942 whilst at Sandbach School. As Bob was Tony's oldest friend, we asked him to speak at Tony's funeral, and we were glad we did as he shared some lovely memories of Colebrooke life. Bob remembered he and Tony playing on the pond at Colebrooke in bright orange, ex-RAF rubber dinghies; of fishing for sticklebacks with their nets in said pond, and the disappointment at Tony's mother, Marjorie, declining to cook them for lunch, but the delight at going to the Dixon Arms for lunch instead!

The boys spent a lot of time together at the weekends and during the holidays, cycling to each other's houses (Bob lived in Middlewich). Their parents became friendly. Tony recalled making model airplanes with Bob, inventing games with toy soldiers and playing Cowboys and Indians together.

Above: From left to right: Tony, Maureen, unknown and Bob Neill at Colebrooke

Bob also remembered challenging Tony's sister, Maureen, and her friends to tennis matches on the back lawn, which, in the summer had a tennis net and a court was marked out. The photo here is taken on the back lawn at Colebrooke with, from left to right: Tony, Maureen, Maureen's friend, and Bob. In the background behind the greenhouse, is the 'Green Shed' which we all loved to play in as children.

The pair shared various holidays, one being in Abersoch, North Wales, staying in the home of a friend of Tony's father. One day the boys set out in a rowing boat and passed between the headland and Saint Tudwall Islands. On deciding to row home, they encountered a strong current pulling them out to sea and, despite their efforts, couldn't make progress home. Luckily for them, a motorboat appeared and offered them a tow home, as the current was too fast for them. They gratefully accepted the help, otherwise Bob joked with me that they could have ended up in Ireland at best!

Tony and Bob shared letters over the years, and three have survived below:

9 February 1949
School House, Clifton College,
Bristol

Dear Tony

Thank you for your letter. I am keeping OK and my weight on Jan 16th was 10/10lbs. So long as the water is only on your knee, I don't suppose it's so bad. The weather down here is not so bad. – No snow yet though – thank goodness. We look like going a long way in the Colts House Matches. In fact, we are in the final on next Tuesday.

We have had one film "Pride and Prejudice". It wasn't bad. All about a family of five girls and how they get married.

I'm sorry to disappoint you but I never got hold of Jaqueline's address. However, all being well, I shall go full steam ahead next holidays. I haven't quite made up my mind who to send my Valentine to. Perhaps I shall send it to Ann Stubbs. I am just wondering what would be the outcome. Dorcie won't have a clue who yours is from. I don't believe she even knows you go to Sedbergh. So, if only 'Yorks' is clear she'll be clueless (on the postmark).

Sorry you're going to lose the shooting match on Saturday. I feel rather sorry also for Yeovil on the 12th as well. I am annoyed they beat Sunderland, because Sunderland beat Crewe in the round before, and there is rather a keen supporter of Yeovil down here.

Have you had the booklet telling you all about the Sandbach School Memorial Fund to build a chapel? I have anyway. What are you going to do about it?

Can't think of much more to say, except that I have started to learn German. It's not bad.

Love from Bobby

7 July 1949
School House, Clifton College,
Bristol

Dear Tony,

Thank you for your letter. Better late than never and all that you know! My birthday happened to be just before Commemoration, and we had wizard hot weather and Dad managed to get the car going and brought Mummy down with him, so we enjoyed ourselves. On the Saturday instead of attending the headmaster's garden party we went and spent money at Weston Super Mare. The dodgem cars are pretty hot stuff.

Our VIII have just gone up to Bisley as well. We don't have a Field Day this term, but I have to attend camp at Aldershot at the end of term. One H-!! of a shag. What on earth did you want *to go up Winder for at ¼ to midnight?! I find study windows, at least like the one I have got on the ground floor at present, are a very useful entry and exit to the house.*

8 July 1949 continuation

Sorry this letter is spread-eagled over so many days. The shooting VIII have come back from Bisley now. They arrived at 11.30 last night. Apparently, you did rather well. 5th or so. We were 20th, but we had the best Cadet pair.

It has just struck me that School Cert starts today. At least the Joint Board one does. I hope you have plenty of good luck in it. Which one do you take? I have to take Higher Cert next Summer. I have dropped Cricket and row now. Much better fun. At present I am stroke in the house 2nd IV with the house races on Thursday. We have a bye in the first round.

Mr Seddon will be feeling very pleased with himself as Cheltenham beat us at cricket at last!! This year we are sending besides a cricket team to Lords a tennis team to Wimbledon. Well, once again I'll wish you luck in School Cert and hope everything goes OK. Hope to see you next holidays.

Love from Bobby

I love the snippet in the letter above detailing Tony climbing out of his school bedroom window to run up Winder Hill (hill behind Sedbergh) at midnight! As a nice continuation, Tony's youngest daughter, Kate also used to climb out of her bedroom window at boarding school to go and get fish and chips!

Sunday 26 November 1949
School House, Clifton College,
Bristol

Dear Tony,

Sorry this is on ordinary school paper, but I have used up all my writing pad, and could only borrow stuff with no lines on, which is no use to me – for I go squint without them. Also, I am sorry I have not written sooner – I meant to before half-term but I got engrossed in fixing up papers etc to get into Bristol University with. It strikes me as being rather curious, that this time next year I shall be started on a 1st MB course as an under-graduate there!

How are things with you? I hope everyone is OK. I believe your Pa was ill in September? Apparently, my mother met yours in Glasgow around the end of September when Dorcie was going back to school.

I guess you must have had a pretty good time at that hotel last summer – it was jolly good fun down in Penzance, especially after enduring 10 days of army life at a Corp's camp at Aldershot. The heat was terrific there – and the dust shocking. Before I went to camp I stayed a night in London with a bloke who was in my form, so that I could take the permitted day off camp to see the school 1st XI play Tonbridge at Lords. As the flat I was staying in was also in St John's Wood – about 200y from the actual ground it was rather good, for you wasted no time in getting there. I also saw Madame Tussaud's wax display. Is it this term you take school cert? It isn't long till the exam starts, is it?

We have had our field day, which consisted of the usual field crawling operations. All the keen militarist platoons – the ones with Cert A etc etc … and those in the naval and air sections had such things as weapon film shows down in Bristol, the technical section went for a ride in some tanks somewhere else, the air sec went for a trip in an Anson, the naval sec left the Sunday before, – went down to Portsmouth, and had a day at sea in a destroyer, but I who have not got cert A had a good rag out on the Mendips.

Our house 1st XV have lost in the first round to what is generally accepted to be the prospective cock-house. The 2nd XV which contains me in the 2nd row has beaten one house and is now in the semi-finals. The school 1st XV has also been doing rather well – I think it has only lost 2 school matches – Bristol Grammar, and Marlborough – we only managed to draw with Cheltenham which I consider poor.

Well – I had better be getting on with some biology now. Hope you get school cert alright – when do you break up? We come home on the 20th. Hope you are OK.

Love from Bobby

Other recollections from their friendship included a chance meeting in Canada whilst Tony was living there. Bob was travelling across the country and happened to stop in Montreal for twenty-four hours. Bob phoned Tony and, on explaining the situation to his boss, Tony was promptly given the rest of the day off and enjoyed showing Bob around the city. What a wonderful surprise it must have been for Tony to see his best friend so far from home.

On Tony's return to the UK, he purchased a Sunbeam Alpine and was very proud of it too; Bob remembered a trip out in the car on the new A1 where the car reached 100mph. They spent a lovely day together at Farnborough Air Show. Bob remembered being impressed that the car had seat belts.

Both Bob and Tony enjoyed supporting their teams in rugby – Bob supported Scotland and Tony, England. On one occasion, they had a trip together to watch the Calcutta Cup at Murrayfield Rugby Stadium in Edinburgh. Bob recalled Tony arriving wearing a dinner plate-sized rosette declaring England across it, which he kept for many years. Scotland won the match, but Tony's disappointment was tempered by several Scottish supporters buying him a sympathetic beer on sight of the rosette. A tale the paid loved to recant.

1951

From Tony's diary of 1951, he started the year with a bang! He went to a party at his good friend Bob Neill's house, in Middlewich, "went to bed at 5:30am". These New Year's Eve parties became something of a fixture in the Neill family calendar – even I remember going to them as a child!

Tony occasionally kept score of the rugby matches he played in, and on Saturday 20 January "went to Shrewsbury won 19–0. Played snooker and watched some wrestling". He was clearly working hard and kept track of all his travel expenses each day. Tony met with his mother on various days and on Saturday 17 February he passed his driving test and wrote, "passed test, took Mummy to Southport".

In the summer of 1951, Tony took a trip to Scotland visiting Inveraray Castle, Loch Fyne and the scene of the Massacre of Glencoe. The photo here is of Tony and his unknown companion on the trip. Tent looks to be basic!

Above: Tony (RHS) and companion in tent

Tony kept his Identity Card from 1951. It shows his signature, which changed dramatically over the years into an almost straight line! Note the address – Peover Road, not Pepper Street. I wonder when the name of the road was changed.

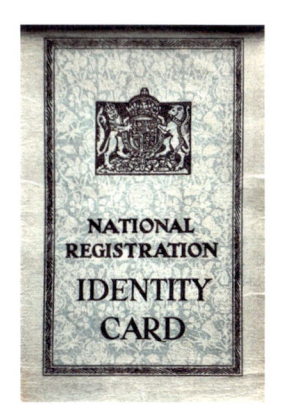

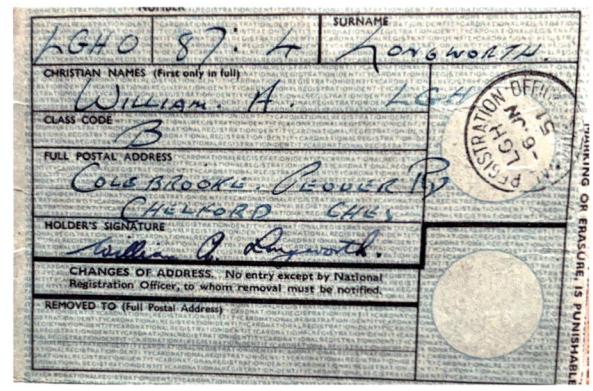

National Identity Cards were introduced as part of the National Registration Act of 1939 as an emergency measure at the start of World War II. They were mainly introduced due to the expected dislocation of the population, from evacuation and mobilisation. Also, for the need of manpower control, to help with planning the war economy, and to support the expected rationing.

Every man, woman and child had to carry a card at all times, and would be expected to present their card, on demand, to a police officer or person of authority. These cards detailed a person's name, sex, date of birth, occupation, address, marital status and whether they were a member of the armed forces. The National Registration Act expired in February 1952, when it was no longer necessary to carry a card.[37]

---

37   https://www.iwm.org.uk/history/what-you-need-to-know-about-rationing-in-the-second-world-war

1952

From Tony's diary of this year, he must have been at a New Year's Eve party at Bob Neill's house again, as on 1 January he wrote: "came home from Neill's and played rugger in the afternoon against Heaton Moor A won 33–3."

On Friday 4 he was back at the Neill's house and headed on the train to London, presumably with Bob. Saturday 5 January, he wrote: "Twickenham. Arrived London 4:15am had breakfast at Euston, look round London in morning went to match in afternoon. Home on 6:30pm train, arrived Chelford 10:30pm. Bob stayed the night. England lost 8–3 after great fight." A full-on, exciting day!

The next day, "Dorcie came [Bob's sister], played cards, darts, billiards. Got up at 12:40. Went to collect turf from Mr R's". The rest of the entries in the diary are solely where he was working and his expenses.

At the start of the year Tony fills out a little 'bio' – it makes for very funny reading. His passions of golf, photography, red wine and roast duck never left him, and he fulfilled his ambition to be a "director of a large firm".

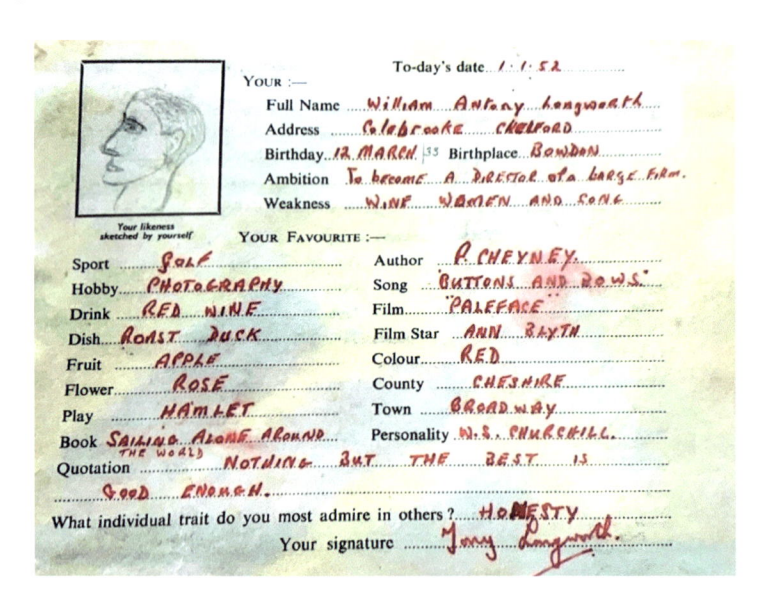

To-day's date: 1.1.52
Your:—
Full Name: William Antony Longworth
Address: Colebrooke, Chelford
Birthday: 12 March 35 Birthplace: Bowdon
Ambition: To become a Director of a Large Firm
Weakness: Wine, Women and Song

Your likeness sketched by yourself

Your Favourite:—
Sport: Golf
Hobby: Photography
Drink: Red Wine
Dish: Roast Duck
Fruit: Apple
Flower: Rose
Play: Hamlet
Book: Sailing Alone Around the World
Quotation: Nothing but the best is good enough
Author: P. Cheyney
Song: Buttons and Bows
Film: Paleface
Film Star: Ann Blyth
Colour: Red
County: Cheshire
Town: Broadway
Personality: W.S. Churchill

What individual trait do you most admire in others? Honesty
Your signature: Tony Longworth

Cycling Holiday to France with Bob Neill

During the summer of 1952, Tony and Bob decided to explore the French Riviera on their bicycles. Tony's father, Bill, paid for this

Above: Bob Neill with broken bike in France

trip, and at the time you could only take £25.00 out of Britain. On arriving in Paris, they took the train to Lyon and set off on their bikes. Unfortunately, two to three days later, three miles past Tain, Bob's three-speed gear jammed, and it was beyond the ability of the village blacksmith to repair it.

Above: Bob Neill (LHS) and Tony in sea and Tony on beach. Bandol, France

They sent the bikes back to Paris and made their way to Marseille. The pair also visited La Ciotat and eventually took a bus to a little holiday resort called Bandol, which Bob recalled as being "delightful". Perhaps this was because the landlord where they stayed gave them free wine with their supper! Tony recalled them spending between five and ten nights here. Their spending money was 3 and 6, which is about 17.5p, and the accommodation cost £2.00 full board.

Both boys were relieved they had purchased return tickets, as they had run out of money and could only afford a cup of coffee at Paris on the journey home. According to a letter from Bob's sister, Dorcie, they left France early and went and stayed with the Neill's for a weekend.

Wilmslow Rugby Cup

At some stage after leaving Sedbergh, Tony joined Wilmslow Rugby Club where his brother-in-law, Ralph Birchenall, played. Tony's position was prop forward, and he remembered that his first beer was at St Helen's Rugby Club with his good friend Pete Poizer, also a member of the club.

Tony recalled that he took part in a trial for the Cheshire Schoolboys team at Wilmslow, and that in the ensuing write-up in the newspaper it stated that Tony was one of the better boys that wasn't picked!

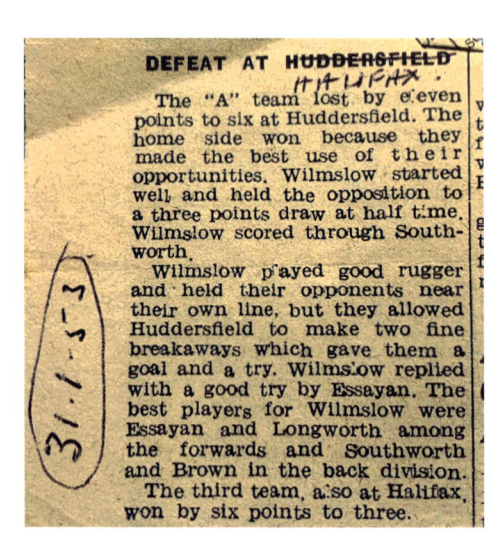

Another article, cut out of the newspaper (left), was found amongst Tony's belongings, dated 31 January 1953. "The best players for Wilmslow were Essayan and Longworth among the forwards."

From School to Accountancy

An article that Tony kept appeared in *The Tatler and Bystander* magazine on 1 October 1952. The article focused on the history of the club and had a photo of the team. Tony and Ralph Birchenall are in the photos below.

Above: Wilmslow Rugby team 1952, Tony middle row, RHS, next to man in trilby hat. Ralph Birchenall, front row, third from right

Above: Wilmslow Rugby team 1952–1953. Tony back row, RHS, second from the end. Pete Poizer is back row, fifth from right

203

Above: Match in January 1953 against Broughton Park, described on back as the "A" team. Tony is dead centre.

1953

The first three months of Tony's diary for this year are full of snippets of his life, and I've tried to weave them into a story. Once again, he "let NY in at Neills. Danced till 3:30am went to bed at 4:15 approx. Very good time was had by all. Played rugger on A versus Old Salions won 22–0".

On Saturday 3 January, Tony's played rugby again at Oldham on the A team and won 6–0. He noted the ground was "very hard". That night he "went to Gates for party saw Dorcie, Bob, Jackie. Came home at 3:30am. Quite good". The next day, Sunday, Tony "took Jean, Peter and Susan home. Averaged 35mph there and 33mph coming back. Went to meeting of YC's [Young Conservatives] elected [proposed to be Vice Chair]". Jean was Tony's mother's younger sister, with Peter and Susan being her children.

Tony spent Sunday 11 January golfing "played with Brian Duxbury v Fred and Pop won 3–2 and 1 up on bye. Played well gross 80. Played 12 holes against Martin finished all square. Played canasta in the evening with R and Pop, then darts, won both". The Tuesday of that week Tony "wrote thank you letters". I remember thank-you letters being a criteria after every birthday and Christmas, and having to sit in the dining room "until they are done". We all moaned about writing them, and whoever finished first was dealt glaring looks of jealousy!

Friday 16 January saw Tony calling in at The Dixon with Ralph and the Saturday he "played A v Broughton Park lost 6–0. Quiet evening went to Knutsford for F & chips came back and watched TV".

The Sunday 18 January was "foggy. Played golf with Pop 15 holes lost 3 & 2. Driving well putting not so good. 1.5hours at washing talking to old woman and Ivy. Very good play in evening. Very bad fog in evening".

Sunday 25 January Tony played golf again and "Ma and Pa went to Aunt Ethel's in afternoon. Very good TV at night". Aunt Ethel Walshaw was Tony's mother's sister-in-law and she lived in Tyldesley, northwest of Manchester. During the week he suffered with "bad back ache", whereupon he used a sun ray lamp which burnt his back!

The following Saturday, his back must have been a bit better as he played rugby again but the weather wasn't great "snow in morning, very cold. Went to Halifax with A lost 11–6. Came back to M/C [Manchester] had meal at Ping Hong then went to Grand with Harris and Pritchard".

Sunday 1 February Tony attended a meeting of the Young Conservatives, and he played golf with Ralph and Brian Duxbury, he won and "Ralph played very well". Guy and I both joined the Young Conservatives in our teens purely for the social side – I don't recall there ever being any political discussions. Meetings were held at The Queen's Gate pub in Alderley Edge, Cheshire.

During the week there were daily problems with electricity

outages and Tony's father, Bill, was in bed ill for a few days. There was heavy snow with drifting. The Friday he "took Ma to the Green Room" – I think this was in Wilmslow. Tony played rugby against Sale on Valentine's Day losing twenty-five to eight and he "played well" but "got [his] fingers hurt". Snow continued throughout the week. Nevertheless, Tony cleaned his car and "went to dentist in evening had injection and two fillings". Going to the dentist wasn't Tony's favourite thing – he never accepted pain relief for any procedure, citing that you can't remember pain – maybe, but it's not pleasant at the time, and in later life he once bit the dentist during an extraction!

Friday 20 February was the OS (Old Sedbergians) dinner, and his friend Tony Adams came to stay. The dinner was "very good. Came home 4am". The next day he played rugby against Rochdale but lost 10–0. In the evening he "went into town with Tony nothing doing so came home about 8pm". The next day he and his friend Tony played golf with Ralph and Neil Goff. They won the match and then the two Tonys went on to play again in the afternoon.

On Friday 27 February, Tony spent the day studying and went to the RUFC dance at The Rex in Wilmslow. On the Sunday Tony hosted the Young Conservatives committee at Colebrooke. The diary goes blank after this but picks up again when he goes on holiday to Ireland in August.

Trip to Killarney – August 1953

In early August 1953, Tony took a trip to Killarney in Ireland. I believe he went on this trip with Ian Lauchlan and Mike Yeadon. Tony's parents kept two postcards he sent.

5 August,
To Mrs M Longworth (Marjorie)

We had a very pleasant flight over. It was very smooth, and one could see a long way until we got above the clouds over the sea. The train journey was not so good however, it was very hot and not too comfortable. The hotel is very pleasant the food is good, and we have a good view from the bedroom right across the lake. We are off to play golf now. Tony

10 August
To Mr and Mrs W Longworth and Mrs Bentley (Bill, Marjorie and Grannie)

We are having an excellent time, the weather has been perfect. Yesterday we watched the Killarney Regatta and I managed to show a profit of 8/– on the afternoon's betting. We have hired a car from the hotel at a £1 a day, the only trouble is that it is nearly falling to bits. The golf course is just wonderful we have

Above: Tony on Muckross Lake, Killarney, 13 August 1953. Tony LHS, Ian Lauchlan behind him and I believe Mike Yeadon on RHS

played there twice. We have been to three dances so far and as yet we have not broken any hearts. The hotel had no water for two days, so we washed in the lake. Tony

The only photo from the trip is above; "August 13 1953, Killarney, Muckross Lake. Taken by Midge" is written on the back. In Tony's diary he noted that he "met Midge" on 12 August and that the following day, he "danced with Midge at Lake". On Sunday 16, prior to returning to England, Tony "met Midge in Dublin [and] went to Hurling match then to the Paradiso". Hurling is a fast Irish sport played with clubs similar to a hockey club, and I think The Paradiso was a restaurant.

Tony, I think, must have been quite taken with Midge, as he kept three letters from her. On 27 August she wrote, "Dear Tony, after your last epistle I feel I would be a positive cad if I did not write". She also references "a wonderful time on Tuesday". From Tony's diary he wrote, "went to Chester to meet Midge. Had meal at Bollands. Very enjoyable evening".

From Midge's next letter we learn that she was an Australian and was on a travelling holiday around Europe. Tony invited her to Colebrooke. Midge was anxious about this:

About staying with you. I can't help thinking it would be an awful lot of trouble for you, and also just what would your family think having a complete stranger from Australia suddenly landed upon the doorstep for no apparent reason. They don't even know me but would probably think me a rather strange type of girl. I don't know quite what to think or say. However as there is no time left now for a battle back and forth of hasty letters, I will admit I would really love to come. See you Wednesday.

Midge arrived on Wednesday 9 September and from Tony's diary he booked a day "off". The next and final letter from Midge is written on 18 September whilst on a ship to Norway and she signs off, "do remember me to your parents Tony and thank them again for me, as they really were very good to me when I was there. All the best for your rugger training, Yours Midge".

It's pretty clear that Tony's parents made all of Tony and Maureen's friends welcome at Colebrooke, something that Tony continued all his life.

Intermediate Accountancy Exam 1953

Above: Tony second row from top, dead centre behind older gentleman

Prior to the Intermediate and Final exams, Tony spent some time at an accountancy school at Caer Rhun Hall, in Conway, Wales. This was required as he got no real training at the firm he worked for. A photo of him at the school is below.

Unfortunately, when Tony took the intermediate exam at Moorgate Place, London in July 1953 he failed all the exams except Book-Keeping and Accounts (Partnership). Tony had another try in January 1954 and, once again, failed, this time with bad failures in Taxation and Cost Accounting and Book-Keeping and Accounts (Ltd Companies). He gained a pass, albeit 'weak' in General Commercial Knowledge.

Years later, Tony recalled these failures, and that his friends Ian Lauchlan and Mike Roff failed as well. They used to meet up at The Whipping Stocks pub in Over Peover, Cheshire, to open their results. Celebrating when passing and leaving swiftly when failing.

1954

1954 kicked off in usual style with a New Year's Eve party at the Neill's house. Tony stayed the night and when he got home on New Year's Day, he "sawed logs"!

During this time, Tony was corresponding with a girl called Rosemarie. The letters that he kept started in October 1953. From what I can gather, she worked at The Egerton Arms and was German. In her letters she described being at Colebrooke and spending time with Marjorie, Tony's mother. When Tony was home from the accountancy school, he spent quite a lot of time with Rosemarie, meeting for drinks, watching TV, going to a "pantomime in village – terrible"! On Saturday 16 January they went to The Hanging Gate up in the hills with a crowd of friends which was "very good". The Hanging Gate, a pub in the Macclesfield hills, was a favourite of Tony's; as children we often went for lunch there, enjoying sausage or scampi and chips in a basket, admiring the wonderful views out across the Cheshire Plain.

The end of January must have been bitterly cold as Tony "went skating on Lindow in afternoon with Rosemarie". Ralph accompanied them on another skating trip the next day. From his diary, Tony was spending quite a bit of time at Maureen and Ralph's house, joining them for meals and to watch TV.

Tony continued to play rugby with quite a few mentions of games in the diary in January of this year. He was fitted for a suit, presumably in preparation for his upcoming twenty-first birthday, and on 12 February he had his photo taken in honour of this milestone.

From School to Accountancy

From his diary, Tony enjoyed his spare time in Wales with friends called John and Martin. They had trips up The Orme in Llandudno, enjoyed drinks in various bars and golfing in the grounds of the hall. Years later, Llandudno became a popular day trip for our family – I particularly enjoyed going – the pier was full of touristy shops selling what I thought to be, all kinds of wonderful things – I remember Tony's frustration when I took forever choosing.

On Friday 5 March, Tony got the train home for the weekend and "Pop met us at Knutsford. Got in row because turned up late after running Martin home"!

Above: Professional photo taken of Tony to mark his twenty-first birthday

Tony's Twenty-First Birthday – 12 March 1954

From his diary, Tony had an exam on his birthday, but "Ma and Pa came to meet [him], took Martin home, arrived 7:30. Picked

Rosemarie up at 8:00, Bridge 8:45. Very good meal. Came home, had champagne went to bed at 4:30. Very very good". The Bridge was, and still is, a pretty swanky restaurant on the banks of the River Bollin in Prestbury, Cheshire – a place to go for a special occasion.

It must have been quite a celebration at Colebrooke. Tony kept his birthday cards from his parents and his grannie. He also took some photos of the table, set out with his birthday cake, champagne and spring flowers.

Above: Tony's twenty-first birthday celebration table

One of the gifts Tony received from his father was a pair of stainless-steel nail scissors in a leather pouch. I still have these. They meant an awful lot to Tony and, years later when my family were travelling with him to Costa Rica, the security guard at the airport confiscated them as per the rules which had been introduced. Tony spent a long time explaining to him what the scissors meant to him and incredibly the guard kept them for him to collect on our way out of the country.

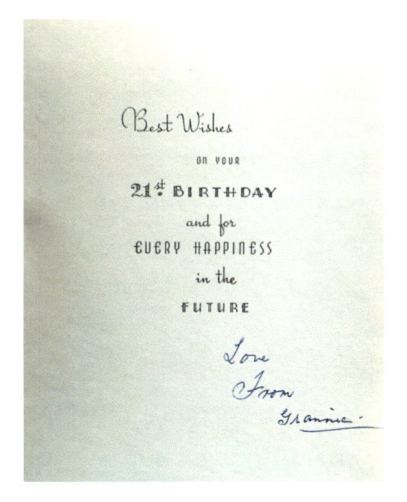

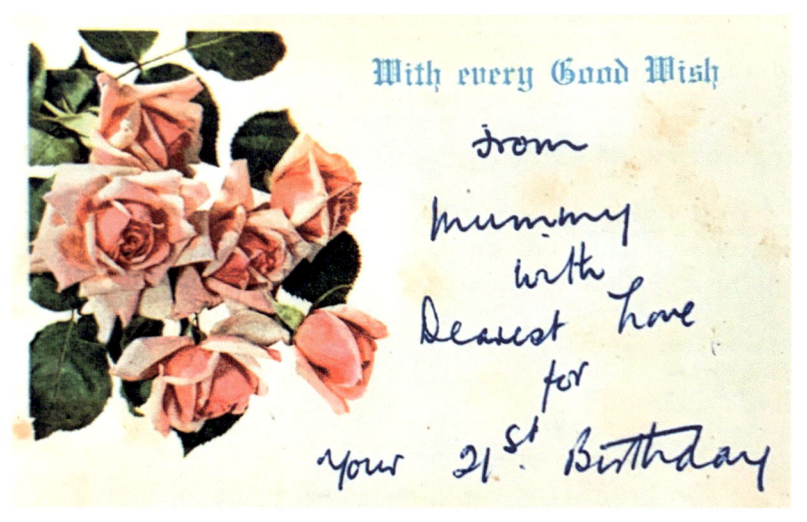

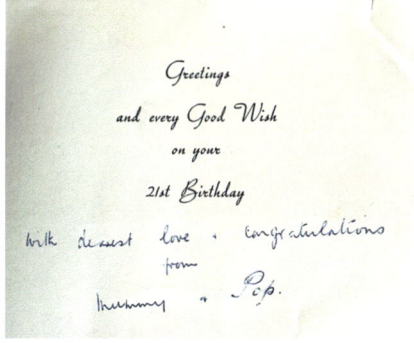

Above: Twenty-first birthday cards to Tony

The relationship with Rosemarie fizzled out not long after his twenty-first birthday. She wrote the following to Tony after his party:

> *I looked deep into the glass* [of champagne], *it was as sweet as I would look into your romantic eyes, oh darling I love to look into your blue eyes, they are so honest and faithful, your words are so true and loveable, you are so good and so attentive to me, darling…*

It seems Tony found the intensity all a bit too much, and by the end of April the short romance ended. Rosemarie was only nineteen years old, and perhaps thought she was in love having found 'the one'. I suspect that Tony would have found this too much at such a young age.

1954 and Intermediate Accountancy Exam

In May 1954, Tony finally passed his Intermediate exams. He must have been pleased with his result as he wrote to his tutor, Ronald Anderson, who had set up the Accountancy School in Wales, and on 28 July 1954 he received the reply below:

> *Dear Tony*
>
> *Thank you for your letter (you old rogue) and congratulations. Any time you are passing regard it as a duty to call in and see us. Most certainly I will take you for your final but for goodness sake do some work in the meantime.*
>   *Yours sincerely*
>   *Ronald Anderson*

A couple of letters were kept during this time:

> Friday, no Date
> Colebrooke, Chelford

Dear Tony,

Just a hasty note so that David can post this. Where is your washing – ? I haven't received any since Angelsey and did you get the pyjamas I sent?

We went to see the last match on Wednesday against Davenport. Wilmslow won 30 points or so easily.

The garden is looking lovely – all the narcissus are out. Rain is likely today, we've had one shower after all this lovely weather. We do hope you are working every minute and really hard to recompense for the fees and we sincerely hope you do well. When do you come home?
Lots of love M & D

Saturday, no Date
Colebrooke, Chelford

Dear Tony,

Here is your laundry and the card from Barbara and Donald Rigg enclosed with the book 'The Ascent of Everest' which I am keeping here until you come home. Their address is Utherstone, Blacks, Nr Nelson.

Grannie thinks your photograph is perfect and that Aunty E and S are mean.

We are hurrying now to get off to the rugger match but it's not a pleasant day. Daddy went to The Egerton for a drink just before lunch and met F Robinson and Dr Thomas who is just recovering from bronchial pneumonia. Hope all's well, with love from both.

Mummy. Ethel sends her regards.

4 May 1954
Colebrooke, Chelford
3 Parsonage, Red X Society,

Manchester
Dear Tony,

We went to Coops on Sunday and Mr Coops very kindly gave me a £5 note to give you for your birthday, so I am keeping it here until you return. Write Grotto House, Over Peover, Knutsford. Hope washing arrives tomorrow.
Love Mum x

12 May 1954
Colebrooke, Chelford

My dear Tony,

I am sitting in the front porch 2pm in the glorious sunshine and heavenly blue sky. It is a perfect day with just a suggestion of a breeze. I expect your part of the world is looking very beautiful too. Actually, we still need more rain as the sweet peas and peas are at a standstill. The narcissus and daffodils are all finished now and are just waiting to have their heads taken off but really it is much too hot to work out in the sun.

I went to my Red Cross class yesterday in M/C and also last week and we have gone as far as covering lampshades in satin.

Neil Fletcher and his wife came about 3:30pm on Sunday and stayed until after 6pm. They were very impressed with the garden and all the lovely views we have from every direction.

We went to watch some cricket at Alderley on Saturday, but it was so pathetic we didn't stay long. In the Egerton the other evening Heal told us he was playing (2nd team) and he has been a member for 28yrs, never played for 1st team.

Lots of people ask after you and are wondering how you are progressing. I expect this week is a very momentous one for you and I do hope that all your term's work will have the desired result.

Mr Coops has sold his Austin Sheerline and is awaiting delivery of a Daimler. He told Papa last night that he had heard from you.

I expect you will be letting us know about what time you wish to leave so until then – I suppose it is work work and work.
With dearest love from Mummy and Pop

Tony started writing in his diary again in July 1954, and on Tuesday 6 July he wrote:

Bob lunch 12:40. Stopped by police on way home never noticed license out of date." On Thursday of that week he *"went to Open Golf"* which was held at Royal Birkdale in Southport. The Saturday 10th was *"Bob's party (21st). Very very good went to bed at 6:45. Dorcie was there looking more beautiful than ever."*

Tony must have stayed at the Neill's house, as the next day he had lunch with them then *"saw Dorcie etc off, took Merlin to Crewe. Went out for a drink in evening to Dun Cow"*. Dorcie was Bob's sister and a lifelong friend of Tony's, they corresponded for a while during their school years.

Tony had a trip to Silverstone on 17 July: *"good racing, meal at Wheatly Arms on way back."* An Argentinian – Juan Fangio – won and set Silverstone's fastest ever lap to that date, breaking the 100mph barrier with a lap of 100.35mph. Stirling Moss was also racing that day and came fourth. From a photo Tony took on the day shown here, is the line-up with No.4. the Ferrari, being the winner. Tony really enjoyed motor racing with fairly regular trips to Oulton Park in Cheshire, and he twice went to Le Mans in 1953 and 1954.

Through the rest of July and August Tony continued to play golf and went to various parties and dances, then on 2 September he set off on holiday to Spain, travelling through Paris, where he stayed with a friend called John en route. From the scant writings in his diary, he had a night in Perpignan, and on Sunday 5 September he arrived in Tossa de Mar in Spain, which, at the time, was a quaint old fishing

Above: Silverstone 1954

village. The Thursday of that week he went to a bull fight and Saturday 11 was his "last night at Miramar", which was the hotel he was staying in, right on the seafront.

The next day, Tony started his journey home travelling along the French coast, where he spent nights in Narbonne, St Maxine, Juan les Pins and Nice, and took a train to Paris before travelling back to the UK, where he ended up with a puncture!

Tony's diary falls quiet again until towards the end of the year when he mentions taking a lady called Pat O'Driscoll out to lunch at The Little Mill, a pub in Rowarth, which is a hamlet on the edge of the High Peak. They had been friends for eighteen months before they started dating sometime in October.

On Saturday 18, Tony and Pat attend a dance at The Midland Hotel in Manchester, and from her letters poor Tony wasn't very well that night, coming down with a bad case of flu, which persisted up until Christmas. However, he was recovered enough to attend a dance at The Cricket Club, a couple of meals out with Pat, a trip to The Opera House with Pat and her friend, Anne, followed by a meal at The Café Royal, before finally attending a New Year's Eve party at a friend's house. Not a bad end to a good year.

1955

There are a number of entries in Tony's diary for 1955. He spent New Year's Day with lunchtime cocktails at Mike Yeadon's house and went to a dance at The Free Trade Hall in Manchester, with Pat, that evening.

On Sunday 2 January, Tony and a group of fourteen friends went to bid farewell to Pat as she departed from Manchester Airport; she was on her way to Liege, Belgium for two years to start a new job. From the tone of Pat's letters, Tony was quite smitten with Pat, so I suspect this parting must have been difficult for him. Over the next few weeks Tony sent red carnations, perfume, wrote her poetry and he was upset that she took a little while to reply. Below is a photo of Tony and Pat (centre) prior to her leaving. The other photo of Tony is taken at a house party at around the same time.

Above: Tony and Pat O'Driscoll centre, and Tony on his own at a party

That first week of January the weather was bitterly cold and windy *"dust bin lids blown about"* and Tony is *"looking forward to rail strike"* – perhaps this meant he couldn't get to work?

On Tony's birthday he had a cocktail party and went to *"Queens"*

Rugby and Rationing

(Queensgate in Alderley Edge), and *"Whippers"* (The Whipping Stocks pub in Peover, Cheshire). He was accompanied by *"Barbro"*, who was from Sweden. I believe she and a girl called Siv Larsson were in England staying with a family in Wilmslow to improve their English, perhaps Maureen and Ralph Birchenall.

From Pat's letter dated 20 January 1955, Tony was selected to speak at The Student's Dinner. *"That must be quite an honour,"* she wrote, and on Friday 18 March, Tony delivered his speech which, again from the letters from Pat, seemed to have gone very well. Tony excelled at public speaking; he spent time preparing and researching and then engaged his audience with sincerity and wit – he commanded attention when speaking.

The correspondence continued with Pat on a regular basis, but gradually became more sporadic as they were each enjoying their lives, Tony in England and Pat in Belgium.

The diary goes quiet until July when Tony set off for a holiday in Sweden to stay with the Larsson family; they had invited him to spend three weeks in Sweden, travelling around the country. Tony sent a postcard from Grays in Essex, on the boat:

7 July 1955,
5–15pm
To: Mr and Mrs Longworth and Granny

B— hot!! 78 degrees fahrenheit in cabin. Have just turned the fan on and had a cold wash. I have the top bunk of 2 which suits me as there is a cold air stream directed onto my head. Regards to Ethel,
　　Love Tony

From his diary, Tony had the most wonderful time, and was really well looked after by the family. On his return he wrote to Mr and Mrs Larsson to thank them and he kept a copy of what he wrote:

2 August 1955

Dear Mr and Mrs Larsson
Since I got back, I have had such a busy time that this is the first opportunity I have had to write to you. I want to thank you most sincerely for giving me the best holiday of my life, it was quite marvelous. I should like to thank you for the great trouble you went to in order to make my stay (holiday) a happy and very interesting one. I feel that I have still a great deal more to learn about your fascinating country and I hope one day to return.

Perhaps it is wrong of me, but I should like to pick out one or two of the things which stick in my mind. The Saturday night we spent looking around Skansen and sat drinking in Solliden. You made me feel very welcome and I at once felt at home. Then I shall not forget the excellent evening we spent at the Grand Hotel Saltjobaden "I love duckling!"

The day Siv and I spent at Sandham will always remain as a highlight of my holiday. It was a most majestic sight watching the yachts as they came over the horizon. The archipelago is certainly a very beautiful place, and I am sure all Sweden must be very proud of it.

Then the first Sunday at the cottage when I became as red as a tomato! The Smorgasbord at the Grand Hotel in Helsingborg. The whole of the trip in the south was so good that I do not propose to single out any one incident.

Last but not least were the wonderfully relaxing days at the cottage. I enjoyed these most of all as I love family life especially when it is with such a wonderfully happy family as yours.

I shall cherish for the rest of my life the memories of this holiday. I hope that you are all keeping well and that Siv is now very brown. Please tell Bodil to "take it easy". My Mother and Father send their kindest regards to you and Siv, and so do Maureen and Ralph. Fiona sends her love to you all.

Please do not hesitate to write and ask for my help when you come to England as I shall be only too pleased to be of some assistance to you. Please give my love to Siv, Bodil and Lars Olof. Once again very very many thanks for a perfect holiday.

With love, Tony

PS we really do throw sour milk away in England!!

Tony wrote about his daily activities in his diary, but rather than just write that up here, the letter above really is a good summary of the trip. From the diary the weather was very hot, and Tony enjoyed plenty of "*bathing*" and relaxing by lakes. He also saw "*the most wonderful sunset [he'd] have ever seen*". The day he left, Tony bought Mr and Mrs Larsson some flowers and they gave him a glass ashtray; he wrote "*very, very sorry to leave nearly chocked*", so clearly, very emotional.

Prior to this trip Tony had been exchanging chatty letters with Siv, who helped with arrangements for the holiday. Then during the trip, Tony and Siv had a falling-out when he thought she was "*laughing at him*". He was deeply angry and upset about this, and although they patched things up, their letter writing became very sporadic, inevitably the letters dwindled after a time.

There is very little in Tony's diary after this trip. He wrote that he finished his Articles on 13 November and there seemed to be plenty of parties and dances to attend, he also went "*carol singing*" the week before Christmas.

1956

There is little information in Tony's 1956 diary, but we do know that in the spring Tony returned to Caer Rhun Hall in Conway, Wales to prepare for his final accountancy exams. Another group photo was taken and Tony, now aged twenty-three, is looking happy and extremely smart in the photo below.

Above: Tony at Caer Rhun Hall, Conway, seated front row, fifth from right

Tony kept four letters that he received from his parent's that spring, transcribed below.

23 April 1956
Colebrooke, Chelford

My dear Tony,

Very many thanks for your letter. I imagine it was quite a thrill driving Richard's car at 80mph. I didn't win anything on the Pools this week so I can't buy you one yet! And there isn't much time left now – or have they finished? The weather here has been really beautiful all week but as you remark there has also been a coolish breeze.

We didn't go to rugger on Saturday as it was only a 2nd team game and the last one was pathetic. Mike Rhodes has been proposed as Captain for next year at the Annual General Meeting last Thursday.

Wendy Roberts has had her baby but whether a boy or a

girl I can't say as on that particular day I didn't look in the M/c Guardian. I see in the Telegraph this morning that Mike Craven has had a daughter – so now they have 2 children.

I do hope you manage to push on with all your studies. I will send you some more shirts and collars – probably tomorrow so please send your dirty linen back, or else you will be short of attached collar shirts.

You'll have to excuse the writing but I'm doing it outside on the wobbly table. Pa sends his love and best wishes. I was glad to hear you were first in one paper – so do try to get ahead with the others.

With dearest love Mummy Shall be looking forward to seeing you.

The "*wobbly table*" was a wonderful chunky oak table that had warped over the years. I remember it being pretty annoying to sit at as, not only did it wobble, but the tabletop was also so warped it was difficult to use!

1 May 1956
Colebrooke, Chelford

Dearest Tony

Here is your laundry. I didn't know whether to send it or not as I was waiting to hear if you were coming home this weekend or not. We went to cricket on Sunday. Ian took 6 wick for Ches Gents against Ches Wayfarers. Frank Robinson was out for a 0. Several of the boys asked how you were doing.

The drive is looking really beautiful now all the flowers are out and the perfume is heavenly. M & R etc went to Angelsey to do some painting at the week-end but I haven't heard from them since their return. Let me know if you are coming as we shan't be able to go to Knutsford on Saturday as it is their May Day.

Hoping you are doing well and keeping fit. With dearest love,
Mummy

1 May 1956
Colebrooke, Chelford, Cheshire
Telephone. 326. Chelford
My Dear Tony

No doubt you will be wondering what has happened to me, I thought it advisable to avoid correspondence and allow you to concentrate on the job in hand. Nothing extraordinary has happened these last few days with the exception of my being snowbound (on Cock Hill between Hebden Bridge & Keighley) last Thursday for a matter of 3hrs in a blizzard.

The snow was about 9" deep in the centre of the road and about one mile from the summit I encountered a 10 tonner and load across the road. I stopped and could not get moving again, the road behind was blocked by two vans following me; not a soul with a spade. Briefly the lorry driver set off to telephone but reported about an hour later all the telephones were down but fortunately he stopped a car ascending the hill and turned back for Hebden to phone the police.

Eventually the home-made snow plough arrived and cleared a single path after having to be dug out 2 or 3 times. I decided after the straightening out process to reverse down the hill until I could find an uphill turning, this I struck after about 1½ miles, returning to Hebden at 1-0pm. The last was to be informed they could not provide lunch at the White Lion, anyhow I managed it for 1-30pm. I ultimately decided to proceed via Halifax, Bradford, Keighley (the Valley road) arriving at Silsden 3-0pm, all being well I should have been there at 10.15am. Needless to relate I travelled home via Colne, Nelson, Burnley, Bury.

You will be sorry to hear that Stewart Livesey lost his wife last Saturday. Thrombosis.

I was gratified to receive your details regarding the exams, and I know you are putting all you can in to it and may God be with you and all good wishes also. Have you decided to come home this weekend? Wedding invitation card arrived from Anne and Mick. Mummy sends all her love.

The very best of health and good wishes, lots of love Pop

15 May 1956
Colebrooke, Chelford

My dear Tony

I have redirected some correspondence to you which I hope you receive safely. I quite thought I should have had your laundry this morning. How many shirts shall I send back, and which day are you coming home?

Maureen went to see Barbara Rigg on Saturday and so we went to stay with Fiona. Pa took Fiona out for a walk, and I stayed in as Barbara Brown was supposed to be coming to use Maureen's machine but she didn't turn up until both Maureen and Pa arrived back.

The weather is not too bad at the moment, quite sunny but changing about midday with a cold n.west wind.

How is the work progressing? I hope you are managing to put in a lot of work.

We went to Knutsford on Saturday to watch some cricket and saw some very fine bowling by Knutsford, but we left before the end as it had gone very cold indeed.

The garden is still looking very lovely. The azaleas and wallflowers and polyanthus are all out and fortunately the birds haven't been up to their tricks of nipping out the buds. I don't think there is any more news at the moment. So, here's hoping you are quite well and working hard,

With dearest love from Mummy

Excuse the writing but I'm doing it on the kitchen table where Ethel is ironing.

William Antony Longworth, ACA

On Saturday 21 July, Tony found out that all his hard work, encouraged by his loving parents, had paid off – he passed his final exams and received his certificate becoming a member of the Institute of Chartered Accountants in England and Wales. The certificate is below, along with a handwritten, excited note by his mother. He also kept a telegram of congratulations from the Larsson family.

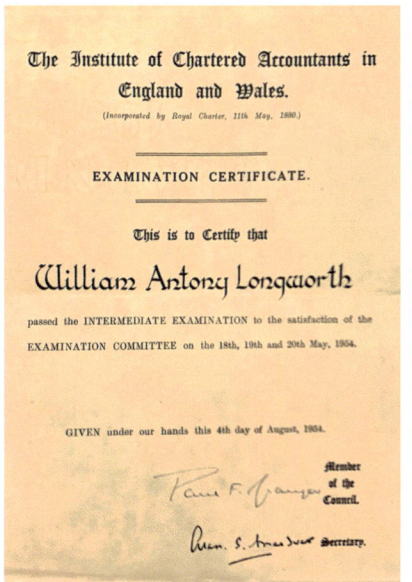

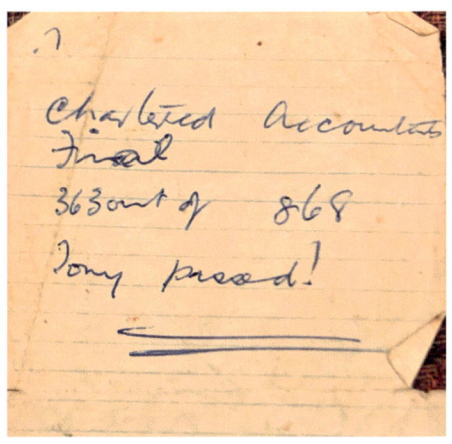

Left and above: Exam certificate from final accountancy exams, and a note written by Marjorie

Trip to Belgium July 1956

The same day Tony received his results he flew off to Belgium on a short trip to visit his friend Pat. From her letters she had made arrangements for him to stay in her digs and planned to take him all around Liege where she lived, as well as trips to Brussels and Bruges. After this trip, either the letters from Pat stopped or Tony hasn't kept them.

From here on the diary remained fairly quiet with the occasional reference to a party or dance and the odd mention of golf, but on Tuesday 18 December there is the first mention of Tony making plans to go to Canada. *"Fiton Shaw interview Manchester re Canada"*. There is nothing else in his diary of note for the rest of 1956.

Bill Haley and His Comets – February 1957

A lovely nugget that jumped out of Tony's diary was a trip to see Bill Haley and His Comets at the Odeon in Manchester on 13 February 1957. I remember him telling me about it every time we walked past the building.

Bill Haley and his band are widely credited with the launch of the rock-and-roll revolution, and although by the time of this tour in 1957, they had become passé in the USA, they were greeted as heroes in Great Britain where rock and roll was only just starting to explode.

The enthusiasm from the war generation teenagers was similar to Beatlemania. Prior to the bands arrival, the film *Rock Around the Clock* was being shown in cinemas around the country. The level of excitement and the resulting *"hooliganism"* behaviour resulted in the film being banned by Rank in all of its cinemas. The band were mobbed on arrival at Southampton and again at London's Waterloo Station later that day – more than five thousand fans formed a crush at the station to greet the group in a raucous display the press dubbed *"the Second Battle of Waterloo"*.

Graham Nash, co-founder of The Hollies was at the same concert as Tony and years later said, *"I've still got the ticket stub in my wallet from when I went to see Bill Haley and His Comets play in Manchester in February 1957 – my first ever concert. Over the years I've lost houses, I've lost wives, but I've not lost that ticket stub. It's that important to me."*[38]

---

38 www.bestclassicbands.com/bill-hayley-first-uk-visit-2-5-16

Tony regularly played his vinyl LP of 'Rock Around the Clock' whilst we were growing up, with classics such as 'See You Later Alligator', 'Shake, Rattle and Roll', and obviously, the huge hit – 'Rock Around the Clock'. We all loved it.

Canada 1957-1960

1957

In 1957, after a discussion with someone at Wilmslow Rugby Club, Tony decided to go to Canada. A girl he knew had been and also worked at a travel agency, so she helped him with tickets. The easiest way for Tony to go was to emigrate, as you only had to pay £50.00 to get there. He initially planned on going for twelve months, and although he was travelling alone, some friends later joined him – Chris Skelton and Ian Lauchlan being two of them.

Above: Tony and his father, Bill, in front garden at Colebrooke

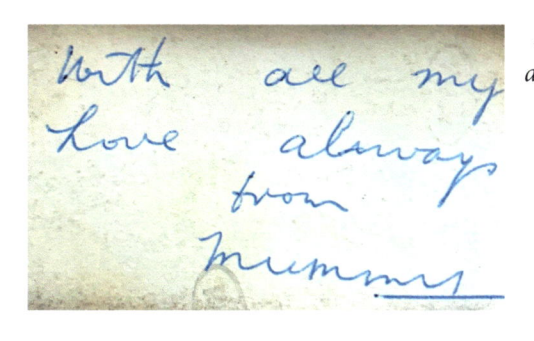

Left: The back of a photo of Tony and his mother, Marjorie, showing the handwritten note

I think the above photo (in front garden at Colebrooke) was taken when Tony departed for Canada; there is also a photo of Tony with his mother (poor quality), and what she wrote on the back of her photo is above.

From his diary, Tony left Ringway Airport, Manchester on Wednesday 20 March at 08:15am, he noted *"small party"*, so I suspect some friends and family saw him off. From London, Tony flew via JFK, New York arriving in Montreal on Thursday 21 March at 1:30pm. He had *"fixed up at YMCA"* to stay and went for a walk that evening, enjoying beautiful weather. We can only imagine his excitement. The following day he made some calls, went to a photo exhibition and the pictures, and on the Saturday, wrote letters and *"in evening went to ice hockey match M Canadians v Chicago, Canadians won 3-0"*. I remember him telling me how much he enjoyed watching ice hockey.

Tony wrote in his diary nearly every day in 1957, so I have weaved a story and included things of interest within this section. A few letters survive from his time in Canada and I have included them as appropriate.

22 March 1957
c/o YMCA 1441 Drummond Street,
Montreal, Canada

My Dear Tony,

News arrived this am of your safe arrival. Trust you had a good journey and no bumps. I have been up to the eyes in work and I am snatching a few minutes 4-40pm in an endeavor to get this letter off to you tonight.

May God Bless you and keep you and all good wishes for the future appointment. I have no doubt you will be in a good position without any great difficulty.

Believe in yourself Tony and the Good Lord go with you,
Fondest Love yours, Father x

Written on the outside of the letter in Tony's hand is a list, which I suspect are notes for his reply to the above letter. The list is:

Ice hockey, tennis, Brian Taylor, Pools, Diver, giving up smoking, M/cr United, staying at YH for 1 month, Jamaica.

26 March 1957
c/o Bank of Montreal, 119 St James St West,
Montreal

My dearest Tony,

Your very welcome letter arrived yesterday. I was very glad you had someone on the plane suitable to talk to. Fiona came here on Saturday, but she may be going back today.

Uncle Fred died on Sunday morning – I don't particularly want to go but your father says I ought to – so will have to see.

I do hope by this time you have made your contacts and I do hope you have hit on a suitable job. It seems so very different when you don't come in at night.

There was a burglary at Barber's on Friday evening, so the police are on the job. They think the man is from Derby.

M Yeadon called on Saturday for the tabards. I don't feel like going down to the rugger match and a policeman called to see if I could give any information, but he got a negative reply.

How expensive the YMCA is! I do hope you have soon managed to find cheaper accommodation. There isn't much happened since you went. I gave M Yeadon your YMCA address.

Look after yourself my darling and try to make the best opportunity of your stay in Canada. Remember I love you always and you all the very best.

Love from Mummy

When Tony arrived in Montreal he didn't have a job, but soon found employment with The Aluminium Ltd Group (ALCAN), which, from Tony's recollection, was the second biggest aluminium company in the world. From his diary he had an interview on Monday 25 March, was offered the job the next day and had a medical on the Wednesday, with a start date of 1 April.

Tony described the job on a later CV:

Senior Internal Auditor for North and South America and Caribbean areas, visiting plants and subsidiaries in these locations, reporting of systems and procedures in use, installing new systems, and amending existing ones where necessary, reporting to management. Consolidation of Group's accounts, including resulting information and statistics for top management. Cost Department, Costs Statements for group and special projects reporting direct to top management.

Tony bought his first car in Canada, which was a Plymouth. He remembered it cost him about £300 and within three weeks he had to buy three new tyres! It did last for some time after that.

Above: Tony's first car, a Plymouth – changing the tyres with unknown friends

On Friday 29 March, some welcome letters arrived from home, and he "*had lunch with Ed at Squash Club. Very good indeed. Smoked salmon, steak, ice, coffee. Drinks before. Very nice guy*".

On Tony's first day at work, he was "*allotted a desk and given a manual to read*". He noted that "*everyone called by Christian names*". The following day at work he got "*stuck in lift and had to climb out*"!

Thursday 4 April was a good day: "*Today everything went right. Had few drinks with the boys at Mount Royal Tavern then went up to see apartment. Move in on Saturday. Rang Joan T up fixed up for Saturday with George McLeod. Had dinner with Ed very enjoyable.*"

The Friday wasn't quite as successful, Tony wrote home, then went to a barbeque for chicken which was "*not very good. Very ill during the night. Also went to the pictures where I saw a fight*".

Tony swiftly found accommodation and on Saturday 6 April

moved into his new apartment at The Linton, which he described as a *"posh"* block of flats on Sherbrooke Street, Montreal. He lived there with Geoff Knight, Peter Brodie Brown and Ian Ruxton. Peter and Ian were Scottish. That night they went out for dinner returning at 2:00am and Tony *"didn't leave the apartment"* the next day. Must have been a big night!

On the Monday work seemed to have really started and he took a train from Montreal to Wakefield (northwest of Montreal) at 08:55am, travelling first class. He noted the weather was very cold, but clear and sunny, and he spent around ten days working here travelling home at the weekend.

Tony quickly got involved with a local rugby team, Mount Royal. His first match was on Saturday 13 April, Mount Royle v Westmount. That night he was at a party and got home around 3:30am and arose at a leisurely 2:30pm on the Sunday – Tony had settled into Canadian life quickly and was already having a fine old time.

"Lots of letters" arrived on 17 April and that night Tony was out with Peter and Geoff to Casino Francoise and arrived home at 3:00am. The following night was another late one with dinner at an Indian restaurant and a *"downtown"* nightclub after. Luckily, he didn't have to get up early the next day as it was Good Friday and Tony played rugby again with Mount Royal winning 6–0.

Easter weekend and beyond was a whirlwind of dinners, drinks and dancing – Saturday he returned home at 5:00am. The following weekend Tony and his friends held a party at their apartment which continued until 7:30am – he noted the following day was spent cleaning!

The beginning of May continued in much the same way and on Thursday 9 May Tony *"got in touch with Chris Skelton"*; that night Tony, Peter and Geoff met Chris for a meal and headed to a nightclub.

Tony collected his golf clubs, which must have been shipped over, on the Friday morning and *"decided [he] had a guilt[y] complex about drink"* that evening!

Tony, Geoff, Peter and Hamish took a trip to Ottawa on Saturday 11 where they watched a rugby match, had a meal out and went to a dance: "*v enjoyable. Drove home through the night arrived M 5:30am. Beautiful sunrise*."

The next day, Tony took an overnight train to Arvida, northeast of Montreal. He "*slept well*" on the train and arrived at 8:30am on the Monday, checked into a hotel, sharing room 253 with Trevor, who must have been a work colleague. The weather was clear, cold and windy and the next few days Tony was working hard and going to bed "earlyish". On that Thursday Tony got home from work and fell fast asleep not waking until 10:30pm – he went to the doctor who said he had "*Spring fever*"!

Perhaps all Tony's hard partying had caught up with him, as written on Friday 17 May is, "*developed German measles!! Saw Dr Raymond in evening. Itched like hell all night long. Felt unwell*". The next day, Tony was told he had "*to go into hospital. B nuisance*". That afternoon he was admitted onto the children's ward where there was "*noise like sheep*", but he had a "*very good meal of steak in evening. Very comfortable, have a good chance to let my system settle down after Montreal*"!

Whilst on the ward, Tony was impressed with Solange and Celine, the day and night nurses. "*Both speak a little English. Very good. Nothing too much trouble*". He is clearly being well looked after and must have had a good view outside as each day comments on the beautiful weather and how he could see the "*very still*" river. He found the ward peaceful, "*except for the noise of the children*", and the food was good. He took time to write some letters.

By the Tuesday he was clearly starting to recover:

Woke up feeling fine at 6am, greeted by a cheerful Celine. Had grapefruit juice. Beautiful morning. Wrote some more letters. Had 2 excellent meals. Rang Peter up in Montreal – amused by my being in hospital. I'm annoyed by not being able to go to Montreal this weekend as he said Mount Royal RUFC are going down to Ottawa, however, have arranged to go following weekend. Sister very good to me. Looked after very well.

Canada 1957-1960

> *Contented. On good form in evening with Celine, wanted to dance etc.*

The following day wasn't quite so good:

> *Woke up at 5am feeling awful… very hot and sticky… Very X with Elizabeth. Finished Boswell's London Journal… was a little out of best humour in evening.*

Boswell's London Journal was published in 1950, it was a daily journal kept by James Boswell, a Scottish biographer, diarist and lawyer, between 1762 and 1793. It's an amusing, educating book, giving a unique glimpse of life into society circles in eighteenth-century London.[39]

Thursday was very hot and sticky again and Tony awoke at 2:00am "*itching like hell*". "*Very X, am annoyed that there has been no post. Solange very good, think I might take her out although she seems a little young. Decided about time I get down to my job. Must conquer fear of losing love… Also keep your thoughts to yourself more.*" Perhaps the time in hospital gave Tony a time to reflect.

Tony was finally discharged from hospital on the Saturday, still a "*little out of sorts*"; he was tired but more talkative and resolved that he "*must make effort to talk more and not be moody*". I suspect he went back to stay in the same hotel and on the Sunday, he hit a few golf balls in a field and went to see *High Society* at the pictures: "*not bad.*"

Monday 27 May was raining and cold and the rash had reappeared. Tony was having doubts as to whether he did have German Measles but resolved to "*keep going to end of week*" and to consult a doctor in Montreal. He was relieved that his firm had agreed to pay his expenses. The rash was extremely itchy that evening and he seemed to be questioning his job: "*can you stick this work for 12 months?*"

---

[39] www.jamesboswell.info

The next day the rash was still very itchy, and Tony was "*still worried about*" it, he resolved to "*pray and wait.*" Luckily by the Wednesday he "*felt much better, am certain prayers heard*", and he wrote that he "*worked hard again today*". The resolutions he made in hospital were holding firm.

Thursday 30 May was a holiday and Tony wrote that he "*felt very good and sure GM have gone at last*". This must have been such a relief for him and the next day he flew back to Montreal where he "*took Judy out to dinner*". Afterwards, they went to Mount Royal and onto a "*very good*" party at Pete Everalls. However, he then wrote, "*tonight lost another very nice girl, too possessive, must try hard not to be*".

Tony and Judy must have remained on good terms as the next night he attended a party at her apartment which wasn't "*too bad, bed 5:30*"! Sunday morning, he went to church and had lunch with some friends before he headed back up to Arvida in the evening. Tony "*can't remember what the hell [he] did*" on Monday 3 June!

Sunday 9 June was a "*wonderful day*" spent at a "*cottage*" with friends where he went rowing and enjoyed some drinks. Tuesday was extremely hot and sticky and Tony was annoyed that he "*wasted the evening, must not do this, must plan evening better, no case walking round streets doing nothing*". He seemed to take this plan seriously as the next night Tony "*went for glass of ale*" with some friends, then to a park and finally for a meal at a restaurant called Fontainbleau.

News of Tony's illness must have reached home as the letter below arrived from his mother; it must have been very welcome. "*Very Important*" is written across the envelope:

11 June 1957
c/o Aluminium Securities Ltd, Box 6090,
Sun Life Buildings, Montreal

My dearest Tony,

I was delighted to know you were fighting fit again and that you were covered for health. You sound as though you had a jolly weekend with the two parties, and I do hope you manage to get your golf in.

Since Dennis has married, he seems to have given up coming and David hardly comes at all so your father had to cut all the lawns on Whit Sunday and Monday and as for the flower beds they are shocking. 1st frost and then wind and they almost all died off. Now we've had some hot days – we haven't been able to plant out – so I don't know what will happen to them.

As for birthdays I can't find the diary with them in. Mine July 30th; Maureen's Sept 7th; Pop's 21st (Sept); Susan's is about 2nd Sept, I think. Peter's Jan 13th? Fiona's April 4th; Rupert's Oct 15th.

We didn't go out at all at Whitsuntide and although we had some glorious days, we were much better off than the south where 7" of rain fell in Cornwall. I am sitting now in the front porch, and it is very hot – less breeze than yesterday.

I was very pleased to hear you had been to church – I am always thinking about you. Are you managing to save anything?

I haven't been out at all during Whit Sat, Sun and Monday as your father was busy on the garden and his eyes and ears have been troubling him a bit and he has to bathe them. He went to snooker last night.

With all my dearest love to you, Mummy

Tony wasn't feeling well later that week and is again annoyed with himself "*must not waste time in evenings again*". But on the Friday night, back in Montreal, he went to a party, a "*very nice evening*", where he met a Turkish girl called Solmay, a nurse at the General Hospital in the city. Tony thought she was a "*really charming girl*" and was sorry to leave her in Montreal, writing, "*it will be nice seeing her again when I get back*". Another very late night going to bed at 5:30am and then up on the Sunday morning to church again before watching a cricket match.

During the week Tony *"went on tour of Lake St John. Very nice countryside"*. This large lake is situated in the Laurentian Highlands, northeast of Montreal. Over that weekend, Tony *"played golf at last with Corbin and was quite pleased with score"*, but noted it was very, very hot and he got sunburnt.

The following weekend, 29 June, Tony took a short holiday and drove south from Montreal to Burlington, then onto Old Orchard Beach on the Maine coast USA, where he had a *"good room in hotel, good evening, pleasant ride through the mountains"*. Over the next few days Tony swam, played soccer, and spent time on the pier, and drove back up to Canada on the Tuesday, having had a *"good holiday"*.

The first couple of weeks of July Tony was continuing to work up in Arvida, where the weather was very hot, and he enjoyed playing tennis and golf in the evenings. The weekend of 19–20 July he was back in Montreal where he took Solmay to the pictures and had a *"very, very enjoyable evening"* with a dinner of *"smoked salmon, chicken and grapes"*. Smoked salmon was one of Tony's favourites, served on brown bread and butter, a sprinkling of black pepper and a squeeze of lemon. It became a staple of any special family event and continues with his children today.

Tony was fed up to be back in Arvida – on the Monday he wrote, *"cold! Very quiet day but I was b–dy miserable and complained far too much. Must try and get out of this habit and be more cheerful"*.

The rest of July and early August continue in much the same vein – work, golf, tennis, parties and seeing Solmay.

Tuesday 30 July was Tony's mother's birthday and he wrote, *"phoned home in evening, very clear, very good to hear familiar voices again"*. Whilst Tony was clearly having a fabulous time in Canada with a group of good friends, he must have sorely missed his family.

Mid-August Tony started working in Isle Maligne, a town north of Quebec City. On his first day he had an *"interesting"* tour of the plant and *"in evening played 3 holes of golf, got very wet. Danced at club got a little tight but very enjoyable. Home early"*. Tony also wrote that he *"must try and be cheerful and work harder"*.

The work in Isle Maligne didn't last long, and on Monday 19 August Tony was told that he was going to be working in Vancouver, but stationed in Kitimat, a town north of the city. He wrote that it was a *"hell of a rush"* trying to get everything sorted and on Wednesday morning he was on a plane heading to the west coast of Canada. He wrote, *"very good flight. Wrote letters. Great thrill to see Rockies"*. He had a walk *"downtown in evening, very interesting. Highly cosmopolitan city"*. Clearly impressed with the place.

During the few days Tony spent in Vancouver, when he wasn't working, he seemed to enjoy himself; on the Saturday he *"went over by boat to Victoria [a town on Vancouver Island] with Vern and Corbin [work colleagues]. Very good trip, had dinner at English Inn, came back by plane"*. That evening, he and Corbin went downtown for some drinks to celebrate Corbin's birthday, and to a club which was *"not too good, all closed down by 12:00pm."* The next day he went on a sailing trip with *"Brian, Mr and Mrs Shelton"* up Howe Sound, which is an inlet north of Vancouver. Tony wrote that he *"had a lovely day, hot and warm. Good"*.

It seems that Tony had been expecting a trip to the Caribbean, as he wrote in his diary that he *"heard not going to Caribbean, very X"*.

On the Wednesday, Tony flew up to Kitimat, writing that the bus broke down between the airport and terrace, that the train was *"like the wild west"*, but he had a very nice apartment, and that evening he enjoyed a good meal, wrote letters and had an early night.

Thursday was *"another very nice day"* and he had dinner with a Mr Radley who took him for a walk around town in the evening which he found very interesting. They called in for drinks with a *"Mr Hopkins who I gather is not liked too well in the town"*. The following day he wrote of Kitimat: *"[a] lot better than I thought would be"* and he enjoyed a long weekend as the Monday was a national holiday (Labour Day). Tony spent time with his colleague, Vern, walking by the river in the warm weather.

Work started on the Tuesday although he was *"doing bugger all at the moment*". He received some letters and spent time "*working out if [he] saved any money in August*"!

Tony continued to enjoy the great outdoors and spent the weekend "*fishing for salmon, no luck but plenty of mosquitoes*", and he continued to try his luck fishing during the week, with a couple of trips to "*the pictures*" and drinks with friends.

The following weekend Tony had a trip to Kemano, a remote settlement situated seventy-five kilometres southeast of Kitimat, built to service a hydroelectric power station, which provided energy for Alcan to smelt ore to produce aluminium. He spent quite a few days working there and spent the evenings playing poker with varying success, and snooker.

Whilst in Kemano, Tony went to "*Horetzky Camp*" in a jeep where he "*saw fish spawning*". From looking at a map, Horetzky Peak is a mountain with a height of 2,162m, with a creek running in one of its valleys, which I suspect is where Tony went. The scenery looks absolutely stunning here – lush and wild, and if you have a spare five minutes a quick google of both the hydro power station at Kemano and the locality is worthwhile.

On Saturday 21 September, whilst in Kitimat, Tony walked down to Minette Bay with a friend. Here he wrote that he "*saw them booming logs*", which is when a barrier is placed in a river designed to collect floating logs timbered from nearby forests. Must have been some sight and he "*got a ride back on a log lorry*". That evening he was off to the pictures and the next day "*climbed mountain back of smelter to lake. Saw Blue Jay, very interesting*". The Monday he needed to go to "*bed early after climb*".

Towards the end of September, Tony's relationship with Kitimat seemed to become frayed as over the coming days he wrote, "*going mad slowly*", "*still going mad*", "*wrote letters almost in state of madness, the sooner I get out of Kitimat the better*". His days were much the same and the weather was very cold with the "*first snow on mountains*" arriving on 2 October.

From the diary, Tony was organising a holiday and made note of his vaccination, a trip to a travel agent, a visa arriving, and, on Friday

11 October Tony was "*on [his] way to Vancouver*". Unfortunately, the next morning he "*woke up feeling lousy, had temp of 102f, saw chemist gave me some pills*". Feeling under the weather, Tony then took a flight to his holiday destination – Mexico City. He noted it was a good flight but "*arrived feeling awful*" and "*went straight to bed*".

Unfortunately, apart from "*walked around town*", Tony doesn't write in his diary where he went on this holiday, but he somehow ended up in New York, as on Monday 21 October he flew from Idlewild (JFK airport) back up to Montreal, where, over the coming days he met up with Solmay, enjoyed seeing his friends for dinner and drinks, and went to the pictures. He noted how cold the weather was and that he "*must endeavour to be better tempered and also better conversant*".

Tony's diary keeping towards the end of the year was sporadic but by the beginning of December he was back working in Chicoutimi, north of Montreal, where the weather was bitterly cold, and, over the course of three days, there a lot of snow – eight inches, twelve inches and twelve inches fell on subsequent days.

1958

From his diary, Tony finished 1957 with a New Year's Eve party at "*Everalls, very good indeed*", and spent New Year's Day with a trip to the pictures. Work continued up in Kemano and the usual round of parties and drinks with friends kept his social diary full.

Trip to The Caribbean

On Friday 17 January 1958, Tony flew to New York for a one-night stay in The Roosevelt Hotel, midtown Manhattan, prior to embarking on a much-talked-about three-month trip to the Caribbean, where he visited Jamaica, British Guiana and Trinidad. From both Tony's diaries and his personal recollections, I have tried to put together an account of this exciting work trip.

Rugby and Rationing

Accompanied by his boss, Chris Allen, Tony flew from New York to Kingston, Jamaica on Saturday 18 and noted in his diary that the US navy were in the port. The following day, after another flight, he arrived in Port of Spain, the capital of Trinidad, staying at the Normandie Hotel (still in existence).

Work commenced on the Monday morning with a tour of the plant, and he went *"to bed early, very tired"*. The next night, Tony enjoyed a show at the hotel in the evening where he *"saw limbo for the 1st time, very interesting"*. In later years, when we were children attempting to limbo, Tony would always recount seeing it *"done properly"* in Trinidad! In this first week Tony enjoyed two parties at the US Naval Base, the second one being described as "big", and noted that he met the *"Federal Minister of Finance and the Acting Governor"*. Many years later Tony recalled this party and that he got on very well with the Minister of Finance, who wanted to confiscate Tony's boss's passport so that he could take Tony to a three-day party, but sadly they had to move on!

On Sunday 26 January, Tony had a trip to Maracas Bay, where he spent his time *"swimming, sunbathing etc"* and *"got badly burnt"*, resulting in *"very sore and painful sunburn"*!

The remainder of January and first two weeks of February were

Left: Tony's passport showing visa stamps

spent working, and going to various parties, dinners and dances. One weekend Tony took a trip to Pitch Lake in the southwest of Trinidad – the largest natural deposit of asphalt in the world.

On Saturday 15 February Tony was up early at 5:30am and headed for the airport to catch a flight to British Guiana (now Guyana). On arrival he took a *"launch up river to Mackenzie"* to a large alumina refinery – Tony recalled that Alcan was the largest company in the country. He was met by a colleague, settled into room sixteen at The Mackenzie Hotel, and that evening went to a party. The next couple of days were spent relaxing in the *"very hot"* weather.

In between working, Tony continued to enjoy all that life had to offer, playing golf, tennis, going to parties, and exploring wherever he found himself to be.

Whilst in Guyana, Tony recalled spending four to five weeks in the jungle; he travelled first class everywhere. He and Chris were able to explore a little, and one day they hired a jeep, drove down a jungle path ending up at a small village of huts. Here they found a small stall which had three bottles of Guinness on its shelves for sale; they found this very amusing, and Tony loved telling the tale. I suspect they bought and enjoyed the Guinness too.

The trip to the Caribbean ended on Saturday 5 April, and he started the long journey back to Montreal. Tony recalled that whilst he was living in Georgetown, Guyana, he got to know one of the airhostesses from Canadian Airways, so on the flight back to Canada, stopping at several islands on the way, she arranged for Tony to have a seat at the back near the kitchen so he could chat to her and was close to the *"booze"*! Another of his favourite stories.

Other Trips in 1958

Tony stopped writing in his diary when he left Jamaica, so we can only speculate that his life continued in much the same vein – work, sport, parties and fun. From the few photos that survive of his time in

Canada, he had a trip to Huntsville, a town west of Montreal in May 1958 – the photo of Tony below in a boat is from that trip.

Above: Tony in Huntsville

Above: Tony and Dick Seall, Terrace Airport, Kitimat

From the photos here, we know that Tony was back working up in Kitimat in November 1958. I particularly like the one that shows Tony with his old Leica camera and leather camera bag over his shoulder – he kept these his whole life, as well as the balaclava he is wearing; I remember the balaclava living in the cupboard in the downstairs loo at Colebrooke, moth-eaten, for years! The other person in both photos is Dick Seall, who must have been a work colleague.

Canada 1957-1960

Above: Tony and Dick Seall, Kitimat with Leica Camera

Above: Tony enjoyed a trip to Old Orchard Beach, Maine, USA with. From L to R: Chris Skelton, Geoff Knight, Tony Burns, Tony and Corlin Bauman. The photo of the same group loading the Plymouth with beers was taken on another trip, unsure where

Rugby and Rationing

The photo of the same group loading the Plymouth with beers was taken on another trip, unsure where

Above: No date or place on this photo of Tony (RHS) with Ian Lauchlan and unknown lady

1959

Tony doesn't write anything in his diary until later in January 1959, but he received a lovely long letter from his father:

9 January 1959
Colebrooke, Chelford, Cheshire,
Telephone. 326. Chelford

My Dear Tony

May God's Blessing be with you in 1959 and the very best of health and success. The weather at last caught up with me and I have just recovered from a bad attack of bronchitis. Fortunately, I never developed a temperature, and the inflammation was kept under control. The contributing factor was 3 out of 4 weeks in December were foggy and on 5 or 6 days real pea soupers. I have never seen worse. I felt the effects as you may imagine but thought I was managing quite well until I conked after Boxing Day.

I was out of bed on Weds and DV hope to resume business on Monday, it would of course be stocktaking with this week absent, anyhow I shall bring the books home next week each night make up for lost time. We finish 19.1.59.

This week we have had the biggest fall of snow for years and very cold with it. At present the lane is like a sheet of glass but having had no wind here we have no snowdrifts. Derbyshire and many other counties are much worse off with roads blocked and in the south west there has been flooding. Still, from photographs in the press of the St Lawrence and New York etc we have no complaints, excuse the scrawl but my hands feel crabbed.

Many thanks for the lovely pull-over, it is delightfully warm and a most unusual and attractive colour. Mummy also asked me to thank you for the lovely woolen scarf. Maureen phoned to enquire about my health last night and mentioned that the parcel of presents had arrived, and they were delighted with them.

Bob the joiner etc will be starting today on the alterations to their new house but from all accounts I should visualize a long job with only one man.

They are all well at Kerry even though they were in contact on Christmas Day with Barbara and family who have nearly all been down with flu which necessitated cancelling the party fixed for New Year's Day at Nelson, a good job they did not go there. Most people glad to see the end of 1958, lousy weather all year, we hope 1959 better.

I sent off a further 2 shirts which I had made thinking they may be useful for the winter weekend wear. I trust the style and size is suitable, the sleeves I had shorter than mine for if I remember rightly, you are a little shorter in the arm length. I hope you like them.

Gratified to hear about the advance in salary, long overdue I should say, may you have further increments in the near future, probe all you can for advice and information, absorb all the knowledge and experience possible and above all keep well in touch with the right people for advancement and progress, do you manage to swot and keep up with good reading? All my dearest wishes go with you.

By the way I posted the C A diary to you before Xmas 2nd class Air Mail, hope you have now received same, also did you received the Times Supplement? Are there any other papers or information you require?

What a battler has been going on for British Aluminium – it looks as though Tube Investments have won and settled the issue, a dam good thing for the shareholders only I should say. Have you had any lucky investments?

Wilmslow RFC have improved greatly the last 3 months and have had a most successful time against the new clubs they have played, particularly Harrogate, Wakefield etc. The Old School have had more write up than for years and the enclosed cuttings give you a reasonably good summing up for the year's end.

Taggart, Dr Thomas, T Ward, Marnot etc expressed their good wishes when I saw them all just before Christmas, Thomas by the way, has been TT and non smoking for 3 months and looks and also says he feels 100% better. I have not given up smoking but apart from an odd drink or 2 at weekends and Tuesday night at snooker, I am not interested, too damned expensive.

I shall be interested to receive my balance sheet for 1958 which has been an extremely trying year. The business never appeared to settle on an even keel at any period but even so my turnover will only approximate 1.25% down, the interesting feature will of course be the profit angle.

With expenses increasing each year it is extremely hard to arrive at the net profit which one strives to attain, even a slight fall in turnover has quite an appreciable effect, unless of course a higher rate of gross profit can be obtained, again a difficult proposition on a very competitive market.

Do let us know how the skiing is progressing, if you have started, the details in The Times speak well of the Laurentians, bit expensive from all accounts.

It is to be regretted you cannot find accommodation at the Linden. We both sincerely hope you find something equally as good if not better, look after yourself and keep fit and well. We both hope there will be no recurrence of the ulcer trouble and you will no doubt find your own method of dealing with any adipose tissue, 182lbs if solid is a useful weight.

M/c United are in top form again having won their last eight matches in succession and look a reasonable bet for the Championship, sorry I cannot say the same for City, they appear to be at sixes and sevens, one half the match they play start football and worse than novices the other half. They will have to do much better to avoid relegation. I suppose the next team will be the Moon Rockets from the Lunar League, what a life!

Here's wishing you all the good things you wish yourself and may God Bless you, lots of love Pop

PS if you get another car go easy on it if you don't want to burn it out! "Nuts did you say!"

The above letter talks about Tony getting another car, so we can guess that the Plymouth was no more; from his diary Tony was looking at cars at the end of January and on Tuesday 3 February he bought a 1956 Power Hawk Studebaker. Tony talked about this car on many occasions – he clearly loved it and kept the manual and this fabulous photo below.

Above: Studebaker manual and Tony in Studebaker car

Also from Bill's letter, it seems that Tony had taken up skiing and was having lessons in the Laurentian Mountains, which lie to the north of Quebec City. In his diary, on Saturday 7 February, Tony wrote: "*took Andy up north to ski hut, dancing in evening. Very cold, car went well.*" On Monday 9 he noted: "*realized I'm broke*"! I suspect the car might have wiped out his savings.

The following weekend Tony was back "up north" for another skiing lesson, and on the Saturday night he went out with friends in the evening: "*very, very enjoyable, danced till 2am.*" The Sunday was a "*beautiful day*" and he "*went on long walk with Katie up to look out. Very very nice girl*". This is the first mention of a young lady who became very significant in Tony's life – Katie Milligan.

After the above weekend Tony stopped writing in his diary until mid-November, but from the many letters that Tony kept from Katie, beginning in April 1959, we know that he spent some time working in St John's, Newfoundland and Shawinigan Falls, a city northeast of Montreal. Aside from that, I think we can safely assume he continued working hard in various locations around Canada, skiing, playing rugby (he became the Captain of Mount Royal Rugby Club, Montreal) and generally enjoying himself.

From Tony's recollections, in the summer of 1959, Tony and Katie embarked on a three-week road trip in the Studebaker covering some 7,500 miles. Commencing in Montreal, some of the places they visited were Chicago, Kansas, Albuquerque, the Grand Canyon, Las Vegas, Los Angeles – including a trip to Disneyland which had only opened in 1955, San Francisco, Reno and back up to Montreal. It must have been an amazing trip.

Sadly, there are hardly any photos from this stage of Tony's life; however, this wonderful one was taken on Metis Beach, "*Duck Shooting*", October 1959, with Ian Rene and Peter Brodie Brown and Tony in his favourite balaclava.

Above: Tony, far right with Ian Rene and Peter Brodie Brown on Metis Beach

In early November, Katie left Canada and travelled back to Edgeware, Middlesex, to stay with her parents. The day after her arrival, Tuesday 10 November, she received a phone call from Tony with a marriage proposal which she accepted. That evening she wrote an excited and happy letter to Tony exclaiming, *"it was such a surprise, I hope you don't have any regrets, I know I won't, I couldn't be happier"*, and how, when she told her parents *"they seemed very pleased, Daddy laughed and said 'well he'll have to ask my permission first', but they have very good impressions of you although they have never seen you"*.

On 27 November, the engagement was formally announced by Bill and Marjorie in *The Manchester Evening News*, and by Katie's parents in *The Telegraph*. They both say pretty much the same thing, so I have just included the one from the MEN here:

They met on skis. It was Catherine Ann Milligan's 21st birthday when she received the transatlantic phone call from Montreal. On the other end, with a proposal of marriage was former Wilmslow Rugby player William Antony Longworth. She accepted.

Canada 1957-1960

Today they announce their engagement. Miss Milligan is still in England, visiting her parents in Edgeware, Middlesex. She returns to Canada, where she is a private secretary in Montreal, after Christmas. The couple met on a skiing holiday in the Laurentian Mountains in Quebec. They plan to be married next autumn in England.

Radar Network: Mr Longworth, who is 26, is a chartered accountant and comes from Chelford. He is with the Federal Electric Corporation of Canada, where he is working on the DEW line, the Arctic radar network. He plans to spend his leave with his fiancée in Montreal.

When he went to Canada in 1957, he joined the Aluminium Company of Canada, and travelled extensively to British Guiana, Trinidad, Jamaica and British Columbia. He has kept up his interest in rugby, and until the Arctic Circle job he was captain of the Mount Royale Rugby Club in Montreal."

In the announcement in *The Telegraph*, Katie's parents got the spelling of Tony's name wrong, and spelt it 'Anthony' rather than his spelling 'Antony' without the 'h' – he wasn't happy about this and wrote to Katie to tell her! It never failed to infuriate Tony if his name was spelt wrong.

From the letters, Katie immediately started planning both the wedding, where they should live and took a short trip to Canada over Christmas to see Tony. It is fairly clear that Tony wanted to remain in Canada, but Katie wanted to stay in England.

Arctic Adventures

November saw another big change in Tony's life; on 16 November he started a new job with the Federal Electric Corporation (FEC), where he was appointed Field Accountant (Eastern Sector) on the Distant Early Warning Line (DEW) in the Arctic Circle, Northern Canada. The FEC were an American firm who operated the DEW

Line. Tony's job involved travelling to all the sites in the eastern sector, checking the accounts and then reporting his findings back to management.

Tony recalled that he took the job for the money, which was very good at $11,000 p.a, including living expenses, which would be roughly $100,000 today. The contract was for eighteen months.

What was the DEW Line and how did it come about? This period was during the Cold War, when the two superpowers – the USA and the Soviet Union – were in geopolitical tensions with one another, and the USA feared being bombed. The USA felt they needed to have a presence in Canadian territory to be able to detect incoming bombers from far enough away, in order to protect their cities, so they asked the Canadian government to partner with them. However, the Canadian government had just finished building two lines further south and didn't have the resources to do another, but they agreed that the Americans could build it if they paid for and constructed it themselves.

The DEW Line was a chain of fifty-seven manned radar stations stretching three thousand miles across the Arctic, from Alaska through Canada over Greenland to Iceland, built between 1955 to 1957, to detect enemy aircraft bombers coming over the Pole, up to an altitude of 50,000ft. The mission was one of observer, to detect and report – it would play no part in any offensive or retaliatory action. There were three types of radar stations on the line: main, auxiliary and intermediate, and they differed in size, function, equipment and manpower.[40][41]

In the course of my research, I came across the DEW Line Training Manual, produced in December 1957, given to employees. It gives a full background into the development of the Line and is very detailed as to what to expect on arrival. It also describes the type of person who "*served*" on the Line:

---

[40] www.dewlineadventures.com
[41] https://lswilson.dewlineadventures.com/planning-design-construction-the-early-years/

> The man who serves on the DEW Line has been screened to meet strict security requirements. His loyalty to the United States and Canada must be unquestionable; he must have no criminal record; he must never have been a member of a subversive group nor involved in any activities endangering our national security.… In personal interviews, this man has shown that he does not regard his DEW Line assignment as just another job… He is proud of the part he plays in our national defense. He must be a healthy man, in excellent physical condition. And he must be able to adjust himself to a life in the Arctic.

Tony seemed fully on board with this act of service, writing to his manager in January 1960: "*I must say I find the work interesting, and it is rewarding to know that one is doing a real service up here.*"

The manual describes the housing, which were prefabricated modules, all furnished identically. As well as bedrooms, kitted out with dressers, lamps, armchairs, rugs, and curtains, there were first-aid and recreation rooms, toilets and laundry facilities as well as kitchen and dining areas. Cooks provided the meals in well-equipped kitchens, with all food having to be flown in regularly.

Keeping the employees entertained when not working was important, and the manual describes all but the smaller stations as having lounges, a hobby room, photographic dark room and library. All the stations were equipped with projectors to show the latest movies. Outdoor activities included fishing, skiing and hiking.

Certain items of clothing were issued, and of these Tony kept his leather mittens, and long woollen socks all his life, as well as a pair of snowshoes, which resembled tennis rackets. I remember trying these out when it snowed at Colebrooke, but they weren't much use in an inch of snow!

Monday 16 November was the day Tony left Montreal to start his new job and he wrote in his diary that "*Peter and Chris saw me off at the airport 11pm. We stopped at Frobisher then went on to FOX where we arrived at 8am. Had letter from Katie*". After arriving he "*had *breakfast then waited until 10 to get a room. Very windy rather cold, zero. Slept in afternoon, missed dinner. Wrote to Katie then walked 1 mile to get a sandwich. Very very cold".*

After the long flight from Montreal Tony touched down at Frobisher (now known as Iqaluit), on Baffin Island, then swiftly took a flight up to the FOX-MAIN station, aka Hall Beach, which was the main transportation hub for the eastern sector of the line. Here he had to wait for a plane to take him to his first destination and he was delayed by severe weather. On the Wednesday he wrote: *"still no plane for CAM-4, place has been closed in for two days now by high wind and snow. Temp was up around 28f at times, wind up to 45mph. Eating is a bit of a rat race. Wrote to Katie."*

The map below shows the extent of the DEW Line and the location of the stations. We know Tony went to FOX-MAIN, FOX-2, CAM-4 and CAM-5, and that he was going to visit all the other eastern stations, including the ones in Greenland.[42]

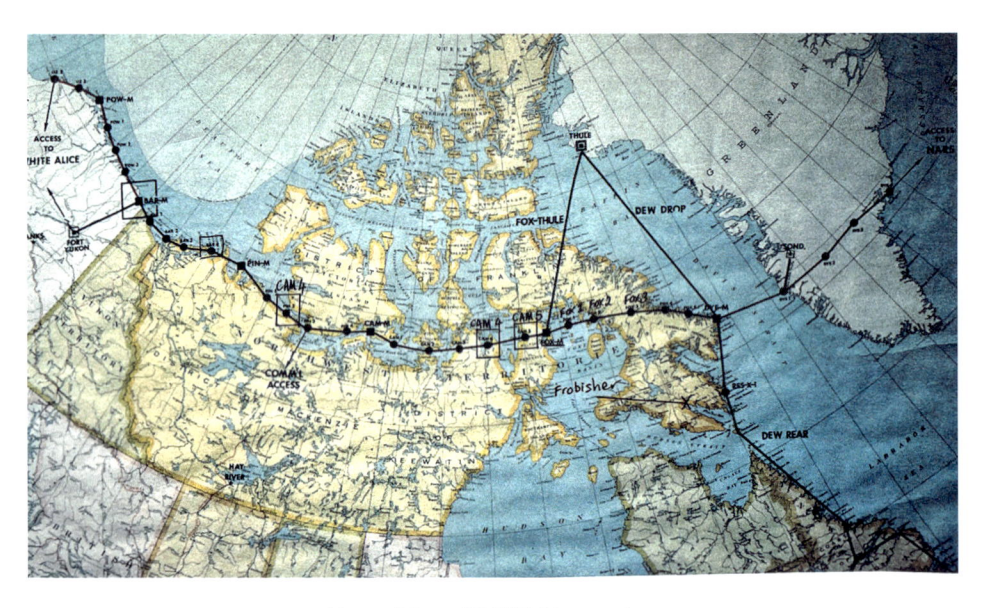

Above: Map of DEW Line stations

---

42   Photo reproduced with kind permission by Brian Jeffery of The DEWLine Museum

Thursday 19 was "*another day waiting… was awoken at 11:30pm to get plane to Cam 4, couldn't make it so am now at Cam 5, arrived Friday morning*" where he met "*John, Ned, Norb, George, Jimmy, Connie etc etc, went down quite well*". The Saturday was a "*beautiful day, the sun shone all day, and the sunset was glorious. Had some drinks in the evening. No mail yet*". Tony was starting to become accustomed to his new life in the Arctic.

The whole of the next week was spent waiting at CAM-5 for a plane to CAM-4, the weather was just too bad. Tony noted that he "*saw a crow*" – must have been an unlikely sight in the wild winter weather. By Friday 27 Tony has still received "*no mail*" and there was still "no plane"; he was clearly fed up with this. Later that day he was called to the airstrip to board the plane; however, things didn't get any easier as the plane had to turn "*back, mechanical trouble, nearly crashed on way in, only one engine, that was failing. Drank until 3am.*" Can't say I blame him after that!

The letter Tony wrote to his manager in January 1960 demonstrates the difficulties in travelling between the stations "*the most frustrating thing I find is transportation. So far, I have been unlucky with planes, but now the temperature is getting lower I hope a lot of the fogs and mists will disappear*". Plane crashes were not uncommon – trying to land in fog, snow and mist, not to mention snowy runways must have made for some hair-raising flights, and clearly Tony had his own near miss.

Tony remained stranded at CAM-5 for a few more days where he wrote: "*still waiting, very cold, no plane, no mail, cold.*" The Wednesday seemed a little better "*very cold minus 35degrees Fahrenheit, hopes of mail today. Today the base of the sun did not get over the horizon. MAIL 3 letters Katie, 1 Ian, 1 Mike, 1 Maureen, 1 Ma, 1 Barbro*". Receiving letters from friends and family must have been a welcome boost and will have given him a boost – much needed with the temperature at negative thirty-five degrees Fahrenheit, which is negative thirty-two Celsius. I had to check that twice as I can't imagine that kind of cold.

Tony's last diary entry was Monday 21 December when he wrote: "*dark all day, at 2pm it was pitch black. Very high winds. Some snow. Sea visible ice flows drifted out to sea. Won $10 bingo, saw movie the Wild and The Innocent.*"

Tony must have eventually arrived at his initial destination – CAM-4. Below is a photo of the station taken in 1960.

Above: CAM-4 on the DEW Line, 1960

Above: Inuit and Americans comparing weapons

Although Tony took his camera to the Arctic, sadly none of his photos have survived, something he deeply regretted. There is a possibility he will have seen polar bears, caribou, Arctic foxes and hares, maybe even an Arctic wolf. Tony met members of the Inuit community, some of whom worked on the Line – he knew and referred to them as Eskimos which was the term in general use at the time. I particularly like the image below of the Americans comparing weapons with the Inuit. The photos here are reproduced with kind permission of Charles Stankievech of www.stankievech.netprojects/DEW/BAR-1. There are some fabulous photos of the living accommodation and the various sites – well worth ten minutes of your time.

I remember Tony talking about the Eskimos, and how in awe of them he was. He talked about their igloos, seeing them fish through holes in the ice, babies being carried in papooses on their mothers' backs, their clothes made from fur and seal skin. He would regularly give us all Eskimo kisses by means of a nose rub, perhaps this is where that originated from. Tony especially remembered seeing and using the dog sled teams, and how incredible the husky dogs were. Many years later in 2006, his oldest son, Guy, took him on a cruise where Tony was, once again, being driven by a dog sled team, this time on the Juno Glacier in Alaska.

The building of the DEW Line had a huge effect on the indigenous population. The Inuit were a hunter/gatherer culture, and many moved from one seasonal camp to another. The DEW Line was built in places where no buildings had ever been, no roads or runways – it must have been a huge upheaval in what had been a very quiet part of the world. During construction 120 ships in two convoys delivered 23,000 construction workers, 42,000 tonnes of steel, 337 million litres of fuel and twelve acres of bedding to the sites. The changes were profound and had a permanent effect on the communities.

The late Bob Williamson of AINA (Arctic Institute of North America) was working as an anthropologist during this period and in 2004 wrote in an article which appeared in *The Nunatsiaq News*:[43]

A lot of the Inuit were quite keen to get work and have money and get housing, as well as medical facilities. Times were pretty hard then. This was the time of the really dreadful TB epidemic. Life was very hard for the people. Fur prices were not good then and the federal government was just starting to assume responsibility." Williamson said

---

[43] https://nunatsiaq.com/stories/article/dew_line_black_hole_in_canadian_history/

it's easy for people to get sentimental about the old way of life before the DEW line and criticize the forces of change, but he doesn't think all the changes that started around the DEW line were bad. For one thing, the DEW line opened up air transportation in the Arctic. And, as a result, the DEW line was ultimately responsible for the development of cooperatives because it made the transportation logistics possible.

The DEW Line was shut down in the late 1980s, and shortly after, the clean-up operation began. The cost was $575 million dollars, and the Inuit played a key part working with the Canadian government to develop what was needed at each site and to ensure it was completed correctly. Soil and water samples are taken on a regular basis to check for any environmental hazards.[44]

Although Tony only spent three months of his life in this job, it made an indelible mark on him, forging lifelong memories, and I'm leaving this section with some of Tony's own words from his letter to his manager in January 1960:

> *Before I came up on the Line, I was a little dubious of the stories, from various people, as to how good conditions were up here. However, I am pleased to be able to report that the stories were not in the least exaggerated. So far, I have enjoyed myself very much finding the people up here very friendly… I can now fully appreciate what you meant when you said I would have to know the DOs backwards, and also be a walking encyclopedia. I think to date I have been asked every question in the book and fortunately in most cases I have been able to give an answer. I must say I find the work interesting, and it is rewarding to know that one is doing a real service up here."*

Photos reproduced with kind permission by Brian Jeffery of The DEWLine Museum and Charles Stankievech of www.stankievech.net/projects/DEW/home.

---

[44] https://www.canada.ca/en/department-national-defence/corporate/video/other/distant-early-warning-line-an-environmental-legacy-project.html

Homeward Bound

1960

1960 was a sad and very difficult year for Tony. Having started his job with the Federal Electric Corporation up in the Arctic, he discovered that his beloved mother was seriously ill.

Several letters from Tony's father, Bill, arrived in quick succession, updating Tony on the sad events:

15 January 1960
Colebrooke, Chelford
Regards from Ethel

Mr WA Longworth ACA, c/o Federal Electric Corp, Montreal Airport, Dorval, Quebec

My Dear Tony

Many thanks for your letters, they are a great comfort to Mummy, and I was pleased to hear you arrived up north safely and trust all goes well with you.

How delightful to have enjoyed such a lovely break at Christmas and the New Year, I had Xmas dinner at Maureen's and Boxing Day with Mr and Mrs Birchenall, but I had to break away at 1:30pm each day to visit Mummy in the MRI.

I have waited until hearing the final result of the many examinations Mummy has been having, before I wrote regarding same. The physician, Prof Black, decided on Thursday that it was definitely an infection of the bowel and would necessitate an operation, this was confirmed by the surgeon Mr Simmons today Friday. The operation will be a serious one, but the surgeon stated it would be more serious if not attended to at once. Mummy was transferred to the surgical ward SR5 this afternoon and will be operated upon early next week. I am of great faith and praying to the Almighty that a successful operation will give Mummy a long period of good health which she so richly deserves.

It is amazing what the surgeons can perform today, in many cases they border on the miraculous. I feel so helpless but comforted in a small degree by the fact that the medical is of the best and without minimizing the effects I must have faith and confidence in the outcome.

The usual gossipy letter I will endeavour to write this weekend, but I am anxious to post this at once. You may be assured as soon as there is anything definite, I will advise you. In the meantime, have faith my Dear Boy and say a prayer for Mummy.

With fondest love yours Pop

PS we received a letter from Katie today will reply Sunday.

25 January 1960
Manchester

My Dear Tony

I have broken my eyeglasses so hope you can read the scrawl. This morning I saw the surgeon Mr Simmons and was grieved to have his report on the result of Mummy's operation last Thursday 21 January. In the first instance I was given to understand (after long investigation) it was a small cancer on the bowel and the impression given to me was that they had removed the growth and a portion of the bowel.

Unfortunately, there were previous conditions which Mr Simmons could not understand, particularly the severe hemorrhage which Mummy had after arriving at the Manchester Royal Infirmary. Consequently, he decided to investigate further during the operation and to his dismay discovered that the small cancer had penetrated a blood vessel which burst and spread the germ cells to the liver.

I am still so stunned I can hardly write these notes. The position is that the germs will spread in the liver and in the surgeon's opinion maybe create a jaundice condition, and there is no known treatment they can hope to give in the future. Today I fully expected to send a cable stating operation successful Mummy doing well, she was so much improved on Sunday. I am heartbroken to write and say that the trouble will continue and with careful nursing we may expect a period of 5 months to 6 months.

The surgeon does not want Mummy to know the full story and should you write to me in reference to the illness, write to the Warehouse, 35 Church Street. I shall not tell Ethel until absolutely necessary, maybe weeks or months.

It is so terribly hard for me to write this letter, but I have always known you are like myself and want the truth, sorry it has to be this way.

Mr Simmons is trying for another week to see what the results are, and I shall immediately write to you on Monday next should there be any development. Please write to Katie for me. Write to Mummy Manchester Royal Infirmary, SR5 Female, Oxford Road until I advise otherwise.

Fondest love, may God be with you, Pop

26 January 1960
Birchenall, 92 Knutsford Road,
Wilmslow

My Dear Tony

You will by now have received the appalling news contained in Pop's letter of the 25th. I couldn't even begin to tell you how deeply sorry I am – not if I sat here all night could I find the right words. It is all very tragic and so unbelievable coming at a time when we all had such high hopes that Mum was going to be completely cured of all from which she has suffered in the last 7/8 years.

Decisions are not taken easily at a time like this and those that you may have to take must, of necessity, be your own. We understand that it was your intention to come home permanently in July or so. If your plans were to try for a job in England whilst still in Canada, may I suggest that you do that without delay, but I feel perhaps that you should not act too hastily.

Bluntly, as you know, we expect Mum to come out of the MRI in perhaps 10 days' time following which Mr Simmons, the specialist who operated, gives her an expectation of not more than 5 – 6 months. During that time, we must all of us do our utmost to make her as happy as we can without arousing her suspicions.

Mum, of course, has been advised to expect that she will feel tired for a few months, and Pop has probably told you that Simmons has said that she will steadily lose weight, reach a jaundiced condition followed by a coma which will precede the end. This follows very closely the pattern of my own Grandpa Walker. He died very suddenly within 36 hours at the end with little or no pain.

Mum, following her depressed condition, for which she went to Cheadle – which Simmons says is no better at all – and following the hemorrhage which preceded the operation on the bowel, is very weak but is now recovering very well. I feel that there is no hurry for a few weeks, but that assuming you intend to return you should not delay too long. No doubt you will want to fly down to Montreal on the first available plane so that you can speak to Pop. Assuming this and not knowing how long the news will take to reach you, may I suggest you phone us just in case by then Mum is already home. If you can cable first to say when you will phone so much the better as we can then arrange for Pop to be with us if Mum is not home. If Mum is home, you could then phone there afterwards but in no circumstances must she be allowed to suspect the truth by word or deed. She thinks she has had an operation for an ulcer on the bowel which perforated and in doing so burst blood vessels which caused the hemorrhage.

I do so wish I could offer you some real advice and sympathy, knowing how isolated you must feel. Maureen and I both have you in our thoughts all the time and send you our very fondest love. We will do all in our power to help Pop as much as we can. We can do no more for Mum than is being done now until she comes home. Please whatever you do, don't ask, or speak in a manner which could destroy her ignorance of the terrible truth.

God bless, very much love from us all,
Ralph

Bill, Tony's father must have been concerned that his letter of 25 January would not reach Tony quickly, so he also sent a telegram:

27 January 1960
Telegram

Mummy very ill but no immediate danger. Air letter posted 25th January giving full details. Important in your letters to Mummy refer to ulcer operation only and not to minor complications explained in letter. Specialist advised.

This telegram is swiftly followed by three from Tony, firstly to his manager requesting *"permission, if necessary, to return home on compassionate leave"*. Then one to his father, Bill: *"Received your* cable Wednesday. Have been stuck at one site for two weeks thus had no mail and have not been able to get any out. Please explain to Mummy. Greatly distressed by your message. Am holding myself in readiness to fly home immediately should the necessity arise. Please advise progress by cable. Give love to Mummy from Katie and myself. Tony."

Finally, Tony sends a cable to his fiancé, Katie: "*Received cable from Father. Mother very ill. Please write or send cable home. Have been stuck in one site for two weeks. Tony.*"

28 January 1960
Kerry, 92 Knutsford Rd,
Wilmslow, Cheshire

My Dear Tony

I know you will forgive me for not writing when I explain that I just did not know what to say about Mummy's illness, until we knew any definite news, and that I could not write and not mention it. I cannot tell you how sad and disappointed we are that after all our hopes, the final verdict should be so tragic and that our news to you is so terrible. You have our constant thoughts and sympathy as we understand too well how hard it is on you so far away. Our biggest concern is that Mummy shall have no knowledge of her illness.

I'm afraid it almost seems irrelevant to thank you for our Christmas presents. We all liked them very much indeed and do thank you really most sincerely. It hasn't been quite the weather to use mine. Ralph is making good use of the wallet and Rupert's car is 'kept for best' – with no chance to let him pull the wheels off. Fiona of course is absolutely thrilled with the Eskimo doll and when we have decorated her room, we hope to get a glass fronted show case for her collection. David gets new clothes with the $5.

I intended to write to you as soon as Katie had gone back but we were up to the eyes in it before Christmas and Mummy's illness was put before everything. We had a lovely weekend with Katie and loved her on sight and the children took to her straight away – even Rupert who was going through a shy stage at the time, followed her around like a lap dog! I can't tell you enough how much we like her and I'm sure she will make you a jolly good wife. I think she enjoyed her visit, it was very brave of her to come alone, but once or twice I could tell that she missed you and wished you could have been here too – still – that's your fault for getting engaged by telephone! In fact, we had quite a good weekend blaming all sorts of things on "Tony"!! It will be lovely to have another sister-in-law – I feel she is more of a contemporary than Barbara! I hope!!!

The children all send their love. We are not telling any of our friends about Mummy in case it should get back to her. Thinking of you both and with all our love,

Maureen

2 February 1960
92 Knutsford Road,
Wilmslow, Cheshire

To try to keep in touch with you lately has not been easy but telephone calls on Friday, Saturday and Monday have been a wonderful help and in addition have been I think something of a morale booster to Pop.

We were all bitterly disappointed that on Monday Simmons could do no better than confirm his suspicions formed at the time of the operation. We had feared the worst, but still clung to the hope that time might prove him wrong. There can now be no hope nor any alternative. Nor does it make it any easier to know that what actually happened in the transmission of the cells to the liver was a long shot of at least 100-1 against.

Pop and Maureen have both been very brave, but it is not easy and the act which will commence next Saturday when Mum comes home will get progressively more difficult to keep up as time goes past. I have tried to convince Maureen, when she breaks down – only very occasionally when we are on our own – and feels so terribly sorry for Mum that that is wrong. We must all of us die once and none of us knows the way by which we must go. Our sympathy, since we have our own little family and you no doubt soon will have the same, must lie with Pop, who, as an essentially family man, must face the future alone.

Tough as he tries to make himself out to be, Pop is very emotional and lives to an increasing extent on his nerves. It was for his sake more than for any other reason that I suggested you came home permanently. He is going very much to need moral support which you can give him more than I can, for obvious reasons.

After you rang, I spoke to Mrs Milligan and gave her your message about Katie. She seemed highly pleased. I did not tell her all about Mum – merely that things had not gone as well as expected following the operation – the cause of which she knew. I told her you had been advised to come home in 4-6 weeks. She took this to be only for a week or two I think and said she hoped she would meet you. I did not tell her your return was for good because I couldn't tell her what Katie would be doing and she might have been upset. I leave you and Katie to advise them of your plans and why.

Many thanks Tony for your Xmas present which is in daily use and came at a most appropriate time as my other was due for the dustbin – apologies for not having thanked you earlier. Re your films (transparencies) have you got a projector? Pop was wondering whether to get one. He has been under heavy expense, and it would be silly to buy one if you have one already. I can borrow one for occasional use and one could be bought later.

Let me know if I can be of any help to you in any way – meeting you, collecting baggage, or any other way. The kids are longing to see you. We shan't mind seeing you ourselves strangely enough.

    Yours always, Ralph

To have received this news, so far away from home, with the added difficulty of poor communication in the Arctic, must have been unbelievably difficult for Tony. We know he was very close to his mother and can only have been devastated by the news. Tony swiftly made the decision to resign from his new job in the Arctic and to return home as soon as possible.

2 February 1960

Dear Mr Schmincke

This is to inform you of the results of the conversation I had with my father on Monday evening. The pathologist confirmed the surgeons' suspicions that my Mother had cancer of the liver. In his opinion she has a maximum of between 3-6 months to live. Under these circumstances I feel it necessary to return to England in March and remain there until the inevitable happens.

    It is therefore with very deep regret that I now have to tender my resignation. I should like this to be effective 5th March 1960.

    Yours sincerely, W A Longworth

15 February 1960
Kerry

My dear Tony

Many thanks for your recent letter. Mum came home 10 days ago, and all has gone so far much as planned. She was of course quite weak and could only walk with assistance but is now much improved, although when we were round yesterday, Pop said she had been very depressed during the morning.

Last week Jean (Thomas) was up with Susan from Monday to Saturday. This week my mother, Maureen, and Joan (David's wife) will be with her during the afternoons. In fact, Maureen spent 3 afternoons last week at Chelford and will, I know, continue to do so – subject to children's health.
Suggestions that occur to me as I write:

Destroy all correspondence of a secret nature, unless there is any which, for sentimental reasons you wish to keep, in which case you could send these to me. I will keep them locked away as I am doing for one or two of Pop's.

Don't suggest yet altering the wedding date without good cause.

Can I do anything to collect you at Liverpool when you arrive? I will gladly come over day or night. March 19th, I note, is a Saturday and if Mum is well enough, I suppose she and Pop would probably collect you. Suggest Katie stays with you for a few days at Chelford if she is agreeable. Perhaps her parents could come up and stay at The Egerton. They badly want to meet you (can't say I blame them!).

Forget about my birthday you've enough on your plate to worry about – my Christmas present is in daily use and although it never has enough, I'll make it do for Xmas and birthday.

I have been having some correspondence with Sedbergh School lately and have had letters from Thornley and Mawby. The latter is now housemaster of Winder and has accepted Rupert and David for May 70 and May 71 respectively – subject, I suppose, to entrance standard and my pocket being deep enough! It is now £122 per term basic! So, I shall also book them at somewhere cheaper as well just in case Littlewoods let me down.

The kids are all looking forward to seeing you, though they still haven't been told the advanced date yet. David is a real stinker. Laughs when you smack him – or glowers, and when I'm really cross with him, he just grins from ear to ear and says "ello Daddy"! Impossible child. Rupert still sweet but getting steadily more aggressive.

Filthy weekend – snow, ice and now snowing hard again at the office (4pm). You are not the only one suffering Arctic conditions, but none the less you have our sympathy. Hope Mum and Pop coming for a meal on my birthday (38) if Mum feels up to it. We are doing all we can and will do more if it is needed.

Love from all, Ralph

25 February 1960
"In bed" (Colebrooke)
Regards from Ethel

W A Longworth ACA, 1509 Sherbrooke St, Apt 68, Montreal

My Dear Tony

Many thanks for your last two letters – the short one arriving this morning. I do hope my convalescence improves before you come home as I am very far from fit yet. I still don't get up until lunchtime and then all I do is sit in the lounge reading or watching television. Yesterday I had to stay in bed as I had a really "off" day and Pa was at home too with his chest. Goodness knows what we should do without Ethel!

On Sunday afternoon I had my first trip out and went to M & R's for tea to celebrate his birthday, Feb 18th. It is David's on March 18th when he will be two.

Yesterday we had a letter from Mrs Milligan and a surprise photograph of Katie taken for her 21st, so we are reciprocating and sending one of you. The 3 colour snaps you sent are lovely too.

This morning there came an invitation to the wedding of Dorothy Clarkson Neill to Mr Alan James Dickenson on April

2nd for you only – I always thought her real name was Dorcie! Mrs Birchenall came round on Tuesday afternoon in her new Red Riley car and very nice it looked too. Ben Evans was here at the time, and he has a new light green Austin.

I have had ear trouble again – pain and swelling. I also get palpitation very easily – so I can't do anything much at all – I have read some interesting and some very amusing books though.

I wrote to Katie earlier on this week asking her to let me know if she was calling here from Liverpool – so that Ethel can get the small room ready for her and Pa will have to join you, as you fortunately, can sleep through any slight noise.

Your bedroom curtains have been washed this morning as first preparations for your homecoming. I dreamt the other night you had returned home unexpectedly bringing with you a most marvelous toy sweet shop for Fiona and I was hurriedly preparing a meal on a rotisserie!!

I was glad to hear your ulcer was behaving itself and I hope it continues to do so too. No more news for now, with dearest love from

Mummy xxxxxx

1 March 1960
Manchester

Mr W Longworth ACA, 1509 Sherbrooke St West, Apt 68, Montreal

My Dear Tony

A hasty note in reply to your letter which arrived yesterday.

I should be only to delighted to be enabled to entertain Mr and Mrs Milligan, but really Tony I do not think the excitement of your homecoming combined with the introduction of Katie's parents at one and the same time would be in the least conducive to Mummy's well-being. "My dear boy" I do hope you understand *my meaning, the last thing in the world I should attempt would be to give either yourself or Katie the impression that we did not wish to see Mr and Mrs Milligan.*

If you will be advised by me let the matter ride for a week or two after your return and you will then be in the position of making judgement on your own account. Naturally we expect Katie to spend a period with us on arrival and you may have my assurance she will be more than doubly welcome.

In the interim I have been making enquiries in reference to the sailing and arrival of the "Sylvania" at Liverpool, but I shall have more complete details nearer the date and after the boat has sailed.

Since Friday last, we have had a glorious spell of warm weather and at times the temp 60/65 degrees has been just a little excessive for the time of year.

May I express the wish that you are keeping fit and well and doing exercises if necessary. Mummy may be able to give you a lesson on the lines of those suggested by her physiotherapist.

At the moment Mummy is looking quite fit and well but inclined to be a little ambitious. In the event I do not write before March 12th may I wish you a very Happy Birthday, with best of luck.

My love to Katie and yourself, yours Pop

Arrival in England

Tony's journey home will have been an arduous one – flying from the DEW Line to Baffin Island, onto Montreal and then to New York, where he boarded a Cunard boat, the SS *Sylvania*, docking in Liverpool on 19 March 1960.

On the passenger manifest under the columns 'Country of Permanent Residence' and 'Country of Intended Future Permanent Residence' both state Canada, and that he only plans to stay in England for six months. We do know how much Tony loved living in Canada and the only reason he came home was to spend time with his mother.

The reunion at Colebrooke must have been a very joyful but emotional one, especially with the knowledge of Marjorie's illness. As was the case in those times, the family – under guidance from the doctors – chose not to tell Marjorie of her terminal diagnosis, and they kept the news within the immediate family for fear of Marjorie finding out.

It must have been very difficult to have been cheerful and to have kept up a pretence, and I find myself wondering when Marjorie must have realised that her diagnosis was terminal. She was an educated, intelligent lady and I suspect she must have guessed.

However, it is comforting to think of the family sharing her last days together at Colebrooke, of having her beloved son, Tony, return home, and her little grandchildren – Fiona, Rupert and David – around her, who must have been a great distraction.

Marjorie Longworth's Death

Sadly, the inevitable happened, and Marjorie died on 30 May 1960, at Colebrooke. Marjorie was just fifty-four years old. I believe she was cremated and suspect this will have been at Altrincham Crematorium.

A couple of letters of condolence survived, one from Tony's old friend Bob, the other from Bill's sister, Cis (Sarah), who had recently moved to Montreal with her daughter, Pat. Bob wrote: "*I shall always remember the times that I stayed at Colebrooke – what a great pleasure those times were, and how much they were due to your mother's kindness and hospitality.*"

Within Cis's letter she talks of their difficult childhood: "*…like as always, it will not be easy, but as we both agreed when last we met, we were brought up in a tough school, so we will cope. Do take care of yourself. God bless you Bill, and may He reward you and help you. I think of you often. Your loving sister Cis xxxxxxxxx.*"

From Marjorie's will she left gifts of money to her sister, Jean, and her children, to Ethel Tomkinson who was the housekeeper and very much part of the family, to Fiona, Rupert and David (Maureen and Ralph's children), with the remainder of the estate being divided between Bill, Maureen and Tony. The total of her estate was £3,178.12.

I've included some holiday snaps of Marjorie and Bill here. Larger photo is taken in Bournemouth. I'm unsure of the beachside photo, maybe from one of their family trips to Blackpool or similar.

Above: Marjorie and Bill on the beach

Above: Marjorie and Bill in Bournemouth

After Marjorie's death, Tony stayed at Colebrooke and spent time with his father whilst considering his next steps. From various letters it's clear he has been deeply affected by his mother's untimely death, a severe blow to a young man, at twenty-seven years of age, still trying to find his place in the world. It put a huge strain on his relationship with Katie, who was keen to continue planning for their wedding and life together, which proved to be too much for Tony – the wedding was postponed and ultimately, they ended their engagement.

Tony made the decision to stay in Cheshire to be with his father, and by September 1960 he had secured a job with Simon Carves Engineers and settled down to life at Colebrooke. He joined the committee at Wilmslow Golf Club and enjoyed playing plenty of golf. The trail of evidence for what Tony was up to starts to run dry at this point, but I know he enjoyed a trip to Silverstone in May 1962, had a holiday to France with friends in July of the same year, and spent a lot of his spare time with his old friend, Ian Lauchlan, including a sailing trip to Anglesey. In the spring of 1962, he took a job as a salesman with the National Cash Register, which required him to spend a lot of time up in Carlisle and the surrounding area.

As Tony's diary writing and letters all dry up around 1963, and evidence of his life becomes scant, this is where I'm choosing to bring this book to a close. Tony packed so much into his first thirty years – an example of a life well lived. He chose to pack them with fun, adventure and hard work, making lifelong friends along the way and never forgetting how important his family was to him.

One of the most enjoyable aspects of writing this book has been learning about Tony's parents and how kind, caring and loving they were – wonderful qualities that Tony inherited. Had Tony not kept that old sports bag filled with his letters, diaries and school reports, this book, and the preservation of those memories, would not have been written.

Whilst trying to add colour and life to the book in the form of relevant social history, I found myself disappearing down various research 'rabbit holes' and found it hard to work out what to leave out rather than what to include – it was all so interesting, particularly the section on Tony's time working in the Arctic on the DEW Line. I so wish I had paid more attention and asked more questions about everything.

I loved writing about the family history; being able to share what I have discovered over the twenty years of research really brings me joy. It's not something that everyone is interested in which I struggle to understand, as we can learn so much about ourselves by finding out about our past. I can't recommend becoming a family history bore like myself, highly enough!

As Tony's eldest daughter, it has been a privilege not just to learn more about his life, but to have preserved his memories in this book and to share it with other people. I feel very lucky that he was my father and incredibly proud to be his daughter.

I hope you have enjoyed reading this book as much as I have enjoyed writing it.

Tony in the Sunbeam Alpine car he bought around 1962, wearing the cowboy purchased in Santa Rosa, New Mexico, kept his whole life and now owned by his grandson, Andrew Longworth

Epilogue

Having finished writing in so much detail about my father's early life, I felt it would be remiss of me not to include a summary of what happened to Tony, and to acknowledge all of the family members that were to come along.

Sometime in 1961/62, Tony was introduced to Judith Milnes – the cousin of his great friend, Ian Lauchlan, and by late 1963 they were engaged to be married. The ceremony took place in Solihull, Birmingham, in July 1964 with Bob Neill as his best man. Together they settled into married life at Colebrooke, with Tony's father Bill moving into a bungalow attached to the house, which had been built for this purpose. Tony secured a good job as company secretary at Milbury Holdings Ltd, 90 Deansgate, Manchester – a firm of house builders.

The pair were blessed with the arrival of Guy in 1966 and me, Sarah in 1967. Sadly, Bill, Tony's father, died in 1972 after a long battle with emphysema, peacefully, in the bungalow.

Tragedy was to befall the family in November 1974, when Judith died suddenly in her sleep. A devastated Tony was left to care for Guy, aged eight, and me, aged seven, as well as a very busy job.

Right: Judith and Tony

Epilogue

The strong family structure came into play, first with Judith's Aunty Mary, her mother's sister, moving in to look after Guy and me, followed by Tony's Aunty Jean, his mother's sister, who resigned from her job, sold her house in Southampton, and moved up to Cheshire to look after us all. We will be forever grateful to both Aunty Mary, Aunty Jean and the countless other friends and relatives who helped with the school runs, lifts to ballet, cubs, football, etc. Thank you all.

Happily for Tony and the children, he met Rosemary Keynes (née Young) who was the neighbour of his good friend Bill Neil. Rosemary was also a widow and had a little boy, Robert, aged two. The pair married at Birtles Church, Cheshire, in 1976, an extremely happy affair, and not long after, they had a daughter, Kate. The family was complete.

A happy family life continued at Colebrooke for Tony, Rosemary and the four children, where it was always open house, and everyone was made to feel very welcome.

Above: Left to right: Guy, Rosemary, Tony, Sarah, Rob and Kate, seated, Colebrooke c.1989

Rosemary, aged just fifty-five, died very suddenly in 2007, leaving the whole family shocked and saddened. Tony's salvation was his children, their partners and his eleven grandchildren, listed here, who gave him such joy until he too died, aged eighty-three years in December 2014.

> Guy, Anne, Daniel, Andrew and Suzanna Longworth.
> Sarah, Richard, Jennifer and James Anderson.
> Robert, Pippa, Scarlett, Martha and Merryn Keynes.
> Kate, Dan, Jack, Cody and Sam Peers.

Below is the last group photo taken of Tony with his family in the garden at Colebrooke, 2014. Only Merryn is missing as she hadn't been born.

Back row: Jen, Guy, Richard, Dan, Rob
Middle row: Suzanna, James, Daniel, Anne, Sarah, baby Sam, Kate, baby Martha, Pippa
Centre: Tony 'Grandpa'
Bottom row: Jack, Scarlett, Cody on knee, Andrew

Epilogue

Not long after Tony's death, Colebrooke, the house that had been at the heart of our family for three generations, was put on the market. After it sold, leaving Colebrooke for the very last time was far harder than any of us imagined. Yes it was just a house, but so many memories and emotions were held within its walls, and it was truly difficult to leave. We are, however, happy that a local family with two children bought the house, and we do, occasionally, drive to the lane at the bottom of the field to peer up to see what's changed and for a hit of nostalgia.

As a family we continue to make every effort to gather whenever we can – quite a challenge with us all living far apart; we remain a close, supportive family – Tony's family's legacy lives on through us all and he is dearly missed.

I'm ending the book with the last group photo of all of Tony's children and grandchildren, taken in June 2016 at my house in Knutsford, this time with Merryn. The book would not have been complete without a photo of all of Tony's grandchildren.

Back row: Andrew, Jen, Sarah, Daniel, Anne, Kate, James
Middle row: Rob, Dan with Sam on knee, Guy, Richard, Jack
Front row: Pippa with Merryn on knee, Scarlett, Martha, Suzanna, Cody

Appendix

Yorston Lodge School, Knutsford
Form 1, July 1941

Yorston Lodge School, Knutsford
Form 2, July 1942

Sandbach School
1942-1946
Forms 1-3 - Various Terms

Sedbergh School
1946-1950
Forms 1-RM

Subjects.	Per cent Exam. Marks	Position in Class	Remarks.
Scripture	62	5	Good. Shows interest.
Reading	66	12	His improvement slowly.
English Composition	80	3	Good work. C.B.
Elocution	58	5	Not used perfects in aspects.
Literature	44	10	Inclined to be inattentive.
Spelling	22	11	Poor. Very poor in spelling recently.
Grammar	40	11	Very fair. C.B.
Dictation	61	9	Shows improvement.
Writing	70	8	With care could be good.
History	60	1	Always interested.
Geography	68	1	Good. Keenly interested.
Nature Study	84	1	Very good. Always interested.
Arithmetic	92	2	Very good.
Mental Arithmetic	92	1	Excellent work done.
Algebra	—	—	
Geometry	—	—	
French	64	9	Could be more attentive. J.O.L.
Science	—	—	Tries to improve. J.O.
Class Singing	—	—	
Music	—	—	
Physical Training			Very good.
Handwork			Much needles work done.
Sewing			
Drawing	40	10	Could work well if not distracted by companions.
Brushwork			Very good.
Kindergarten Games			
Dancing			Excellent progress made. N.B.
Swimming			

GENERAL REPORT.

Reading is still slow, worst subject. He must try to read everything he can in the holidays. He is a good little worker and his progress has been very satisfactory in all other subjects. D.B.

CONDUCT.
Good.

Position in Form on Examination 4th
Position in form for Year 3rd

C. Neal Boydon, Principal.

The School will re-open September 24th.

Subjects.	Per cent Exam. Marks	Position in Class	Remarks.
Scripture	80	3	Good. Always interested.
Reading	65	11	Still a fair subject with Tony.
English { Composition	47	9	Fairly fair. G.B.
Elocution	84	4	Good.
Literature	31	9	Always interested. G.B.
Spelling	54	10	Fair. Could work harder.
Grammar	57	3	Very fair. G.B.
Dictation	50	10	Fair. This very hard.
Writing	53	9	Shows a little improvement.
History	50	10	Very fair. J.R.
Geography	56	4	Very fair.
Nature Study	82	3	Very good. Always interested.
Arithmetic	80	1	Very good.
Mental Arithmetic	86	1	Very good.
Algebra	—	—	
Geometry	—	—	
French	—	5	Could do much better. J.R.E.
Science	—	1	
Class Singing	—	—	Always tries. G.B.
Music	—	—	
Physical Training	—	—	Very good.
Handwork	—	—	Very fair.
Sewing	—	—	
Drawing	50	5	Fair. J.R.E.
Brushwork	—	—	
Kindergarten Games	—	—	Very good.
Dancing	—	—	
Swimming	—	—	

GENERAL REPORT.

Tony's progress in most subjects has been satisfactory, but he is still poor in Reading and Spelling — he should read a little every day during the holidays. D. Brydon.

CONDUCT.

Very fair.

Position in Form on Examination 6th

Position in form for Year 6th

G...t-td Brydon, Principal.

The School will re-open September 24th

N.B.—This Report should be kept. It may be required as a 'Reference' by a boy leaving School, when applying for an appointment.

Parents are requested to talk over this report with their son, and to express to him their satisfaction or dissatisfaction with it.

SANDBACH SCHOOL.

Autumn TERM, 1942.

Name Longworth, M.A. Age 9 Yrs. 4 Mths.
Form I No. in Form 30. Av. Age 9.6. Form Order 4.
Absent 1 half-day; Late / times.

There are three lessons to be prepared for each day's work. There is only one lesson (Scripture) to be prepared for Monday. Parents of day-boys are particularly requested to see that evening preparation work is not neglected; and, as far as possible, to fix a regular time for their sons. The time given to this work each evening should be from 1 to 2 hours according to the age and strength of the boy. Parents are requested to communicate with the Headmaster if much more, or much less, time is given to preparation work. This work should not require the *assistance* of parents, but its general *supervision* is beneficial and desirable.

SUBJECT.	TERM ORDER.	EXAM. ORDER.	REMARKS.	
SCRIPTURE.	10.	2=	Has improved and worked steadily.	
ENGLISH.	13.	15=	Moderately Satisfactory.	
HISTORY.	8=	1	Has worked very well.	L.C.
GEOGRAPHY.	6	15	Good progress on the whole.	
MATHEMATICS.	2	12	Has worked well.	M.H
SCIENCE.	11=	24	Disappointing examination work.	F.G.H
DRAWING.	11=	7	He has worked steadily & made progress	
FRENCH.	5	14	He has made a promising start.	W.G.H.
LATIN.				
PHYSICAL TRAINING	...	...	Fair.	
WOODWORK	...	...	Fair progress.	EB.

HEADMASTER'S REMARKS (where considered necessary).
Conduct, unless otherwise reported above, may be considered satisfactory.

A very satisfactory first term's work.

H.H.C.

A. Winanthorp Form Master. H.H. Crockett Headmaster.

Next Term begins at 9.15 a.m. Wednesday, January 20th 1943.

N.B.—This Report should be kept. It may be required as a 'Reference' by a boy leaving School, when applying for an appointment.

Parents are requested to talk over this report with their son, and to express to him their satisfaction or dissatisfaction with it.

SANDBACH SCHOOL.

Summer TERM, 1945

Name: Longworth, W.A.   Age: 12 Yrs. 4 Mths.
Form: IIA   No. in Form: 36   Av. Age: 12.3   Form Order: 5
Absent: 7 half-days;   Late: — times.

There are three lessons to be prepared for each day's work. There is only one lesson (Scripture) to be prepared for Monday. Parents of day-boys are particularly requested to see that evening preparation work is not neglected; and, as far as possible, to fix a regular time for their sons. The time given to this work each evening should be from 1 to 2 hours according to the age and strength of the boy. Parents are requested to communicate with the Headmaster if much more, or much less, time is given to preparation work. This work should not require the *assistance* of parents, but its general *supervision* is beneficial and desirable.

SUBJECT.	TERM ORDER.	EXAM. ORDER.	REMARKS.	
SCRIPTURE.	1=	6=	Term work very satisfactory. Examination somewhat disappointing.	J.S.
ENGLISH.	14	14=	He loses many marks through carelessness.	R.W.R.
HISTORY.	14=	21=	He can do much better work.	R.W.B.
GEOGRAPHY.	9=	2	He does not always make quite his best effort.	J.S.
MATHEMATICS.	1	16=	Term work good. Examination work very disappointing.	H.K.C.
SCIENCE.	4=	1	Good.	O.G.W.
DRAWING.	1	7	Very good	
FRENCH.	4	17	Far too easily satisfied	
LATIN.				
PHYSICAL TRAINING	...	...	Showing promise.	J.S.
WOODWORK	...	...	A good term's work.	R.B.

HEADMASTER'S REMARKS (where considered necessary).
Conduct, unless otherwise reported above, may be considered satisfactory.

He does not seem to work equally hard at all subjects. He should remember that all subjects should have the same amount of time given to them at home.   H.K.C.

M. Wood   Form Master.   H.K. Crockett   Headmaster.

Next Term begins at 9.30 a.m. Wednesday Sept. 12th

N.B.—This Report should be kept. It may be required as a 'Reference' by a boy leaving School, when applying for an appointment.

Parents are requested to talk over this report with their son, and to express to him their satisfaction or dissatisfaction with it.

SANDBACH SCHOOL.

Christmas TERM, 1944

Name: Longworth, W. A.   Age: 11 Yrs. 9 Mths.
Form: VA   No. in Form: 35   Av. Age: 11·8   Form Order: 4
Absent: 1 half-days;   Late: 0 times.

There are three lessons to be prepared for each day's work. There is only one lesson (Scripture) to be prepared for Monday. Parents of day-boys are particularly requested to see that evening preparation work is not neglected; and, as far as possible, to fix a regular time for their sons. The time given to this work each evening should be from 1 to 2 hours according to the age and strength of the boy. Parents are requested to communicate with the Headmaster if much more, or much less, time is given to preparation work. This work should not require the assistance of parents, but its general supervision is beneficial and desirable.

SUBJECT.	TERM ORDER.	EXAM. ORDER.	REMARKS.	
SCRIPTURE.	—	—	Has worked satisfactorily.	J.S.
ENGLISH.	7	22=	His examination paper was very careless	R.W.B.
HISTORY.	9=	16=	His work is marred by carelessness.	R.W.B.
GEOGRAPHY.	12	6=	A very fair examination but he has not always done his best.	J.S.
MATHEMATICS.	2	17=	Term work, good. Examination work, disappointing. Must work more neatly.	H.L.C.
SCIENCE.	3	8	Good.	O.G.W.
DRAWING.	7	11=	Quite satisfactory work & progress.	
FRENCH.	9	7	Rather disappointing	M.W.
LATIN.				
PHYSICAL TRAINING	...	...	Keen and active	J.S.
WOODWORK	...	...	...	Satisfactory.	

HEADMASTER'S REMARKS (where considered necessary).
Conduct, unless otherwise reported above, may be considered satisfactory.

With more careful work, he could do better still.

H.L.C.

M. Wood, Form Master.   H. Crockett, Headmaster.

Next Term begins at 9·15 a.m. Wednesday 17th January.

N.B.—This Report should be kept. It may be required as a 'Reference' by a boy leaving School, when applying for an appointment.

Parents are requested to talk over this report with their son, and to express to him their satisfaction or dissatisfaction with it.

SANDBACH SCHOOL.

Spring TERM, 1943.

Name Longworth, W.A. Age 10 Yrs. 0 Mths.
Form I. No. in Form 30. Av. Age 9 yrs. 9 mths Form Order 15.
Absent 10 half-days; Late — times.

There are three lessons to be prepared for each day's work. There is only one lesson (Scripture) to be prepared for Monday. Parents of day-boys are particularly requested to see that evening preparation work is not neglected; and, as far as possible, to fix a regular time for their sons. The time given to this work each evening should be from 1 to 2 hours according to the age and strength of the boy. Parents are requested to communicate with the Headmaster if much more, or much less, time is given to preparation work. This work should not require the *assistance* of parents, but its general *supervision* is beneficial and desirable.

SUBJECT.	TERM ORDER.	EXAM. ORDER.	REMARKS.	
SCRIPTURE.	10.		Satisfactory.	ALW.
ENGLISH.	14		Very fair – somewhat erratic	AHW.
HISTORY.	19		Very fair.	E.C.
GEOGRAPHY.	8.		Steady progress.	J.L.
MATHEMATICS.	12.		He can do the work: but is not neat enough.	ALW.
SCIENCE.	14		Very fair.	F.G.H.
DRAWING.	15.		Fairly satisfactory.	ALW.
FRENCH.	12.		Quite satisfactory work.	W.G.H.
LATIN.				
PHYSICAL TRAINING	...	...	Fair.	JS
WOODWORK	...	...	...	Satisfactory.	RM.

HEADMASTER'S REMARKS (where considered necessary).
Conduct, unless otherwise reported above, may be considered satisfactory.

A satisfactory term's work. I should like to see him in higher positions in a number of subjects. H.C.

A. Lumanthorpe Form Master. H.H. Crockett Headmaster.

Next Term begins at 9.15 a.m. Wednesday, May 5th 1943.

N.B.—This Report should be kept. It may be required as a 'Reference' by a boy leaving School, when applying for an appointment.

Parents are requested to talk over this report with their son, and to express to him their satisfaction or dissatisfaction with it.

SANDBACH SCHOOL.

Name _Longworth, W.A._ .... Spring .... TERM, 1944. Age _11_ Yrs. — Mths.

Form _IIB_ No. in Form _35_ Av. Age _11-7_ Form Order _3_

Absent _1_ half-days; Late — times.

There are three lessons to be prepared for each day's work. There is only one lesson (Scripture) to be prepared for Monday. Parents of day-boys are particularly requested to see that evening preparation work is not neglected; and, as far as possible, to fix a regular time for their sons. The time given to this work each evening should be from 1 to 2 hours according to the age and strength of the boy. Parents are requested to communicate with the Headmaster if much more, or much less, time is given to preparation work. This work should not require the *assistance* of parents, but its general *supervision* is beneficial and desirable.

SUBJECT.	TERM ORDER.	EXAM. ORDER.	REMARKS.	
SCRIPTURE.	4		A satisfactory term's work.	J.S.
ENGLISH.	14=		Very fair progress. Neater work required.	C.J.
HISTORY.	4=		He has made good progress	AHW.
GEOGRAPHY.	2.		He has worked well. Map reading very good.	P.J.
MATHEMATICS.	1.		His work has been well done, his homework particularly.	O.E.W.
SCIENCE.	3=		A conscientious student.	J.S.
DRAWING.	2=		He works tidily and well	
FRENCH.	6		A satisfactory term's progress	O.E.H.
LATIN.				
PHYSICAL TRAINING			Fair progress.	J.S.
WOODWORK			Satisfactory.	ZB.

HEADMASTER'S REMARKS (where considered necessary).
Conduct, unless otherwise reported above, may be considered satisfactory.

A very good term's work except in English, which is not so good. H.K.C.

J. Sproule Form Master.   _H.K. Crockett_ Headmaster.

Next Term begins at _9.15_ a.m. Wednesday, 26 April, 1944.

N.B.—This Report should be kept. It may be required as a 'Reference' by a boy leaving School, when applying for an appointment.

Parents are requested to talk over this report with their son, and to express to him their satisfaction or dissatisfaction with it.

SANDBACH SCHOOL.

Spring TERM, 1945

Name: Longworth, W A Age 12 Yrs. 0 Mths.
Form: II A No. in Form 35 Av. Age 11yr 11mths Form Order 3
Absent 3 half-days ; Late — times.

There are three lessons to be prepared for each day's work. There is only one lesson (Scripture) to be prepared for Monday. Parents of day-boys are particularly requested to see that evening preparation work is not neglected; and, as far as possible, to fix a regular time for their sons. The time given to this work each evening should be from 1 to 2 hours according to the age and strength of the boy. Parents are requested to communicate with the Headmaster if much more, or much less, time is given to preparation work. This work should not require the *assistance* of parents, but its general *supervision* is beneficial and desirable.

SUBJECT	TERM ORDER	EXAM. ORDER	REMARKS	
SCRIPTURE.	2		Satisfactory progress.	J.S.
ENGLISH.	3 =		Good progress.	RWB.
HISTORY.	19		He can do much better work.	RWB.
GEOGRAPHY.	3		Good.	PS.
MATHEMATICS.	1		A good term's work.	H.L.C.
SCIENCE.	6		He shows satisfactory progress.	O.G.W.
DRAWING.	5		Very good.	JA
FRENCH.	8		Could do better.	M.W.
LATIN.				
PHYSICAL TRAINING	...	...	Showing promise.	J.S.
WOODWORK	...	...	Satisfactory.	RM

HEADMASTER'S REMARKS (where considered necessary).
Conduct, unless otherwise reported above, may be considered satisfactory.

A very satisfactory term's work in most subjects. History and French need more attention.
H.K.C.

M. Wood. Form Master. H.H. Crockett Headmaster.

Next Term begins at 9.15 a.m. 18th April 1945

N.B.—This Report should be kept. It may be required as a 'Reference' by a boy leaving School, when applying for an appointment.

Parents are requested to talk over this report with their son, and to express to him their satisfaction or dissatisfaction with it.

SANDBACH SCHOOL.

Summer TERM, 1943.

Name: Longworth, WA. Age 10 Yrs. 4 Mths.
Form: I No. in Form 30. Av. Age 10 Yrs. 1 mth. Form Order 10.

Absent / half-days; Late / times.

There are three lessons to be prepared for each day's work. There is only one lesson (Scripture) to be prepared for Monday. Parents of day-boys are particularly requested to see that evening preparation work is not neglected; and, as far as possible, to fix a regular time for their sons. The time given to this work each evening should be from 1 to 2 hours according to the age and strength of the boy. Parents are requested to communicate with the Headmaster if much more, or much less, time is given to preparation work.

SUBJECT.	TERM ORDER.	EXAM. ORDER.	REMARKS.	
SCRIPTURE.	9=	16.	His examination was careless. I know he can spell better than he did.	AHW
ENGLISH.	18	22=	Fair	AHW.
HISTORY.	16=	11=	Fair; is not sure of the work.	EC
GEOGRAPHY.	8	5=	Very fair. Examination creditable.	S.J.
MATHEMATICS.	2.	8.	I am pleased to report on all-round improvement.	
SCIENCE.	23=	15=	Fair only.	F.C.H.
DRAWING.	16=	15.	Fair. to be still inclined, at times untidy.	AHW.
FRENCH.			a very willing trier indeed.	W.S.H.
LATIN.				
PHYSICAL TRAINING			Fair.	J.S.
WOODWORK			Satisfactory.	RB.

HEADMASTER'S REMARKS (where considered necessary).
Conduct, unless otherwise reported above, may be considered satisfactory.

A satisfactory term's work on the whole. Will have to work hard next year in the main School to make good progress.
H.L.C.

A. Linanthorp Form Master. H.L. Crockett Headmaster.

Next Term begins at 9.30 a.m. Wednesday, September 8th 1943.

N.B.—This Report should be kept. It may be required as a 'Reference' by a boy leaving School, when applying for an appointment.
Parents are requested to talk over this report with their son, and to express to him their satisfaction or dissatisfaction with it.

SANDBACH SCHOOL.

Summer TERM, 1944

Name **Longworth, W.A.** Age 11 Yrs. 4 Mths.
Form **IIB** No. in Form 35 Av. Age 11 yrs. 11 mths. Form Order 2
Absent 5 half-days; Late — times.

There are three lessons to be prepared for each day's work. There is only one lesson (Scripture) to be prepared for Monday. Parents of day-boys are particularly requested to see that evening preparation work is not neglected; and, as far as possible, to fix a regular time for their sons. The time given to this work each evening should be from 1 to 2 hours according to the age and strength of the boy. Parents are requested to communicate with the Headmaster if much more, or much less, time is given to preparation work. This work should not require the *assistance* of parents, but its general *supervision* is beneficial and desirable.

SUBJECT.	TERM ORDER.	EXAM. ORDER.	REMARKS.	
SCRIPTURE.	2	1	Satisfactory progress.	J.S.
ENGLISH.	11=	9	Made good progress. Neater work required.	C.J.
HISTORY.	12	9=	Very fair work & progress this term	A.H.W.
GEOGRAPHY.	5	4	Good work spoiled by great untidiness	P.S.
MATHEMATICS.	4	4	Satisfactory.	O.G.W.
SCIENCE.	2	6=	Progress satisfactory.	J.S.
DRAWING.	3=	14	His examination was somewhat below his usual term standard.	
FRENCH.	4	12	Has worked and made progress.	
LATIN.				
PHYSICAL TRAINING	...	...	Fair.	J.S.
WOODWORK	...	...	Satisfactory.	R.J.

HEADMASTER'S REMARKS (where considered necessary).
Conduct, unless otherwise reported above, may be considered satisfactory.

A very satisfactory term's work. Must pay attention to his neatness.
H.L.C.

J. Sproule Form Master. *H. Crockett* Headmaster.
Next Term begins at 9-30 a.m. Wed., 6th September.

N.B.—This Report should be kept. It may be required as a 'Reference' by a boy leaving School, when applying for an appointment.

Parents are requested to talk over this report with their son, and to express to him their satisfaction or dissatisfaction with it.

SANDBACH SCHOOL.

Name _Longworth. W.A._ Summer TERM, 1946

Age _13_ Yrs _4_ Mths.

Form _III A_ No. in Form _36_ Av. Age _13.5_ Form Order _8_

Absent _4_ half-days; Late _—_ times.

There are three lessons to be prepared for each day's work. There is only one lesson (Scripture) to be prepared for Monday. Parents of day-boys are particularly requested to see that evening preparation work is not neglected; and, as far as possible, to fix a regular time for their sons. The time given to this work each evening should be from 1 to 2 hours according to the age and strength of the boy. Parents are requested to communicate with the Headmaster if much more, or much less, time is given to preparation work. This work should not require the assistance of parents, but its general supervision is beneficial and desirable.

SUBJECT.	TERM ORDER.	EXAM. ORDER.	REMARKS.	
SCRIPTURE.	17	7	Fairly good	
ENGLISH.	15=	17=	Satisfactory progress.	W.R.H.
HISTORY.	8=	14=	Satisfactory progress.	W.H.
GEOGRAPHY.	15	19	Satisfactory.	C.E.H.
MATHEMATICS.	8	3	Good work and good results	J.Q.
SCIENCE.	14	8	Satisfactory progress	I.A.H.
DRAWING.	3	6	Good.	WB
FRENCH.	8	14	Satisfactory.	RWB.
LATIN.	12	19	Fair.	WRJ.
PHYSICAL TRAINING	..	..	Good progress.	WB.
WOODWORK	..	..	Satisfactory	RB.

HEADMASTER'S REMARKS (where considered necessary).
Conduct, unless otherwise reported above, may be considered satisfactory.

A very satisfactory term's work. I wish him every success at Sedbergh.

H.L.C.

W.R.Jones . Form Master. _H.L. Crockett_ Headmaster.

Next Term begins at 9.30 a.m. Wed. Sept. 18.

Sedbergh School.

Lent Term, 19 47 Name W.A. Longworth
House Winder Age 14

Form.	Av. age.	No. of boys.	Starting Place.	Final Place.	Height	Weight	Girth	
II	14.2	17	12	8	5'5"	8.4½	33"	Commencing Term
					5'5"	8.8	35⅛"	Ending Term

Form Subjects.

English 9.
History 7.
Divinity

He is doing quite well and making reasonable progress, but he works rather unimaginatively and without real attack. He is a pleasant character to have around. JMS

Latin 16th — Finds the work difficult but he stuck to it well and was improving towards the end of the term.

Set Subjects.	Set.	No. in Set.	Place.	
Mathematics	6.	16.	9.	Quite good. A.D.B.
French	7.	17	9	Capable, and would be much higher placed if he concentrated and took things more seriously. E.S.
Greek or German				
Latin History Geography		17	5	He seems interested and quite keen, though he doesn't always hit his nails on the head. A.S.

Music: Piano. Fair. Scales need more care. Ctc. pp &p.   Art:

Housemaster Good. RCHC.

Headmaster He has done quite well on the whole but he must not be content until he has acquired that extra bite which makes all the difference. JHB

1 MAY 1947

Next term begins on .... 19...

All boys must return on that day, unless they have leave of absence from the Headmaster. Parents can obtain this leave through the Housemaster, to whom the earliest possible information of any serious illness should be sent. Each boy must bring with him a certificate that he has not been exposed to infection.

Sedbergh School.

Lent Term, 19 49   **Name** W. A. Longworth
House Winder   **Age** 16

Form.	Av. age.	No. of boys.	Starting Place.	Final Place.	Height.	Weight.	Girth.	
Vb.M	15·7	24	6	11	5·8	10·1	38	Commencing Term.
					5 8¼	10 4	38	Ending Term.

Form Subjects.

Chemistry 9 = Quite good after a poor start. *[initials]*

Physics 4. Steady effort + satis. progress. *[initials]*

English 12 Sensible + industrious. *[initials]*

Divinity 12. He tries hard and has made progress, but he must work harder to improve his literary subjects. More reading of good authors might help him to become more articulate on paper. *[initials]*

Set Subjects.	Set.	No. in Set.	Place.	
Mathematics	δ	30	4	Good work and very satisfactory progress, but he ought to be becoming more spontaneous. *[initials]*
French	Form	24	18	Very weak. He must work with more determination if he is to get a certificate. *[initials]*
Greek or German				
Latin History Geography	O Q.	17 17	13 13	Not at all strong. A determined effort is needed to fill the many gaps in his knowledge. Some appreciable effort ... the work ...

Music | **Art**

Housemaster A useful term of effort and some progress; except in the matter of literature, the weakness in English seems to be becoming less marked. *OTTF*

Headmaster Good in patches but not altogether convincing. *[initials]*

Next term begins on **28 APR 1949** 19...

All boys must return on that day, unless they have leave of absence from the Headmaster. Parents can obtain this leave through the Housemaster, to whom the earliest possible information of any serious illness should be sent. Each boy must bring with him a certificate that he has not been exposed to infection.

SIXTH FORM

Sedbergh School.

Lent Term, 1950   Name W.A. Longworth
                       House Winder   Age 17

Form.	Av. age.	No. of boys.	Starting Place.	Final Place.	Height.	Weight.	Girth.	
R.M	16.5	21			5 8 7/8	10 8½	39	Commencing Term.
					5 8 7/8	10.9	40½	Ending Term.

PRINCIPAL SUBJECTS.

Chemistry 13/17. He has made a fair start with the more advanced work. NJM.

Mathematics Set A 4/10. A good term's work.

Physics 12/18. He is attentive & tries & will come on. CRS

SUBSIDIARY SUBJECTS.

1. Political Geography: There has not been very much development from his School Certificate standard but he tries hard. RAC.

2. English. Improving now.

3. General Classics. Satis. CPM.

4. Divinity. A very moderate term's work. MFR

MUSIC

ART

HOUSEMASTER

Fair progress, but nothing very striking. OMF

HEADMASTER

A very creditable output. J.M.

Next term begins on **2 MAY 1950** 19...

All boys must return on that day, unless they have leave of absence from the Headmaster. Parents can obtain this leave through the Housemaster, to whom the earliest possible information of any serious illness should be sent. Each boy must bring with him a certificate that he has not been exposed to infection.

Sedbergh School.

Winter Term, 19 49   Name W.A. Longworth
House Winder   Age 16.9

Form.	Av. age.	No. of boys.	Starting Place.	Final Place.	Height.	Weight.	Girth.	
Vb.M	16.4	24	17	15	5'8⅜"	10.8	39	Commencing Term.
					5'8⅜"	10.5	39	Ending Term.

Form Subjects.

He gets fewest marks in literary subjects. His work for me has been quite good but spoilt by his inattention at times. CRS

Physics. 6.

English. 11. Has worked well. DOW

Chemistry 3. Much improved. A very good term. NJM

Divinity. Very intelligent and keen. ALM

Set Subjects.	Set.	No. in Set.	Place.	
MATHEMATICS	8	22	8	Mainly good, but occasionally lapses into inaccurate work. DSW
FRENCH	Form	22		I think there has been more effort on his part this term, but his French is still desperately weak. KB
GREEK or GERMAN				
LATIN HISTORY GEOGRAPHY	P Q.	17 17	9 6	Rather better, but I'm afraid his knowledge is still rather sketchy. LC Steady work. RAC
MUSIC			ART	

HOUSEMASTER He takes quite a good place in his "Modern" subjects, any way; and English, his old bugbear, seems improved. He is growing up sensibly in the House. OMF

HEADMASTER He has worked well.

Next term begins on .17 JAN 1950. 19...

All boys must return on that day, unless they have leave of absence from the Headmaster. Parents can obtain this leave through the Housemaster, to whom the earliest possible information of any serious illness should be sent. Each boy must bring with him a certificate that he has not been exposed to infection.

Sedbergh School.

Term: Summer, 1949 **Name:** W. A. Longworth
House: Winder **Age:** 16.4

Form	Av. age	No. of boys	Starting Place	Final Place	Height	Weight	Girth	
Vb.M	15-11	24	12	17	5.8¼	10.4	39	Commencing Term.
					5.8¼	10.5	39¼	Ending Term.

Form Subjects.

Exam Results:

Not a satisfactory term. His literary subjects are still pulling him down and his efforts to improve seem at the best half-hearted. KB

5 — Divinity :- Poor KB

English 23. A weak start - but has improved recently. DSW

8th — Chemistry 12 Fair progress. NJM

4th — Physics 15. He has dropped from 4th in this subject & it was only lately that he recovered last term's standard. CHG

	Set Subjects.	Set.	No. in Set.	Place.	
7	Mathematics	8	26	12	Not bad. He has progressed in a rather aimless kind of way. AaJ
	French	Form		23	Terribly weak. He must work very hard between now & December if he is to get a certificate. KB
	Greek or German				
10th	Latin	0	18	12	Not strong. IC
	History				
	Geography	0	18	15	very slow progress. RAC
	Music				Art

Housemaster: This is depressing; he seems to have slipped back everywhere, though as a member of the House I still find him keen, cheerful, and quite effective. STTF

Headmaster: I find it hard to believe this is the best he can do. He certainly could improve his English if he took the trouble to. JMM

Next term begins on 20 SEP 1949 19...

All boys must return on that day, unless they have leave of absence from the Headmaster. Parents can obtain this leave through the Housemaster, to whom the earliest possible information of any serious illness should be sent. Each boy must bring with him a certificate that he has not been exposed to infection.

SIXTH FORM

Sedbergh School.

Summer Term, 1950.   Name......W. A. Longworth......

House......Winder......   Age..17.5.

Form.	Av. age.	No. of boys.	Starting Place.	Final Place.	Height.	Weight.	Girth.	
R.M.	16·8	19			5 8½	10·11¼	39	Commencing Term.
					5 8½	10·12	40	Ending Term.

PRINCIPAL SUBJECTS.

Chemistry. 12/15 Progress only moderate — he seems to find the work difficult. NWT

Mathematics. Sets 6/9 Reasonably good. He is not very quick. [init]

Physics. 6/15 I have been pleased with the way he has tackled work that he often found difficult. CHW

SUBSIDIARY SUBJECTS.

1. English. He has made great strides in every way, & ends his time here having reached a very respectable standard. DOW

2. Political Geography: A sensible term's work. RAC

3. General Classics. Very fair. CPM.

4. Divinity. Satisfactory, though he could well find more to add to general discussions. MFR.

MUSIC	ART

HOUSEMASTER   He has always tried his best, and it is a pity that he is leaving before his efforts have had quite time to be crowned with success. SMF

HEADMASTER   A very good last lap is always a sign of the right spirit. Good luck & good wishes to him. J.H.MS.

Next term begins on 21st Sept. 1950.

All boys must return on that day, unless they have leave of absence from the Headmaster. Parents can obtain this leave through the Housemaster, to whom the earliest possible information of any serious illness should be sent. Each boy must bring with him a certificate that he has not been exposed to infection.

Sedbergh School.

Winter Term, 19 46   Name W. A. Longworth
House Winder   Age 13.9

Form.	Av. age.	No. of boys.	Starting Place.	Final Place.	Height.	Weight.	Girth.	
FIRST	14	15	6	6	5.4	7.13½	30¼	Commencing Term.
					5.4½	8.4½	32	Ending Term.

FORM SUBJECTS.

Latin....... 15. Weak.
English..... 10. Fair.
Divinity.... 10. Fair.

His set subjects are largely responsible for his position in the Form. I have found him somewhat lacking in drive and determination. He must put every ounce into his work next term.
JHW.

Geography. 7. Satisfactory work. RJC
History.... 5. Fair. He is a good worker and sets himself a creditable standard. JMS

Set Subjects.	Set.	No. in Set.	Place.	
MATHEMATICS	φ	25	1	Excellent work, he has constantly maintained a high standard. LPee.
FRENCH	8	20	7	His French is very sound but he is too content with a low standard of work. KB
GREEK or GERMAN				
LATIN HISTORY GEOGRAPHY				

MUSIC: Has made a promising start. Seems interested, but should take his music more seriously into advantage now.

ART: An average performance. A.T.

HOUSEMASTER: I have been pleased with all I have seen of him. RCHC.

HEADMASTER: This Latin in which I remember that he failed in the Entrance looks like proving a heavy handicap. It would be worth his while to get some help with it in the holidays. That is a thing I very rarely recommend but in this case I feel it is advisable if possible. He cannot move up a form until it gets better. JHB

Next term begins on **21 JAN 1947** 19...

All boys must return on that day, unless they have leave of absence from the Headmaster. Parents can obtain this leave through the Housemaster, to whom the earliest possible information of any serious illness should be sent. Each boy must bring with him a certificate that he has not been exposed to infection.

Sedbergh School.

Winter Term, 19 47.   Name W. A. Longworth
                       House Winder   Age 14 : 9

Form.	Av. age.	No. of boys.	Starting Place.	Final Place.	Height.	Weight.	Girth.	
III B	14.2	22	1	10	5 6¾	9.2	36	Commencing Term.
					5 7	9.2½	37	Ending Term.

Form Subjects.

Latin 13 — He is still handicapped by his writing of English, which, though purged of its worst inaccuracies, still lacks precision and imagination. His Latin, however, is clearly better: apart from a bad fortnight around half-term, it has been of reasonable quality. I should like to see a slightly livelier attitude in school; but at least he has worked carefully and sensibly. *FHD*

English 17

Divinity 21

Geography: 11 — There is still room for improvement. *RAC*

History 20= — He could do well at this subject, but is content at present with work which is less than his best. *DB*

Set Subjects.	Set.	No. in Set.	Place.	
Mathematics	P	16	10	He is a keen worker; not a very high position but he has done his best. *ADB*
French	5	20	13	He has worked steadily and made a satisfactory advance without having much flair for the subject. *Ames*
Greek or German				
Latin History Geography				

Music: Piano — He must work harder to grasp the fundamentals of music. *CD*

Art:

Housemaster A hopeful and quite satisfactory term; he is coming on adequately both in House and School. *OMF*

Headmaster Definitely an improvement but still short of whole-hearted energy. *JMB*

Next term begins on .... 19...

All boys must return on that day, unless they have leave of absence from the Headmaster. Parents can obtain this leave through the Housemaster, to whom the earliest possible information of any serious illness should be sent. Each boy must bring with him a certificate that he has not been exposed to infection.